South-East England

D1077884

The principal sights

< Lift flap for map

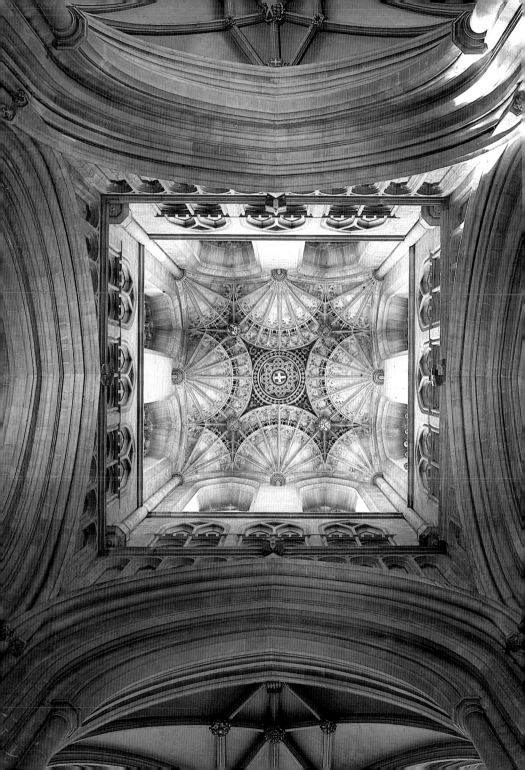

Peter Sager

South-East England

KENT, SURREY, SUSSEX, HAMPSHIRE AND THE ISLE OF WIGHT

Translated by
David Henry Wilson

PALLAS GUIDES

Contents

Colour plates 1-20: Kent – between pages 64 and 65
Colour plates 21-43: Sussex – between pages 128 and 129
Colour plates 44-61: Surrey – between pages 160 and 161
Colour plates 62-81: Hampshire – between pages 208 and 209

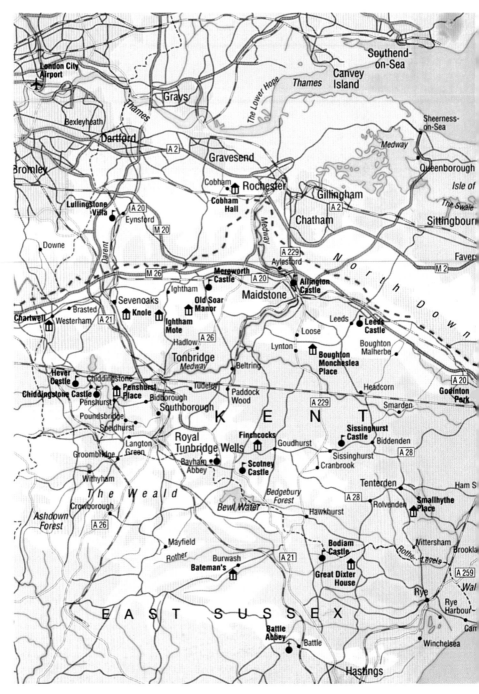

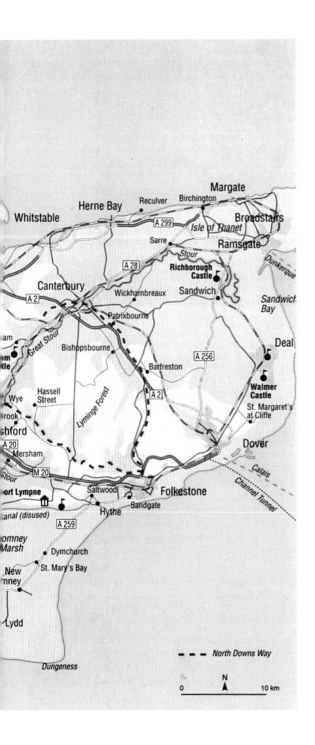

Margate
Herne Bay   Reculver   Birchington   Broadstairs
Whitstable   A 299   Isle of Thanet
                          Sarre   Ramsgate
                              Stour   Dunkerque
                    A 28
                         Richborough
                            Castle
Canterbury   Wickhambreaux   Sandwich
    A 2   Sandwich
         Patrixbourne   Bay
am
         Bishopsbourne   Deal
am   A 256
tle   Walmer
    Wye   Hassell   Castle
            Street   Barfreston   St. Margaret's
rook   A 2   at Cliffe
hford   Dover
    A 20   Calais
Mersham   Channel Tunnel
tour   M 20
ort Lympne   Saltwood   Folkestone
anal (disused)   A 259   Sandgate
                  Hythe
omney
Marsh   Dymchurch
         St. Mary's Bay
New
mney
Lydd
                              --- North Downs Way
Dungeness
                         N
                    0   ▲   10 km

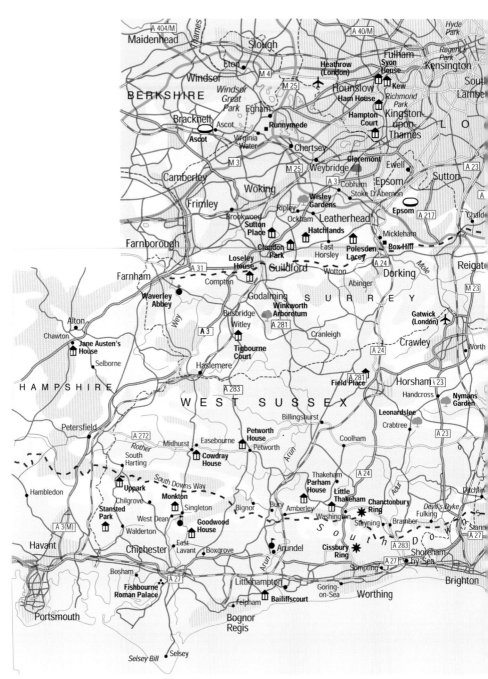

Foreword

This is not simply a guideboook to the sights of Southern England, because there are some places and some people that you can't just go and see. Andrew Lloyd Webber in Hampshire, for example, or Ralph Steadman in Kent. Why have they chosen to live in this part of England, and what do their surroundings actually mean to them? I have tried to write a guide to the inner life of this region as well as to its surface appearance.

Our journey will proceed geographically from east to west, beginning in Kent, staying south of London, and ending in Hampshire, for the West Country has a book of its own. Only in the yellow pages does geography give way to an alphabetical register of counties and places.

For their generous support in this venture, I am deeply grateful to the British Central Tourist Office in Frankfurt – in particular Claudia Ritsert-Clark – to Catherine Althans of the British Tourist Authority in London, Bob Koenig in Surrey, and Inge Hesel of Scandinavian Seaways in Hamburg. My thanks are also due to my German publishers, DuMont Verlag. For this English edition, I have to thank Alexander Fyjis-Walker and his team for their commitment, enthusiasm, and thoroughness, while my translator David Henry Wilson has, as ever, given my German words an English flavour of their very own. Lastly, and most importantly, I thank my wife Else Maria and my daughter Laura, to whom this book is dedicated with all my love.

Peter Sager

The arms of England, as carried by St George in a stained glass window, Tenterden, Kent

Kent

Kent, Sir, – everybody knows Kent –
Apples, cherries, hops and women
Charles Dickens, Pickwick Papers, *1837*

Kent is variously known as *The Garden of England* and *The Gateway to England.*
Today conservationists fear that the gateway is ruining the garden. As the land
corridor linking the continent to the capital, this county of hops and orchards has
in fact never been a pure garden of delights. But not since the Norman invasion of
1066 has it undergone an upheaval quite as dramatic as that caused by the building
of the Chunnel. New roads and railways, extensions to the M20 and A20, and in
inevitable attendance a new spread of industrial estates and shopping centres – all
this livens up the economy while at the same time killing off the landscape.

Since Cæsar's legions first stepped onto British soil in 55 BC, Kent has always
been the most popular point of entry for Europeans, and the most jealously
guarded outpost of the island fortress. Kent has more castles than any other
English county except Northumberland. The first one in the country was and is
Dover Castle. The present castle was begun in 1133 by Henry II; it towers high on
the cliffs above the town in all its medieval majesty as the key to England and the
most advanced fortress of its time in Western Europe. Newly imported from
Constantinople by the crusaders was the use of curtain walls built onto the Iron
Age ramparts, and equally new were the concentric fortifications around the keep.
The walls are about 20 foot thick, spacious enough to contain whole suites of
rooms. We know the name of Henry's military architect: Mauricius; and we also
know the enormous cost of the 12th century building: £7,000.

The chalk cliffs below Dover Castle contain a network of tunnels and casemates
nearly four miles long. These were begun during the Napoleonic Wars and
extended during the Second World War. A few years ago, English Heritage
restored them. What is now a tourist attraction was formerly Churchill's bomb-
proof headquarters during the Battle of Britain. In May 1940, this Hellfire Corner
was also the command post for Operation Dynamo – the evacuation of allied
troops from Dunkirk shortly before Hitler's army reached the coast.

In the grounds of the castle stands the little church of St Mary-in-Castro, an
outstanding example of late Anglo-Saxon architecture (around 1000). There are

St Margaret at Cliffe, by Noël Coward

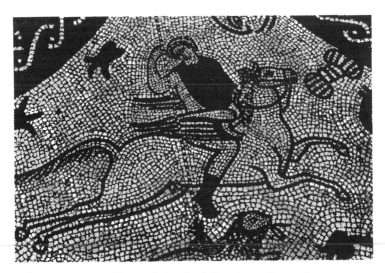

Lullingstone Roman Villa: mosaic showing Bellerophon on Pegasus in the struggle against the Chimæra

Roman tiles in its walls, and at the western end is the Pharos, an octagonal lighthouse mainly dating from Roman times (1st century AD) and thus the oldest building still standing in the country. The most substantial remains of the Roman Empire, however, are to be found further north: *Richborough Castle* on the edge of the Isle of Thanet – Rome's equivalent of the Rock of Gibraltar. As a naval base, after the Emperor Claudius's troops landed here in 43 AD, Rutupiæ was more important than Dover, and it remained the principal port for Gaul right up until the end of the Roman occupation in 407. At the western gate you can step on the oldest cobblestones in England, the Roman *Watling Street*, which went via Canterbury all the way to London (partly following the same route as today's A2 and M2), and from there on to Chester and North Wales. At the end of the 3rd century, Rutupiæ became one of the ten fortresses along the *Saxon Shore*, built by the Romanized Britons as a coastal defence against the Anglo-Saxons.

The landscape now, however, is no longer dominated by Roman remains; instead the skyline offers the three cooling towers of Richborough's power station. And the ruins of *Reculver*, the Roman Regulbium, have been even more ruined by a caravan park. Reculver and Richborough marked the two ends of the Wantsum Canal, now silted up, which separated the Isle of Thanet from the mainland. Once again, as in Dover, the grounds of the Roman castle contain an Anglo-Saxon church, St Mary's Abbey, built in 669 and demolished in 1809, apart from the 12th century twin towers of its western façade, standing high on the cliffs – an unmistakeable landmark for the ships in the Thames Estuary. The rest can only be supplied by the imagination: a cruciform ground plan with apse and archway separating the choir from the nave – typical of 7th century Anglo-Saxon church architecture in south-eastern England. There is, incidentally, an exact copy of the Reculver church in Parramatta, Australia. Emigrants built it to recapture their last impressions of England.

To follow the Romans on their way from Kent to London, you must stop off south of the A20 beside the fish-filled River Darenth, where you will find the Roman villa of *Lullingstone*. This is the most impressive of all the forty or more Roman villas so far discovered in Kent. It was built in the 1st century, and was probably destroyed by fire in the 5th, but in addition to its foundations and its hypocaust heating system, there are floor mosaics in the apse-shaped dining-room showing Europa on a white bull, and in the reception room showing Bellerophon riding Pegasus into battle against the monstrous Chimæra. The reconstructed murals of water sprites, people at prayer, and the Christian monogram chi-rho, all testify to the high artistic standard of this villa, which is believed to be the first Christian place of worship in England.

The Eurotunnel: An Underwater Prologue

If Candide were travelling to England today, he would probably use the Eurotunnel. But in 1758 Voltaire's hero sailed across the Channel from Dieppe, in the company of his learned friend Martin. 'You are acquainted with England,' said Candide. 'Are they as great fools in that country as in France?' 'Yes, but in a different manner,' answered Martin.

There is no seductive Loreley singing from the white cliffs of *Dover*, but they exude an enchantment of their own, evoking a romantic sense of island magic that captivated the Roman invaders as much as the modern army of tourists. 'At the end of the winter I travelled to England again, and was as moved by the white cliffs of Dover as any Englishman returning home from the colonies,' confessed the Austrian Expressionist painter Oskar Kokoschka who, having been branded a 'degenerate' artist, found asylum for a while in England.

The White Cliffs: From here Richard Lionheart set sail in 1190 on his third crusade; Charles II landed here when the Stuarts were restored to the throne in 1660; and Field-Marshal Blücher landed here in 1814, greeted by cheering crowds as he went on his way to London. For returning natives and visiting foreigners, in times of war and peace, these cliffs have always represented more than just a slice of the coastline. Albion, the ancient name for Britain, was derived precisely from the radiant white of these rocks. John of Gaunt's 'precious stone, set in the silver sea' helped make them into a metaphor for the whole nation, protected from 'the envy of less happier lands.' In times of danger they have become a symbol of

Shakespeare Cliff, by George Cruikshank

defiance and of hope, as exemplified by Vera Lynn's promise during the hardest days of the war: 'There'll be bluebirds over/The white cliffs of Dover'.

The Shakespeare Cliff to the west of Dover is generally considered to be the setting for Act IV of *King Lear*, ('How fearful/And dizzy 'tis to cast one's eyes so low! The crows and choughs that wind the midway air/Show scarce so gross as beetles!') and until 1987 the North Downs behind the cliffs had remained virtually unchanged since Shakespeare's day. Then the tarmac ribbon of the new A20 made its way through Farthingloe Valley, and a deep hole was drilled in the base of Shakespeare Cliff: the Chunnel. When on 6 May 1994 the Queen sat in her Rolls Royce and rolled royally along the 31 mile tube in 32 minutes, the enthusiasm of her subjects was somewhat muted. For many Englishmen, the opening of the Channel Tunnel meant the closing of a long, long era. Their island was no longer an island, their splendid isolation was gone forever, and *The Times* would never again be able to indulge in the classic headline: 'Fog in Channel, Continent cut off'.

This engineering feat of the century has been beset by technical and financial problems, and it was preceded by some 5,000 petitions and lawsuits as the fears of an island people were mobilised – perhaps for the last time. The good people of Dover reflected the nightmares of all their compatriots with visions of weapons, drugs, rabies, foreign immigrants, terrorists and Aids all being smuggled through the tunnel to England. Nor has this been an idle fear. The Chunnel has encouraged cigarette and alcohol smuggling on a scale unknown since the 18th century, and it has become the number one goal for desperate immigrants worldwide.

Quite how ancient this trade is was dramatically reconfirmed in 1992, when archæologists checking the site of the Dover-Folkestone road uncovered a boat dating back to the Bronze Age – fully 3,000 years old, and so roughly contemporary with Stonehenge. It is the world's oldest known sea-going boat; one might almost call it a vessel, since it may have been 60 foot long, and powered by 18 oarsmen. People, livestock, general cargo would have comfortably crossed the Channel in her; perhaps even the scrap-metal merchants who abandoned another find, the Langdon Bay hoard of axe heads. Both boat and hoard are now to be seen in the Dover museums.

Britain was no island-fortress then, and did not fully retreat within her cliff-tops until the loss of Calais in 1558; its name, she declared, would forever be written on her heart. She died shortly after and it seems symptomatic that the loss of the French Channel fortress should coincide with the beginning of the heroic Elizabethan phase of what the British used to call 'our island story'.

Churchill saw the Channel not as a waterway but as a philosophy of life. After the Reformation in the 16th century, Protestant England regarded it as a bulwark against the Papist powers of the continent. France, Spain and Portugal were her greatest enemies and her fiercest competitors in the battle for imperial supremacy. Morally, too, Shakespeare's 'other Eden, demi-paradise' developed an almost atavistic aversion to all things European, fostering a sense of superiority that made distance into virtue. And so for some stout English folk, the Chunnel meant a literal undermining of their national identity.

The first comprehensive plans for a Channel tunnel were unveiled by a French engineer, Thomé de Gamond, in the 1840's. Prime Minister Palmerston showed no enthusiasm; there was no need, he thought, to shorten a distance already dangerously short. Nevertheless, in 1880 drilling actually began near Calais and at the foot of the Shakespeare Cliff. The guiding spirit was the railway magnate Sir Edward Watkin, who had dreams of a line joining Manchester, Dover, Nice, and ultimately India. Queen Victoria, famously prone to sea-sickness, would have loved such a tunnel, but her generals invoked the old phantom of invasion – visions of the French army marching underneath the waiting British Fleet. And so in 1882 the project was scrapped. Three years later, Winston Churchill's father, Lord Randolph, stood in

Plotting the war under Dover Castle

the House of Commons and repelled the threat of another such scheme with the words: 'England's reputation depends on remaining as it were, *virgo intacta*.' The English Channel became the nation's chastity belt.

The Second World War confirmed the Great British feeling of moral superiority. Almost every state on the continent had been conquered and occupied, and only the island fortress stood firm. So why should England suddenly be joined to this same Europe – and by a tunnel, of all things? For us continentals, the island mentality is hard to understand. We are more inclined to side with John Donne: 'No man is an island' – and no country should be an island either. The poet Waller, a Kentish man, was closer to English feeling however, when he wrote in 1655:

> Whether this portion of the world were rent
> By the rude ocean from the continent,
> Or thus created, it was sure designed
> To be the sacred refuge of mankind.

In 1973, there was more frantic digging on both sides of the Channel, but in 1975 the Labour government called a halt to that as well, for financial reasons. It was, astonishingly, the arch Eurosceptic Margaret Thatcher who finally achieved the breakthrough. For her, the tunnel – paid for solely by the private sector – was to be a symbol of economic success. It was not meant to signal the end of glorious British isolation. With ever increasing construction costs (estimated at some £13 billion), now converted into horrendous debt, Europe's longest railway tunnel may well prove an economic millstone deep into the 21st century. Nevertheless, Eurostar has cut journey times between London and Paris or Brussels to three hours. Now you can enter the tunnel at Coquelles, south of Calais, and 35 minutes later, out you come at Folkestone, and you will have felt nothing of the salt sea air above you or the long tunnel history behind you. You will also, alas, have missed the finest sight of all: the White Cliffs of Dover. Dorothy Wordsworth in 1802 turned back in Calais to see 'far off in the west the coast of England like a cloud crested with Dover Castle, which was but like the summit of the cloud.'

On the East Cliff Promenade in Dover is a monument to Captain Matthew Webb. In August 1875, wearing red swimming trunks and covered with whale-oil, Captain Webb became the first man to swim the 21 miles between Dover and Calais. It took him 21 hours and 45 minutes. Since then, swimming the Channel has become the classic test of the marathon swimmer – an heroic and eccentric battle against container ships, jellyfish, seaweed, swelling surge, sucking currents, oil slicks, cold, and sheer fatigue. The world record is held by Chad Hunderby, a Californian, who in September 1978 swam the Channel in 7 hours and 17 minutes.

Soon perhaps someone will set the first record for running through the Chunnel.

Henry's Castles and Wellington's Bed: From Deal to Dymchurch

If you want to play an historically and scenically perfect game of golf, then go to Sandwich Bay, also known as *Millionaires' Corner*. One of the three golf courses there is called *Royal Cinque Ports*, and the very name sends us straight back into the middle ages, when the five ports – Sandwich, Dover, Romney, Hythe and Hastings, later to be joined by Rye and Winchelsea – guarded the Channel for England's King, and in return received trading and legal privileges. Lion and ship conjoined – these were the symbols that adorned the flag of the Cinque Ports, from the time of their foundation under Edward the Confessor in the 11th century to the end of their federation in the 15th century. But even today the lords of the Cinque Ports still have the right to special places at all coronations in Westminster Abbey, and they also have their own Lord Warden, whose residence since 1730 has been at Walmer Castle.

Sandwich, the most northerly of the Cinque Ports, was once a bustling seaport, but now nestles picturesquely on the River Stour. Its medieval charms are best enjoyed by strolling round the Butts – the old fortifications – or through the cobbled lanes that follow the old Anglo-Saxon streets. William the Conqueror's *Domesday Book* of 1086 lists this tiny town as the fourth biggest in England, after London, Norwich and Ipswich. It was the gateway to England from the 11th till the 13th centuries, the main port for monarchs and merchants, priests and pirates,

Seal of Sandwich, one of the Cinque Ports

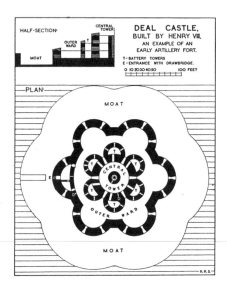

Deal Castle, plan

saints and sinners. Thomas Becket sailed from here into exile in France, and Richard Lionheart landed here after his two-year imprisonment in Austria, and proceeded to walk barefoot to Canterbury. This is the coast of historic landings. In Ebbsfleet, north of Sandwich, the legendary Hengist and Horsa led the first Anglo-Saxons onto English soil in 449, and here too in 597 St Augustine began his mission, on behalf of Pope Gregory the Great – an event commemorated by a Celtic Cross. Sandwich has three churches, dominated by the mighty Norman crossing tower of St Clement's, with its hundred arches inside and out. In St Peter's (13th century) Tom Paine married a local girl in 1759, while he was still working for his father as a corset-maker at No. 20 New Street, and before he started campaigning for American independence. Virtually all the buildings in Sandwich are listed, including many medieval half-timbered and brick buildings, like The Dutch House (King Street) or Manwood Court (Strand Street), which has splendid Dutch gables. After 1560, Elizabeth I granted asylum to Protestant weavers who were fleeing from persecution by the Spanish ruler of the Netherlands (and Elizabeth's brother-in-law), the Catholic Philip II of Spain. This led to a flourishing textile industry and a final golden age for Sandwich. One of the last links with the middle ages disappeared only recently: you no longer have to pay a toll to cross the narrow 'Dutch' drawbridge which crosses the Stour between the two chequered towers of the Barbican.

The Barbican was built as a blockhouse in 1539/40, part of Henry VIII's coastal defences, which included more fortifications in nearby Sandown, Deal and

Walmer. Along the coastline between Hull in Yorkshire and Pendennis Castle in Cornwall, Henry built a total of twenty fortresses, using the money and also the stones from the monasteries he had dissolved in 1538. This chain of gun emplacements was only surpassed by the defences built against Napoleon, and they were still in use during the Second World War. Henry feared a Catholic invasion led by his arch-enemy the French King Francis I at the instigation of Pope Clement VII. The latter had excommunicated Henry shortly before, because he had defied the Pope by divorcing Catherine of Aragon and declaring himself supreme head of the English Church in 1534. The cause of this mighty European upheaval was in Kent – to be precise, in the idyllic setting of Hever Castle. Her name was Anne Boleyn (see p. 77).

Deal Castle is the largest of the three castles Henry built in Kent within a radius of three miles. It stands between the other two, and is a masterpiece of Renaissance military architecture. The German Stephan von Haschenperg designed all three in the most modern style imaginable: very low and large, to provide effective resistance against the new artillery. The round central tower is surrounded by six crescent-shaped bastions with battlements, and these in turn stand within six more semi-circular bastions, one on either side of their smaller fellows and equidistant from the central tower itself. The whole complex is ringed by a wall and a moat, forming an æsthetically perfect military reproduction of the Tudor rose. The Italians took up this form of broad, low fortress, and Dürer also recommended it in 1527.

With the beach in front and a sea of flowers behind, *Walmer Castle* – which once bristled with Henry's cannons – has long since settled down as a well-furnished holiday home. For 23 years it was occupied by the hero of Waterloo, the Duke of Wellington, who as Prime Minister helped to bring about Catholic emancipation, thereby inflicting a late defeat on Henry VIII, in whose castle he died in 1852. The Wellington Room contains his death mask, shaving mirror, legendary black boots, black Wedgwood teapot, red field marshal's uniform, and the armchair in which he died at the age of 83. The iron campbed he used at Waterloo may explain the Iron Duke's exhortation: 'If it's time to turn over, it's time to turn out.' There is another important campbed: that of Pitt the Younger, one of Wellington's predecessors as Lord Warden of the Cinque Ports. Winston Churchill also held this honorary post for a quarter of a century, but he rarely closed his eyes for England here, preferring the softer beds of Chartwell. From 1979 until her death the Queen Mother was the 118th Lord Warden, the first woman to have held an office established by Henry III in the 13th century.

The promenade along the cliffs of *Folkestone* is called the Leas, an elegant mid-19th century quarter which supplied one of the settings for H. G. Wells's novel *Kipps: The Story of a Simple Soul* (1905). Wells himself lived in neighbouring *Sandgate* until 1909, in Spade House (Radnor Cliff Crescent), which was designed by Charles Voysey in 1899. As you get your blood circulation going by taking your brisk walk along The Leas, you will come across a bronze statue of William Harvey, without whom you might never have known that your blood was circu-

lating in the first place. He was born in Folkestone in 1578, and became physician to both James I and Charles I. If you prefer to take your walk in *Deal*, you may be reminded of Edward Lear's enigmatic limerick: 'There was an Old Person of Deal,/ Who in walking used only his heel;/ When they said, "Tell us why",/ He made no reply,/ That mysterious Old Person of Deal.' Not so secret are the intentions of the first Martello Towers, which were built here

The Old Person of Deal, as seen by the Brighton-based illustrator John Vernon Lord

between 1803 and 1808 as a defence against the threat of invasion by Napoleon. Between Folkestone and Seaford there were originally no fewer than 74 of these round, three-storey towers, and 27 of them are still intact. The name Martello is a distortion of 'Torre della Mortella' in Corsica, which the English captured with much ado in 1794. One of these towers is now a museum: No. 24 in *Dymchurch*. A more pressing need for defence is answered by the 'vast and dreary length of sea wall' at Dymchurch, which dates back to Roman times and was a formidable source of inspiration to the war artist Paul Nash.

Port Lympne: The Salon Lions of Romney Marsh

The Royal Military Canal (1804–06) begins in the middle of *Hythe*, makes a wide sweep round Romney Marsh, and finishes in Rye. It's another somewhat curious means of keeping out the dreaded Napoleon. On this canal lie the ruins of Stutfall Castle, the Roman *Portus Lemanis*, whose name is preserved in *Lympne Castle* (14th-15th century) a little higher up, and the neighbouring *Port Lympne*. The main attraction there now is the zoo, but Port Lympne owes its gardens and its legendary fame to a man whose wealth and taste were equally expansive: Sir Philip Sassoon.

He was the son and heir of two great Jewish families, the Sassoons of Baghdad and the Rothschilds. He was born in Paris, and educated at Eton and Oxford and in the salons of a society that no longer exists. Through the untimely death of his parents, he came into an immense fortune at a very early age. In 1912, when he was 23, he became the youngest MP at Westminster. He had inherited two houses, but then proceeded to build himself a third in his constituency of Hythe. Port Lympne stands on a hill overlooking Romney Marsh, and is a mixture of Roman villa and South African estate. It was designed by Sir Herbert Baker, a Kentish architect who had done a great deal of work for Cecil Rhodes in Cape Province before developing his imperial neoclassicism in competition with Edwin Lutyens in New Delhi. After the First World War Philip Sassoon made elaborate extensions to his house. Philip Tilden, a popular architect at that time who was also employed by Churchill for work on Chartwell, decorated rooms at Port Lympne like sets from the *Ballets Russes*: the dining-room has walls of lapis lazuli, with a pink ceiling and a frieze by Glyn Philpot; the guest wing contains a Moorish inner courtyard with fountain, marble columns, and green glazed tiles.

Port Lympne took its character from the eccentricities of a Jewish aristocrat who subtly combined an equal measure of taste and luxury. In the park of his Hertfordshire estate, the stags provided a glittering display – he had the tips of their antlers painted with gold leaf. The gardens of Port Lympne surround the house like an elaborate frame, and they too bear witness to his penchant for extremes. In order to make sure that his gardener composed the flowerbeds in precisely the right colours, Sir Philip bought him a complete collection of Cartier cigarette cases. This was not to be a garden, but a cataract of gardens: a 'harmony seemed to be established in terms of incongruity, the whole swimming in the golden summer light', to reflect the resplendence of Sir Philip himself, an artist who was 'avid of colour and life', in the words of Russell Page, who played a major part in restoring the gardens during the 1970's. Rare lilies grow there, with magnolias, fig-trees and vines. The Trojan Stairway with its 125 steps, flanked by monumental hedges of yew, descends the terraced gardens like an imperial relic of Port Lympne's Roman origins.

This was the setting where Sir Philip welcomed his illustrious visitors: Lloyd George, whose private secretary for a while he was; the Prince of Wales (Edward the Quitter); George Bernard Shaw, Lawrence of Arabia, Charlie Chaplin, and other luminaries of the time. In the summer of 1920 Port Lympne hosted three conferences at which Lloyd George and his French counterparts discussed the post-war world order against the background of an allegorical mural (no longer there) by José-Maria Sert, the conservative Catalan artist, depicting German aggression towards France. Just as he did at No. 25 Park Lane, his London residence, Sir Philip ran a salon at Port Lympne in the very best, and most lavish Edwardian style. The masterpieces produced by his French chefs and his German pastrycooks were served by liveried lackeys, and in the summer meals were taken in the gardens, in marquees of white and gold brocade. In 1933 Sir Philip commissioned Rex Whistler to paint a room in the house as a marquee, complete with tent-poles and trompe-l'œil architecture from 18th-century London and Dublin.

Æsthete, politician, amateur pilot, Commissioner of Works for all public buildings, this extraordinary man died in 1939. His death marked the end of an era and a class. 'The picnic really was over,' wrote Kenneth Clark, Director of the National Gallery, who happened to be his neighbour at Saltwood Castle.

Autre temps, autre mœurs. Port Lympne was bought in 1973 by a gambler named John Aspinall. Born in India, the son of a professional soldier, he was sent down from Oxford, and made his millions running casinos. Eventually Aspinall (who died in June 2000) became one of the 300 richest people in Britain – a man who had come a long way, and didn't hesitate to let you know it. Next to gambling, and friends (including Lord Lucan), his great passion was wild animals, and he owned two zoos, one at Howletts near Canterbury, and one at Port Lympne. Few people have had greater success at breeding endangered species, especially gorillas, and no one gave them more freedom to move than Aspinall. But this love of animals had its price. Four of his keepers were victims of tiger attacks. The fact that he believed techniques of selective breeding and eugenics should also be applied to human beings was just one of the many strange sides of this social Darwinist. His gorillas in Port Lympne often enjoyed the same delicacies as his house guests, the social lions. Parties with dwarfs and magicians, polar bears made of ice with caviar in their laps – this was the sort of thing that established John Aspinall's reputation as a true eccentric. Certainly no one could accuse Sir Philip Sassoon's successor of being a bore, though one might question his taste. Tigers in gold frames and gaudy jungle murals have replaced the exquisiteness of the Sassoons.

From the terraced gardens of Port Lympne, one can look down over the coast and the wide green expanse of *Romney Marsh*. For a long time it was an isolated world of its own, 'the fifth quarter of the globe', as the Reverend Richard Barham of Snargate described it in the *Ingoldsby Legends* (1840). 'The World, according to the best geographers, is divided into Europe, Asia, Africa, America and Romney Marsh.' The marsh was notorious for its smugglers, and famous for its sheep and its churches. The glory of the latter reflects the former wealth of this area: All Saints in *Lydd*, the 'Cathedral of Romney Marsh' where Thomas Wolsey was nominally Rector for eleven years; St Nicholas in *New Romney*, one of the Cinque Ports; and above all, St Augustine's in *Brookland*, with its outstanding tower and font, belfry and decorations. The labours of the months and the twelve signs of the zodiac form a double arcaded frieze round the Norman font, which is made of lead and has no equal in Kent or anywhere else in the country. It was probably made by Norman or Flemish craftsmen around 1200. The octagonal belfry (13th–15th century) stands detached from the church, and consists of three tapering pyramids, one on top of the other, all covered with cedar shingles. There are many theories about why the belfry stands alone. My own favourite is that once upon a time a notorious bachelor and an old spinster from Brookland got married, and the belfry was so surprised that it fell off the roof of the church.

The Last Garden: Derek Jarman in Dungeness

South-west of Dover, a spit of land reaches out into the sea like a giant sickle. Its name is *Dungeness*, a no-man's-land consisting of nothing but wind and stone. Every tide builds up new walls of shingle, and these constantly move eastwards. Dungeness, say the locals, is the biggest pile of shingle in the world. Well, at least that makes it different. For miles the coastal road makes its way past shabby bungalows built between the wars, some of them made out of old railway carriages, as temporary as the whole treeless, lifeless, hopeless landscape. Even birds of passage touch down and take off again as quickly as possible.

Derek Jarman

At the end of the promontory stand a few fishermen's huts, two lighthouses, a pub, and a nuclear power station. In the shadow of the giant blocks of concrete and the high tension cables and pylons is the terminus of a narrow-gauge railway. Miniature steam engines bring tourists from Hythe to visit this Atomic Disneyland by the Sea. Dungeness is weird – a surrealist nightmare. And it was here that the British painter and film-maker Derek Jarman created his last and most improbable work: a garden. It presents itself to the road quite unannounced, with no hedge, no fence, no gate – a sudden, totally unexpected splash of colour, a flowering oasis in the grim stony desert of Dungeness. The garden surrounds a fisherman's cottage made of wood, tarred black, with bright yellow mullions. When Derek Jarman bought Prospect Cottage in 1986, he was a man with no prospects at all. He had Aids.

At first he had no thought of creating a garden in this wilderness. Shingle without a crumb of soil; a biting east wind whose salty spray rots everything it touches; storms in winter, scorching heat in summer – what could possibly grow here? He went down to the beach and brought back some flint to create a stone border, 'like dragon's teeth – white and grey'. Behind the cottage he planted a wild rose, using a piece of driftwood as a support, with a chain of perforated stones. And thus, more or less by chance, he began to build his garden.

Even on the beach of Dungeness it turned out that there were more things growing than the casual observer could ever suspect. One plant especially fascinated Jarman: *Crambe maritima*, or sea kale. In March its leaves sprout purple and inky dark, but in May it bursts forth into thousands of tiny white blossoms with a yellow centre. The seeds grow as big as peas, first green and then bone-white. In the autumn winds, the leaves rot, dry, and are blown away. In November nothing is left of the whole plant except its corky stem. It survives because it sinks its roots more than twenty feet down into the shingle. Its dogged determination to go on living made a profound impression on Jarman, and his own fight for survival against all the odds became bound up with that of his garden. Gradually he succeeded in transplanting the wild flowers of Dungeness all round his cottage: straw flowers, thrift, milkwort, cornflowers and corn poppies, rest-harrow, fennel, scabious. For Jarman there was no such thing as a weed. Every plant, even the ugliest, had its own distinctive charm, and some – like the common valerian that flourishes by the roadside in Dungeness during the early part of the summer – could release memories just like Proust's madeleine: 'It grew in the garden of the bomb-damaged house at the end of the road which the airman Johnny, my first love, took me to on his motorbike, with my hands in his trouser pockets – so valerian is a sexy plant for me.'

Be warned, you fans of Sissinghurst who worship the harmony of perfectly designed, beautifully groomed flowerbeds, Derek Jarman's garden is not for you. It has as little to do with the classical English garden as his films had to do with Hollywood. The rubbish alone will put you off: driftwood, rusty poles and chains, and whatever else he could find on the beach, Jarman would lay out among his plants – symbols of some other, wilder, more fantastic Nature. An anchor chain winds its way through herbal beds, ending up in lobster claws. Iron triangles dangle from wooden posts – the æolian harps of Dungeness. A spade handle pokes out here, a washed-out rubber glove flexes its fingers there, as if reaching forth from a garden long buried beneath the stones. Rusty forks and springs, charred timbers, boathooks, empty cartridges, corks from fishing nets – Jarman saw them all as landscape: *Modern Nature*, which is the title of one of his diaries.

Derek Jarman's garden has a rough, melancholy beauty all its own. Stones and flowers – the hard and the tender – keep each other company here in a manner you will find nowhere else. Where can one draw the borderline between the sweetness of contact and the violence of injury? The posts and stelæ and phallic timbers may be taken as symbols of the homosexuality that gave Jarman's films a special, anarchic poetry and pathos, but more than anything else, this is the garden of a painter. There are subtly gradated circles of white, grey and greyish blue shingle, and of gorse and sage. The blue of the cornflowers, hyacinths, bellflowers, borage, lavender and viper's bugloss echo the cobalt blue of the sea. His last film was called *Blue* and was made solely in that colour – a picture to end all pictures. It was dedicated to the painter Yves Klein, who once said that behind the blue there was more than met the eye.

'Paradise haunts gardens, and some gardens are paradises. Mine is one of them.' In his last years, Derek Jarman spent more and more of his time in Dungeness. Prospect Cottage, which had once been his weekend retreat from London, now became his permanent home. There he painted, wrote, planned new films, and tended his paradise garden. The knowledge that he had Aids seemed to give him extra energy. He knew that brooding wouldn't help. 'I don't think it's much help to think: "This is my last year." It could well be, but I've been living my last year for the last six, and I'm still just here.'

Bees hum round the garden, and lizards scurry over the stones. Gulls, crows, and in wintertime cormorants fill the air with their cries. Even in darkest Dungeness, Derek Jarman was seldom alone. Friends were constantly popping in, and acquaintances and even total strangers wanted to say hello. As film-maker and self-confessed gay, he had become an institution, whether he liked it or not – a holy heretic who acted out his role with typical British self-irony: St Derek of Dungeness. Together with a young photographer he visited Great Dixter and other famous gardens in the south of England, bringing back new plants. He installed a beehive, surrounded by herbs and vegetables. The garden was his therapy and his pharmacopœia. 'I can look at one plant for an hour, this brings me great peace.'

Jarman's gardening book, botanically precise and accurate, is also the diary of a slow death. His garden prose is constantly interrupted by verses that movingly capture the loss of friends and of himself. 'I walk in this garden / holding the hands of dead friends. / Old age came quickly for my frosted generation, / cold, cold, cold, they died so silently.' In his film *The Garden* (1990) he speaks this line himself: 'Cold, cold, cold, I die so silently.' In a scene on the beach he lies naked on a bed, racked with pain, with waves washing around him, and men and women dancing with torches. *The Garden* is a version of the Passion, autobiographical like all his films, shot under the pylons of Dungeness and in his garden: 'Gethsemane and Eden'.

One of the paradoxes of this garden is the fact that the weaker Jarman became, the more it flourished. As long as he could, he went on devotedly tending his plants, even when he himself was beyond nursing. He even succeeded in rescuing a plant that had long since disappeared from the English coast and was threatened with total extinction: *Crepis fœtida*, stinking hawk's beard. In the final stages of his illness, he became almost blind as a result of the drugs he was taking. He could no longer see the colours of his plants, but he could smell their scents, and inhaled them like a bee sucking nectar: the heavy sweetness of the gorse and the sea kale, the sharpness of the tulips, the fragrance of the sage and wallflowers. And the lavender smelt blue. When the storms came, they blew away the scents, leaving only the smell of seaweed and algæ.

Derek Jarman died in London in 1994. Before he died, he had the south wall of Prospect Cottage decorated with lines from John Donne's *The Sunne Rising*, which starts: 'Busy old Foole, unruly sun...' a complaint by a lover annoyed at being woken too early by the interfering orb. Donne was a kindred spirit – a metaphysical poet whose Baroque imagery and analysis of emotion greatly appealed to Jarman. In a poem called *The Paradox*, Donne wrote his own epitaph, which might apply equally well to a man dying of Aids: 'Love-slaine, loe, here I lye.'

Since Jarman's death, his partner Keith Collins has been living in Prospect Cottage. In Jarman's film of *Edward II*, he played the part of the assassin who gives a last kiss to the dying King. Now he looks after the garden, which is no easy task since the garden has no fence but very many admirers. They come from London and Liverpool, Holland and Japan – film-fans, tourists, horticulturalists, gays, and plain and simple gardeners. Reverently they pick their way through the stones, wonder at the plants that grow there, gaze through the windows, and take their photos and make their videos. Some also bring items with them – objects found on the beach, strange shapes of wood and iron, offerings to St Derek of Dungeness. In the evening, when the fans have gone, Keith quietly carries them all back to the beach.

From Broadstairs to Rochester: Dickens was here

Jane Austen once said that Kent was 'the only place for happiness'. Sir Noël Coward had a farmhouse in Romney Marsh, Richard Ingrams a cottage near Camber Sands, and the Kent coast was Charles Dickens's favourite holiday destination. Between Ramsgate and Margate, he found his favourite holiday spot: Broadstairs, one of the 'freshest, freest watering places in the world'. When he first went there in 1837, it was a simple fishing village. Today it is an open-air Dickens museum. In the 'Charles Dickens' restaurant, you can drink as he wrote – namely, in instalments. There is an 'Oliver Twist Bar', a 'Nickleby Lounge', and a 'Pickwick Bar' – all named after novels which he began or finished in Broadstairs. Dickens fans who wish to use his novels as pub-guides to Kent may go for a drink in the 'Barnaby Rudge' in Albion Street, and can spend the night in the same street at No. 40, a hotel where apparently the master stayed no fewer than five times.

Nearby is the Dickens Museum, where the resolute Mary Strong once lived, immortalised as Miss Betsy Trotwood in *David Copperfield*. Disappointment will await you in Harbour Street, though, where The Old Curiosity Shop is nothing but a Tatty Souvenir Shop.

In June Dickens-lovers descend on Broadstairs for the Dickens Festival. A week of readings, plays, films and dance brings together the members of the *Dickens Fellowship*, founded in 1902, plus countless other fans dressed up as Scrooge, Sam Weller, Pickwick himself, Mr Micawber, and a host of other loveable goodies and baddies. But the highlight for any true aficionado is the house on the cliff, Dickens' favourite nest after

Mr. Pickwick

1850. Bleak House, named after the novel rather than the other way round, is a museum with atmosphere and a stunning view. It also contains the glass he drank

Mr. Bumble and Mrs.
Corney take a cup of tea:
illustration by George
Cruikshank for
Oliver Twist

from, the last collar he wore, historic photographs, theatre programmes, illustrations by George Cruikshank, and of course his legendary writing chair, completely worn out. There is also a genealogical tree of later owners. Upstairs, in the room with the bay window looking out on Viking Bay, Dickens would work every day from nine till one on *David Copperfield*. In the afternoon he would go down to the beach for a swim, like 'a kind of salmon-coloured porpoise', as he put it. Of course he used the bathing-machine constructed in 1753 by the Quaker Benjamin Beale of *Margate*, in order to shut out the prying eyes and gossiping tongues. (Perhaps Margate was worse than other places: Thomas Gray sniffily called it 'Bartholomew Fair by the seaside'.) The bathing-machine was a wonderfully English invention – an island within an island.

Turner thought the peninsula of Thanet had the finest sky in all Europe. Little wonder, then, that it was in Margate that he met the love of his life, Sophia Booth. The town is still tacky enough to appeal to young lovers, but plans are afoot to make it more up-market by building a large modern eyesore on the front – a Turner Museum, naturally. Neighbouring *Ramsgate*, another resort much beloved of the bathing classes, claims a milder climate than its close rival and a superior list of visitors. In 1876 the 23-year-old Vincent van Gogh spent a miserable year in Ramsgate as a teacher. Before him, in 1827, the German poet Heinrich Heine was here, but in his *Englische Fragmente* never deigns to mention the fact, preferring to rail against Wellington, who had dared to defeat his idol Napoleon. While German neo-Gothic was reaching its peak in the building of Cologne Cathedral (for which all that was needed was to follow the original plans), A. W. N. Pugin was conducting his own Gothic Revival in Ramsgate – starting from first principles. Or so he would have had us believe; in fact England's Gothic Revival came in two waves, like the Pretenders; Horace Walpole was the principal mover in the first (spelt with a k) and Pugin in the second (much more serious and godly). Pugin's genius as a medievalist can be seen throughout the Palace of Westminster, where he designed everything from sculptures and decorations of the façade to the wallpaper, inkwells and hatstands inside. He moved to Ramsgate because he loved sailing and messing about in boats. He also had scope for fulfilling his religious and artistic dreams right next to his own house, *The Grange* (1843). St Augustine's (1845-50) is a church designed by him, and financed by him. With it Pugin rejected contemporary neoclassicism and harked back to the Catholic Middle Ages (Pugin, ever consistent, had converted to Catholicism). According to him, Christian architecture could only have pointed arches. In 1851, worn out by incessant work and travelling, Pugin became mentally deranged, and he died at The Grange in 1852 at the age of 40. He was buried in his own church. The Grange lay empty for years, but is now in the care of the Landmark Trust, who are planning to repair it.

Another illustrious Victorian died on Thanet – the poet and painter Dante Gabriel Rossetti, son of an Italian political refugee and free thinker. Like Pugin he was an advocate of medieval Christian art – the name he originally wanted to give to the Pre-Raphaelite Brotherhood, of which he was a joint founder. Again like Pugin he was tormented by depression in his later years. His paintings and sonnets depict the typical Pre-Raphaelite *femme fatale*: a gallery of consumptive, scarlet-lipped, red-haired Madonnas and Medusas, Botticellis and Androgynæ greatly detested by Dickens. In the southern nave of the church at *Birchington* is a memorial window for Rossetti, painted by one of his friends. Another, Ford Madox Brown, carved a Celtic cross for him near the south door. Pre-Raphaelite enthusiasts will make their way from Rossetti's grave straight to *Bexleyheath*. In former times this was still part of the country, and not a suburb of the great metropolis, and there, in Red House Lane, Philip Webb built a red-brick house for his friend William Morris (1858). Rossetti said it was more of a poem than a house. Morris – Topsy to his friends – wanted something medieval in style, but in fact it turned out to be entirely Morris in feel, and has in turn inspired generations of architects, from Arts and Crafts to our own time. The interior decorations by Morris and his friends have only survived in fragments, including a cupboard painted by Edward Burne-Jones with scenes from the German Nibelungenlied. After decades in the

Chatham Naval Base: The Clocktower

devoted hands of one family, who entertained architectural visitors to tea on the lawn, Red House (Morris always dispensed with the definite article) is now in the hands of the National Trust, who can always be relied upon to keep tea traditions going.

Chatham is a port and an industrial centre, and it was here in 1817 that the painter Richard Dadd was born. After murdering his father, he spent 43 years in madhouses, where he painted powerful, hallucinatory pictures crowded with sinister fairy figures, which today hang in the Tate Gallery and other museums. The Medway here was the site of one of the major battles of the Roman invasion, won after two days by the future emperor Vespasian. It has remained a key military site, and after Portsmouth, Chatham was once the most important dockyard for the royal fleet. One of the most brilliant naval exploits in all history happened in June 1667, when the Dutch admiral Tromp penetrated the defences to sink or burn fifteen of the greatest ships in the British navy without a shot being fired, and – ultimate humiliation – to tow the 100-gun *Royal Charles* to Holland, where its magnificent stern can still be seen in the Rijksmuseum. Recovery was swift however, and the Royal Dockyard at the mouth of the Medway is said to be the biggest and most perfect complex of Georgian and Victorian marine architecture in the world. 'The buildings here are indeed like the ships themselves, surprisingly large, and in their several kinds beautiful,' wrote Daniel Defoe in 1720. Nelson's *Victory* and many other famous ships were built here, but after four centuries of continuous use, the docks were finally closed in 1984.

It was in Chatham, where his father worked as a clerk in the navy pay office, that Charles Dickens spent some of the happiest days of his childhood ('the birth-place of my fancy'), and on the other side of the Medway in his country house Gad's Hill, he spent his last, restless years. Dickens had loved this Georgian brick house since childhood: 'my poor father used to bring me to look at it, and used to say that if ever I grew up to be a clever man, that perhaps I might own that house or another such.' Dickens eventually bought it in 1856, and built a tunnel under the main road to a patch of wilderness where he installed the Swiss chalet in which he liked to write, and where he enjoyed some moments of domestic content. The painter Frith found him one day surrounded by a troop of grandchildren. '"What do they keep calling you?" said I. "They are obedient children," replied Dickens. "Their infant lives would not be worth five minutes' purchase if they called me grandpa. My name is *wenerables* to them." As the word alternated between wen-bull, winible, wenapple etc. in the infantine chorus,' wrote the puzzled Frith, 'I was obliged to ask for an interpretation.'

Dickens' older friends were treated just as imperiously: a visit to him was 'slavery' wrote one friend, with work compulsory before 2 pm, a ten mile walk followed by orange brandy compulsory in the afternoon; games, drinking and smoking equally enforced in the evening. And for the host even more than the guests it was generally a frantic, driven life, as Dickens – separated from his wife, – was conducting a secret affair with a young actress, Ellen Ternan, writing incessantly and embarking on his exhausting though lucrative reading tours. Small wonder that he was only 58, and still writing *Edwin Drood*, when he collapsed with a stroke at his desk at Gad's Hill, and died the next day.

That main road through Gad's Hill to Dover was the haunt of highwaymen for centuries; the most famous was Falstaff, who robbed and was robbed here in *Henry IV, Part 1*. The pub opposite Dickens' House is called the Falstaff, but the reality behind Shakespeare's fat knight was one Sir John Oldcastle, whose own old castle still stands, in part, at *Cooling*, just to the north. It was in the lonely churchyard there that Pip met Magwitch in *Great Expectations*; Pip was communing with his little brothers and sisters, for whom Dickens was inspired by the graves of thirteen small children, when he was collared by the convict, who had just escaped from the nearby hulks (decommissioned boats used as prisons). This ghostly place has just escaped being turned by New Labour into yet another airport to serve the growing 'needs' of the 'boom economy' south-east.

In neighbouring *Cobham*, which according to Mr Pickwick 'for a misanthrope's choice… is one of the prettiest and most desirable residences I have ever met with', even teetotallers are seen to descend on 'Leather Bottle Inn' (1629), a Dickens pub museum *par excellence*. And directly opposite, in the church of St Mary Magdalene, even confirmed atheists are seen to fall on their knees, for in the floor of the chancel are no fewer than eighteen brass figures, memorial slabs to priests, knights and their ladies, and you are allowed to do rubbings and carry them home with you. Kent is the land of brass, but no church has as large a collection of these monumental slabs as Cobham. They go from 1320 to 1529, and together they make up a unique history of families, costumes and weaponry. The figures, nearly always seen straight on, tend to be types rather than portraits, like the knight in his armour, or the priest in his cassock. These brasses seem to be a form of art as peculiarly English as the Perpendicular or cricket. But the use of engraved brass slabs as monuments was in fact imported from the Low Countries at the end of the 13th century. The English achievement was two-fold: to create drama (and economy) by cutting the figures out of the square brass plates; and to have fewer wars and commotions when men would find it expedient to rip up old bits of militarily useful metal. Over 10,000 brasses survive in England; not even a tenth of that number survive in the whole of the Continent.

The centre and E-plan of Cobham Hall (1580–1670) are late Elizabethan. Built of red brick, with four domed towers and surrounded by cedars and oaks, it lies in the midst of Humphrey Repton's landscaped gardens. Repton designed some 200 gardens and parks. Unlike his predecessor Capability Brown, he never allowed the picturesque freedom of Nature to come too close to the house, but preferred a more controlled approach, with terraces and flowerbeds. Cobham Hall is now a girls' boarding-school, but some of its finest rooms are still intact – especially the Gilt Hall, converted into a Music Room in 1779. Among its splendours are the gilded plaster ceiling of 1672, James Wyatt's wall decorations in the style of Adam (1790), and a Baroque organ built by Johann Snetzler, who came from Passau and settled in England. If you toss a 50p coin, you have a 50-50 chance of finding a connection with Cobham Hall: before she became Lady Cobham, and while she was still serving at the court of Charles II's wife Catherine of Braganza, the beautiful Frances Theresa Stewart posed for the copper engraver Roettier as Britannia. When 'La Belle Stuart' delivered a basket to the King, it was he who called upon her to be the model. If he couldn't have her in his bed, at least he could put her in his pocket.

There is no proof that Charles II spent the night before the Restoration (1660) in Restoration House, Maidstone Road, *Rochester,* but there is no disputing the fact that Charles Dickens had his Miss Havisham (*Great Expectations*) reside there. Dickens fans, like the Pickwickians, will of course spend the night at the 'Royal Victoria and Bull' (18th century), though they should not be surprised if the 'silent High Street' has in the meantime become rather less silent. At the end of this street,

Rochester from the Medway,
by Joseph Pennell

opposite a Tudor half-timbered house, Dickensians will at once recognize Eastgate House as 'Nun's House' (*Edwin Drood*). Today this Elizabethan red-brick build-ing houses yet another Dickens museum, with spectacular theme rooms and an audiovisual 'Dickens Dream'. The Swiss chalet from Gad's Hill is also here. Dickens hated all pomp and circumstance, and wanted to be buried in 'Cloisterham', the name he gave to Rochester, but *The Times* demanded that he be buried in Westminster Abbey. And so now his ghost restlessly searches for peace among the gravestones of St Nicholas. While on the subject of Rochester ghosts, pride of place must certainly go to Lady Blanche de Warenne. Her husband fired an arrow that was meant to hit her lover, but hit her instead, and now she can be seen alone and palely loitering at the top of the Norman keep – the tallest in England (after 1127). "'Ah, fine place!'" says Jingle in *Pickwick Papers*, "'glorious pile—frowning walls—tottering arches—dark nooks—crumbling staircases—.'" From the castle, once an important junction between Watling Street and the Medway, we can look down on the Cathedral, not grand but ancient and loveable (see p. 40), the cement works in the valley, and at the end of the bay the houses of Sheerness.

A Strange German Charles: Uwe Johnson in Sheerness

Sheerness, observed Samuel Pepys in his diary of August 1665, is 'a most proper place – but only for docks.' Today the naval dockyards have gone, and the port is England's biggest handler of motor cars. *Sheerness-on-Sea* lies ahead of the mouth of the Thames, on the north-western edge of the flat, almost treeless Isle of Sheppey. 'It's not very nice,' wrote the famous German author Uwe Johnson in August 1974 to his friend Max Frisch. One month later, he and his family moved to Sheerness. Ten years later he died there. What, then, attracted him to such an apparently unattractive place? Was it the lure of the unfamiliar? The search for new experiences, as when he went to New York, to enable him to write the last volume of *Jahrestage* ('The Anniversaries')? Or simply the desire to get away from West Berlin, where he never felt at home? 'What brought you to Sheerness?' asked a local. 'That's what I'm trying to find out,' replied the stranger from Mecklenburg.

No. 26 Marine Parade stands behind a high concrete wall built to keep out the floods. It's a white plastered terrace house with a bay window and a pointed gable. Only from the living-room on the first floor could Johnson actually see the sea, and gaze at Southend across the Thames Estuary. In the evening he could see the two flashing light-buoys that mark the wreck of the *Richard Montgomery*, an American munitions ship which ran aground in the summer of 1944 and is still highly explosive. The locals regard it as their only tourist attraction, while for Uwe Johnson it was a piece of German history, which he described, in great detail, in *Das Schiff* ('The Ship', 1979).

His writing-desk was in the basement, under an enormous station clock with Roman numerals. On the walls were maps of Mecklenburg and an ærial view of Manhattan. On the bookshelves, 160 reference books, collected issues of *The New York Times*, telephone directories, textbooks, town plans – relics of an author who was obsessed with detail. There he sat, shutters closed, conjuring up memories, surrounded by the raw material of his autobiographical character Gesine Cresspahl. His wife and daughter entered this cellar

Uwe Johnson

study 'as rarely as if it was a no-go area'. At first the locals called him the Shakespeare of Sheerness but later even his neighbours thought this quiet man had simply retired here. 'They don't want to know anything about me as a German. They just want to talk about fishing and the weather.'

Nothing ever happened in Sheerness, which made it the ideal place for writing. But eventually Sheerness became a living hell. Anyone who reads *Skizze eines*

Unglücklichen ('Sketches of an Unhappy Man') will get a good idea of married life at No. 26 Marine Parade. After three traumatic years, Elizabeth Johnson moved out in 1978 to a house just a few streets away. There was no divorce, but they never spoke to each other again. The domestic crisis led to a creative crisis, and writer's block led to depression, drink, and self-destruction.

At half past six in the evening he would enter 'The Napier', sit down on his customary stool on the extreme left of the bar, and drink eight pints of Hürlimann Lager, topped off with a double whisky and tomato juice. Generally he would say nothing and just note down odd turns of phrase on his cigarette packet. A strange fellow, always dressed in black – black leather boots, black peaked cap, keeping himself to himself, often quite brusque, but also generous. He called himself Charles, and sometimes even signed himself Charles Uwe Johnson. At around nine o'clock he would get up and go. Then back in his living-room, he carried on drinking Spanish red wine, and gazing out of the window at the water and the light-buoys over the wreck of the *Montgomery*. Thus he lived in Sheerness much as Gesine Cresspahl lived in New York, 'with relentless homesickness for Mecklenburg'. Sometimes he had visitors: Max Frisch, Günter Kunert, or his publisher Siegfried Unseld. Sometimes he travelled. As Charlie, he would take a train to London and from there fly to Frankfurt or New York, where as Uwe Johnson he would give public readings. This was the double life he described in letters to friends. From such trips he would always return with relief to his writer's cubbyhole in Sheerness. At last, it seemed, he had come through the crisis. He wrote a few *Inselgeschichten* ('Island Stories') and the Frankfurt lectures on poetics, and in 1983 the fourth and final volume of *Jahrestage* was finally published and hailed by the critics as his masterpiece. It seemed like a rebirth.

A few months later, on 12 March 1984, Uwe Johnson was found dead in his house. He had actually died 17 days before of a heart attack, while sitting in his armchair in the living-room, gazing out at the night sky and the black sea. He was 49. In accordance with his will, he was cremated 'without music, speeches, flowers and any sort of religious or other sermon.' His urn was buried in the cemetery behind the marshlands, in double grave Nr. 53/54, sector XD. Siegfried Unseld and Suhrkamp Verlag, the author's sole heirs, set up an Uwe Johnson Archive at Frankfurt University. It includes a reconstruction of his basement study, complete with station clock over the writing-desk, just as it was at 26 Marine Parade.

Becket, or The Glory of Canterbury

Kent is the only county with two dioceses: Rochester and Canterbury. Rochester Cathedral is mainly Norman, consecrated in 1190, and initiated by Bishop Gundulf, who built the White Tower in London. The west door (*c.* 1160) is

*Two of Chaucer's pilgims, after the Ellesmere MS: the Man of Law, who 'rood but homly',
and the Priest, whose horse was in 'greet estaat', and whose bridle men might hear
'Gynglen in a whistlynge wynd als cleere/ And eek as loude as dooth the chapel belle'*

flanked by two of the oldest church sculptures in England: *Solomon* and the
Queen of Sheba. Together with the tympanum and archivolts, the doorway harks
back to French models such as St Denis near Paris. The wide, low nave is Norman,
but architecturally more impressive is the crypt, with its Early English vault. The
choir contains two notable features: the wheel of fortune, a well preserved fragment from a 13th century fresco, and some of the oldest choir stalls in England (*c.*
1227). The sarcophagus of Bishop Walter de Merton, founder of Merton College
Oxford, replaced that of a baker: St William of Perth, a Scottish pilgrim, who was
attacked by robbers just outside the city in 1201, and murdered – just like
Archbishop Thomas Becket, whose grave he was travelling to see.

Becket's bloody end was the beginning of a pilgrimage boom in Canterbury.
The crowds visiting the Cathedral will have been no smaller than the flocks of
tourists who go there today, for in the Middle Ages such pilgrimages, whether on
foot or on horseback, were the only common form of group travel. Some idea of
the numbers can be guessed by looking at the width of the ambulatory around
Becket's shrine in the Cathedral: it looks as if it were designed for maximum
throughput and visibility for pilgrims in rows eight deep. The mixture of piety and
pleasure was immortalised in Chaucer's *Canterbury Tales*. 'And specially from
every shires ende / Of Engelond to Caunterbury they wende.' Chaucer's twenty-

Drawn by G. Cattermole.

Engraved by J. Le Keux.

CANTERBURY CATHEDRAL CHURCH,
VIEW OF THE WESTERN TOWERS.

TO THE REV? GEORGE D'OYLY, D.D. F.R.S. *DOMESTIC CHAPLAIN TO THE ARCHBISHOP OF CANTERBURY* &c. &c. &c.
This Plate is inscribed by the
AUTHOR.

nine pilgrims meet at the Tabard Inn in Southwark, and leave London along the Roman Watling Street. The merchant rides alongside the prioress, whose brooch bears the inscription *Amor vincit omnia*. The monk seduces the merchant's wife, the canon turns out to be an alchemist, and the Wife of Bath entertains the company with the story of her five marriages. Chaucer (1343-1400) had a day job as customs officer, but he was considered a national treasure for his poetry in his lifetime, and the reputation has never really faded. Caxton called him 'the worshipful father and first founder and embellisher of ornate eloquence in our English'; James Joyce said he was 'the clearest master in the language: he is as precise and slick as a Frenchman'; Dryden simply said 'Here's God's plenty.' And it was to Chaucer that another great printer turned when he wanted to revive the greatness of the craft, and recreate its medieval richness: William Morris made his *Canterbury Tales* a veritable bible of the art of printing, with medieval illuminated borders, and 87 woodcuts by Edward Burne-Jones – the *Kelmscott Chaucer* (1896).

The English equivalent of the great continental pilgrim routes from Vézelay and elsewhere to Santiago de Compostela was the Pilgrims' Way from Winchester to *Canterbury* – a path used even in prehistoric times along the slopes of the North Downs. After many long days, the weary traveller would suddenly be confronted, through the mists of the Stour Valley, by the silver-grey glory of the Cathedral rising high above the red roofs of Canterbury. If the name of this route has now shrunk to the symbol A2, the vision itself remains intact. Pilgrims used to enter Canterbury through *Westgate* (1; numbers refer to map on the inside back flap), which is now a museum and is the only surviving gate (1375–81) out of seven. Rich people found lodgings in the vicinity of the Cathedral itself, but the rest went to *Eastbridge Hospital* (3) (c. 1190) in the High Street, or to one of the two monasteries on the Stour: Blackfriars, run by the Dominicans, or Greyfriars (4), which was the first monastery built in England (1224) by the Franciscans. It is now a ruin. Pilgrims can still get rooms in Eastbridge Hospital, opposite the half-timbered houses with pointed gables where immigrant Huguenot weavers once plied their trade in the 16th century. Chaucer's pilgrims slept in some of the 100 beds at 'Chequers of Hope' in Mercery Lane. The lane has survived intact, with its medieval narrowness and its overhanging walls, a needle-thin line of shops and souvenirs threading its way between the High Street and the Cathedral. Here you could buy your pilgrim's gear – your hat, lead Beckets of all sizes, and phials of the saint's blood, which the monks managed miraculously to keep diluting from 1170 till the dissolution of the monasteries in 1538. The final destination, of course, was the *Cathedral* (10), and a touch of the martyr's sarcophagus. Becket's

The West Front of Canterbury Cathedral at the beginning of the 19th century, before the drastic restoration which replaced the original Norman tower on the left with a reproduction of the Gothic tower on the right

golden shrine was covered with jewels, 'glittering more than Midas' gold,' wrote Erasmus of Rotterdam when he came here in 1512. But what, he wondered, would Becket have said about the poverty of the people all around?

The treasure was the spectacular relic of a spectacular story. Thomas Becket embodied the conflict of his time. In his youth, he was chancellor and drinking companion to Henry II, whose policies he supported unconditionally, even if they were in opposition to the church. But when Henry appointed him Archbishop of Canterbury in 1162, Becket proved equally intransigent in defending the interests of the Church against the King. The conflict over matters of law, church livings, and privileges ended on 29 December 1170. Becket had just returned from exile in France, and at the King's behest – 'Will no one rid me of this turbulent priest?' – was murdered by four knights in the north-west transept. Four years later Henry II, who had been excommunicated, had himself scourged by monks at the martyr's grave – an act of political humiliation that was to seal the triumph of Becket and the power of the Pope in England. A king and a prince were buried on either side of the saint: Edward, the Black Prince, the 'flower of English knighthood' in the Hundred Years' War, with his armour (now, alas in replica) above the bronze figure of the Prince himself, armed cap-à-pie; and opposite him, magnificent alabaster sculptures of another king in search of absolution, Henry IV, and his queen consort, Joan of Navarre (d. 1437). The fact that the Archbishop's shrine was considerably richer than those of his royal neighbours would not have escaped the attention of Henry VIII when he welcomed the young Emperor Charles V here in 1520. Unlike Henry II, Henry VIII got himself an Archbishop of Canterbury, Thomas Cranmer, who gave him everything he wanted: a divorce, supremacy over the church, and all the treasures of the monasteries including Becket's shrine – some 26 cartloads containing over 3000 pounds of gold. But even this archbishop ended up as a martyr, under the Catholic Mary, though he was not regarded as a holy martyr since he had been on the wrong side. It was Cranmer who introduced the Book of Common Prayer in 1549.

What happened to Becket afterwards? It is said that his remains were burnt in 1538, and the ashes strewn to the winds. Henry VIII had his name struck from the list of saints. There was to be nothing left of this Catholic 'traitor' who had been venerated by the people because he had defied the authority of the State. And yet the rumour persists that the holy bones are still in existence, hidden in a secret place known only to the faithful few. This, at any rate, is the theory of John Butler, Professor at the University of Kent, who has written a book called *The Quest for Becket's Bones* (1995).

Since the Reformation, the Archbishop of Canterbury has always been appointed by the reigning monarch (as the sole and supreme governor of the Church of England), and as primate with responsibility for some 70 million Anglicans worldwide, he must swear allegiance to the Crown. As compensation,

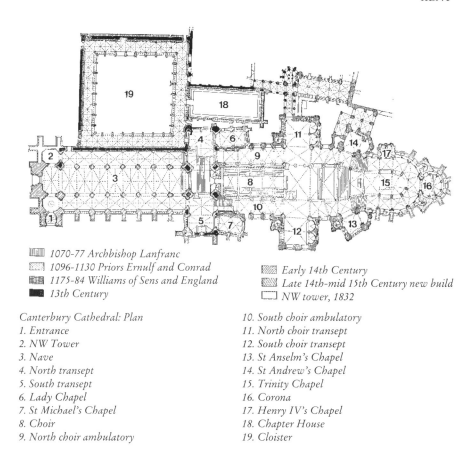

IIIIIII *1070-77 Archbishop Lanfranc*
▨ *1096-1130 Priors Ernulf and Conrad*
▦ *1175-84 Williams of Sens and England*
▮ *13th Century*

▧ *Early 14th Century*
▨ *Late 14th-mid 15th Century new build*
☐ *NW tower, 1832*

Canterbury Cathedral: Plan
1. Entrance
2. NW Tower
3. Nave
4. North transept
5. South transept
6. Lady Chapel
7. St Michael's Chapel
8. Choir
9. North choir ambulatory

10. South choir ambulatory
11. North choir transept
12. South choir transept
13. St Anselm's Chapel
14. St Andrew's Chapel
15. Trinity Chapel
16. Corona
17. Henry IV's Chapel
18. Chapter House
19. Cloister

however, it is he who places the crown on every new monarch's head.

The feet of countless generations of pilgrims have worn down the steps of this great cathedral, tramping from the nave to the choir, from the choir to the Trinity Chapel (15). Here, behind the altar, nothing remains of Becket's shrine except some marble tiles worn smooth. The Becket windows in the ambulatory of the Trinity Chapel managed to escape both Henry's vindictiveness towards 'this mock saint', as Defoe called him, and the vandalism of the Puritans: the windows depict the miracles of St Thomas and are themselves miracles of medieval stained glass (*c.* 1220), as are the windows of the northern aisle of the choir and the south-west transept. The glowing colours and expressiveness of the figures match the very best French stained glass windows in Chartres and Bourges. One of the finest wall paintings of English Romanesque is the fresco in the apse of the St Anselm Chapel (13) (*Paul and the Snake on Malta, c.* 1160), in form and colour much akin to

45

Canterbury Cathedral from Mercery Lane

English illuminations and the Norman mosaics in Sicily. This chapel is devoted to the father of medieval scholarship and mysticism, Archbishop Anselm of Canterbury, who came into conflict with successive kings by defending Pope Gregory VII's ideas on investiture. The frescos (*c.* 1130) of St Gabriel's Chapel in the crypt are less well preserved than the figured capitals of fighting men and animals, archetypal expressions of the fantasy and vitality of the Norman conquerors. This crypt (begun in 1096), with its alternating plain and ornamented columns, is more spacious and more majestic than any of its predecessors in England. It is probably the only part of the whole cathedral that Thomas Becket would recognize today.

The history of the cathedral's construction is fairly complex. On the ruins of the Church of Christ, St Augustine's Anglo-Saxon church, the first Norman Archbishop of Canterbury, the scholar Lanfranc, built a cathedral (1070–77) similar to that of his former Abbey of St Etienne in Caen. The choir burnt down in 1174, and was rebuilt by the stonemason William of Sens with pointed arches, three bays and a clerestory, in the Early Gothic style of the Ile de France. Canterbury Cathedral is the first example of the new Early English style, but it also reveals the independence of Early English Gothic with its double transepts.

When the French William fell from the scaffolding in 1179, an English William took over the eastern extension of the Cathedral that was to house Becket's shrine: the Trinity Chapel with its polished coupled columns, and the corona (16) – the round chapel with the white marble throne which, since the 13th century, has been used for the installation of all the Archbishops of Canterbury. Under Henry Yevele, the King's architect and builder of Westminster Hall, the Norman nave and transepts were demolished and new ones built (1391–1405) in the Perpendicular style. In 1500 Bell Harry, the crossing tower (so-called because of its bell), with its intricate tracery, finally soared above the rest of the great edifice – a sight never seen by Chaucer's pilgrims. Nor did they see the Perpendicular magnificence of Christ Church Gate (1517) with its grandiose oak door, right beside the entrance to Pizzaland. Since 1995 you have to pay at the gate of Cathedral Close, as is the case now with many museums. This is no bad thing. A city of some 30,000 inhabitants is invaded every year by some 2.5 million visitors, and virtually every one of them heads for the Cathedral. Restoration has been going on systematically since 1908, and that is an expensive business. All the stonemasonry is done in Caen, Normandy, with the grey stone that is quarried there. A poster in the Cathedral succinctly sums up the long history and the present crisis: 'St Augustine founded it. Becket died for it. Chaucer wrote about it. Cromwell shot at it. Hitler bombed it. Time is destroying it.'

There are plenty of heraldic shields to be seen on the *Christ Church Gate* (9), but nowhere near as many as on the 825 brightly painted bosses of the Cloister's lierne vaults (1397–1411). To the east is the Chapter House (begun in 1304), where in 1986 Margaret Thatcher and François Mitterand signed the agreement for the construction of the Channel Tunnel. The Chapter House was also the setting for the first performance of T. S. Eliot's *Murder in the Cathedral* in 1935, commissioned for the Canterbury Festival – a modern version of a medieval tale which Elizabethan dramatists never dared to tackle. Even the bold Christopher Marlowe, who was born in 1564 (the same year as Shakespeare), the son of a Canterbury shoemaker, steered clear of the local saint and preferred to tell the story of the less than holy Dr Faustus. Based on a translation of the German legend published in the *Volksbuch* (1587), the

Dr. Faustus, from the first edition of Marlowe's play

play became part of the repertoire of English companies touring Germany during the 16th century. Marlowe's critique of Christianity – 'the first beginning of Religion was to keep men in awe' – made this darling of the Muses highly suspect,

both for his atheism and for his politics. He is believed to have been a secret agent, but no one knows whether it was politics, love, drunkenness, or what we would now call 'aggro' that led to his being stabbed to death in a Deptford pub in 1593. He was just 29 years old. In St Margaret's Street is the hulking Marlowe Theatre, where productions of contemporary English plays must of necessity seem meagre, set against the lavish scale of a *Tamburlaine*.

Marlowe was educated at King's School, which claims to have been founded in 598 and thus to be England's oldest school. Later students included Walter Pater and Somerset Maugham. Maugham hated the place, which he described with vivd satire in his autobiographical *Of Human Bondage* (1915). But he still had his ashes buried here, in a malachite container in the garden of the Library which he had endowed. Lawrence Durrell went to school in Canterbury as well, at St Edmund's in the north-west of the city, which also boasts a university founded in 1965 and built on St Thomas Hill. Here the architecturally outstanding building is Chaucer College, designed by John Partridge in 1991, and built with Japanese finance as a residence for 200 students from Japan.

Font in St Martin's, Canterbury

The fact that King Ethelbert gave St Augustine some building-land outside the city walls may be regarded as an act of far-sighted planning. Augustine, the first Archbishop of Canterbury, founded an abbey there in 598, and next to Monte Cassino this became the most important Benedictine monastery in Europe. Its rival, the Cathedral monastery, only came out of its shadow when Becket was murdered. Then pilgrims decided that they might get greater miracles out of the new saint than out of the old one buried in the abbey church. The foundations of *St Augustine's Abbey* (12), as well as of three Anglo-Saxon churches, can be seen in the grounds of St Augustine's College (1844-73 by William Butterfield, but incorporating medieval buildings), an Anglican mission school. On the hill above stands *St Martin's Church*, where Augustine and King Ethelbert's wife, the Frankish Princess Bertha, are said to have prayed together. Parts of the chancel are of Roman brick, and there is a Norman font with arched and circular ornamentation. This is perhaps the oldest surviving place of Christian worship in England, surrounded by graves and ancient yews, and away from the hustle and bustle of the Cathedral City, where the walls of Agnes' house lean out even more than they did in David Copperfield's day, 'so that I fancied the whole house was leaning forward, trying to see who was passing on the narrow pavement below.'

Canterbury Cathedral: Cloister

Pilgrims Without a Church: Walking as Art

Right of way is fundamental to an Englishman. England may well hold the world record for the number of signs indicating 'footpath', and one might say that the nation's sacred cow is not the monarchy but the countryside. There is no corner of this earth that has not been trodden by British feet. It is therefore no coincidence that two Englishmen have declared walking to be an art form: Hamish Fulton and Richard Long. They both studied at St Martin's School of Art in London in the late 1960s, and they swiftly jettisoned traditional concepts. Since 1969 Hamish Fulton has practised the art of roaming the countryside. He now has thousands of miles of art behind him. He can cover up to 35 miles a day, generally alone, through unin-habited regions in Britain, Iceland, Lapland, Nepal, Mexico, Australia.

Fulton calls his works *Walks*. His motto: 'No walk, no work.' Unlike his Bristolian friend Richard Long, Fulton does not exhibit any natural objects, because 'Art that brings natural objects into galleries is against nature.' While Long's stone circles may create an atmosphere of their own, Fulton pointedly pro-claims: 'The Rocks are Alive in Their Homeland.' The one radically rejects all conceptual art, whereas the other combines action and sculpture, nature and gallery. Fulton is the purist, the pilgrim on the road to true *Arte Povera*; Long is the shaman, working in magic circles. Fulton captures the essence of his walks in photographic sequences, simple drawings, and ever more concise writings. Walking is the most elementary dialogue with nature: 'Being in nature for me is direct religion.' Such personal, metaphysical experience cannot be shown through pictures, but is best captured by evocative, sketchlike blocks of words: 'Walking / Beyond Imagination / In the Memory / Nowhere to be seen.' One of his greatest influences is the Japanese monk and poet Santoka Taneda, who between 1926 and 1940 walked more than 25,000 miles – a life in haikus.

Fulton's early British walk-works, collected in his book *Skyline Ridge* (1975), took him along historical and pre-historical paths, in tune with the generations of traders and travellers that had trodden the same paths before him. The perfect route for this artist (born 1946), who lives in Canterbury, is the Pilgrims' Way. To this he dedicated one of the most beautiful of his walk-works: 'Winter Solstice, Full Moon: an uninterrupted 125 mile walk (rapid, purposeful) without sleep along the Pilgrims' Way from Winchester to Canterbury), road, paths and ancient tracks.'

Artists like Hamish Fulton and Richard Long are pilgrims without a church. The journey is their goal. What else could drive them constantly to uproot them-selves, and take off sometimes for months on end? In homage to his friend, Long, Fulton quotes as a sort of motto for art and life a sentence taken from a book by Sebastian Snow, *The Rucksack Man* (1976): 'It's the going-for-ever-on-ness that I find the attraction.'

SHADOWS OF LEAVES

SONG THRUSH

DANDELIONS

FIRST CUCKOO HEARD ON THE LAST DAY OF APRIL

WAITING FOR THE SWALLOWS

A TWO MILE CIRCULAR EVENING RUN ON MAY 12 1981

TRACKS WITH PUDDLES
FADED DANDELIONS

Kent Aglow: Stained Glass by Burne-Jones and Chagall

Kent's most beautiful churches are to be found in country villages, and sometimes you can make the most astonishing discoveries there. For instance, St Nicholas in *Barfreston*, between Canterbury and Dover, amid the fertile fields approaching the North Downs. This village church of flint and sandstone (12th century) is not even 50 feet long, but its proportions and its decorations are matchless. The corbels are graced with 70 monstrous heads to ward off evil spirits, and in the gable of the rectangular choir at the eastern end is a magnificent wheel window with animal heads. But the *pièce de résistance* is the south doorway, a masterpiece of late Norman stonemasonry, influenced by the very finest craftsmanship from over the Channel. In the tympanum is Christ in a mandorla; above are three richly sculptured arches, with medallions depicting profane and fantastic scenes: miller, forester, falconer performing the labours of the months, a bear playing the harp, and a monkey playing Pan-pipes. It's a little world theatre, carved in stone, and hidden away in a tiny Kent village. St Mary's, in *Patrixbourne* near Canterbury, also has a richly decorated south portal from the same period, quite possibly carved by the same masons that worked on the churches of Barfreston and Rochester. In *St Margaret's at Cliffe*, a cove nicely hidden away from the popular beaches, stands the biggest Norman parish church in Kent (west door *c.* 1150).

I found Marc Chagall between apple orchards and hop fields. Chichester Cathedral and All Saints in *Tudeley* have the only stained glass windows Chagall made in England, and his first commission was here in this unassuming Kent village near Tonbridge. A local art collector named Sir Henry d'Avigdor-Goldsmid lost his daughter Sarah Venetia in a sailing accident at the age of 21, and this was his memorial to her. Swirling, radiant watercolours cover the round-arched east window; at the bottom is a woman in a surge of blue, and over her the crucified Christ, surrounded by angels and a rider on a red horse. When Chagall came to the church in 1967 and saw his work, he was delighted: 'C'est magnifique, je les ferai tous!' And indeed he went on making designs well into his 90th year for the eleven remaining windows: abstract paintings with angels and saints, insects and sea creatures, a turtle, a butterfly wing – it was as if Chagall had decided to go through the full repertoire of his pictorial biblical world. From the Russian shtetl, via Paris, the crucible of modern art, to this tiny village buried in the English countryside – quite a journey.

Just as exceptional in its day was the great east window of St Andrew's in *Wickhambreaux*, bizarrely an American Art Nouveau work in a Victorianised 14th-century village church east of Canterbury. John LaFarge's window of 1896 depicts the Annunciation, with glowing white lilies and a heaven composed of pure art nouveau curves, designed by Arild Rosenkrantz, and donated by a Count James Gallatin from New York. This window is believed to be the first European commission given to an American glassmaker.

A highly distinctive place is St Mary the Virgin in *Speldhurst* near Tunbridge Wells, with what is almost a church window art gallery. This village church of 1871 has not only the conventional Victorian windows that one can see anywhere, but it also contains Pre-Raphaelite stained glass designed by Edward Burne-Jones and made in William Morris's studio. Burne-Jones, son of a Welsh frame-maker, initially wanted to be a priest, but then became a painter instead and designed over 100 church windows. His stained glass windows in Speldhurst are a feast of colour and stylised emotion, of curved lines and dramatic light. The windows over the southern aisle show the sharply profiled, Michelangelesque figures of the four Evangelists, Matthew and John wearing purple haloes; beneath are scenes from the life of Jesus painted in grisaille panels framed in ruby-red. Above the font are Mary and St Elizabeth, heads lowered, with that typical Pre-Raphaelite intense gaze at nothing-in-particular. The two windows on the south side of the choir are studies in blue, green and brown. In the eastern window is Christ crucified on the tree of life, with a red serpent below him, and at his sides John and Mary against a deep blue background; above in three quatrefoil windows are angels with flame-red wings. More poetic and less theatrical is the west window over the northern aisle, which is perhaps the most translucent picture in this translucent

Window by Morris and Burne-Jones (1875) in Speldhurst

church: six angels with ancient musical instruments against a blue background; in their bright robes are flowers that shine like stars. This window is the first that Morris designed himself.

In *Bidborough* and *Langton Green*, two villages near Tunbridge Wells, there are more examples of Pre-Raphaelite stained glass, including a communal work in keeping with the medieval spirit that first animated the Brotherhood; this is in the west window of the southern aisle in All Saints, Langton Green. Mark was designed by Burne-Jones, Luke by Morris, and John and Matthew by Ford Madox Brown (1865/66). The abundance of Burne-Jones's church windows in Kent would not have been possible had it not been for the proximity of his friend William Morris's firm, which had been founded in 1861 but moved from London to Merton Abbey in 1881; wallpaper and textiles with Morris's ever-popular patterns continued to be made there until 1939.

The main attraction of *Tunbridge Wells* is not the single Burne-Jones window in the choir of Christ Church, but the Pantiles. This 17th-century promenade was originally paved with Dutch 'pan-tiles', rectangular bricks that have long since been replaced by grey slabs of Purbeck stone. On one side are the shops and bistros of Upper Walk, beneath colonnades of wood, stone or cast-iron; on the other side you can wander beneath the lime trees of Lower Walk – the overall effect being infinitely more harmonious and more charming than any of our modern pedestrian zones. Here on the Pantiles, in the 17th and 18th centuries, anyone with name or rank or a minor illness could be seen taking the air. 'Company and Diversion is the main business of the place,' wrote Defoe; 'and those people who have nothing to do any where else, seem to be the only people who have any thing to do at Tunbridge... As for Gaming, Sharping, Intriguing; as also Fops, Fools, Beaus and the like, Tunbridge is as full of these, as can be desired, and it takes off much Diversion of those Persons of Honour and Virtue, who go there to be innocently recreated...' The raison d'être for these fashionable gatherings, and the means of innocent recreation is the mineral spring up in the green hills, whose 'steel water' was said to do wonders for nervous complaints, poor digestion, and the after-effects of excess alcohol. As long ago as 1637 these claims were put to the test by Queen Henrietta Maria (and the connection survives in the church dedicated to her husband King Charles the Martyr, to which both Pepys and Evelyn gave money, and which remains one of the finest Carolean interiors in the country). Tunbridge Wells became a spa, and by 1735 had become the fashionable resort for London Society. In that year the dandy Beau Nash came from Bath to make a guest appearance as Master of Ceremonies. Even if the water tasted like 'rusty horseshoes', the *eau de scandale* was always sweet. 'You can't imagine how much people lye with one another here,' wrote Thomas Gray's friend William Mason. 'I had the narrowest escape in the world.' And if it wasn't one thing, it was another. Cobbett was, predictably, disgusted. 'In looking back over "the Wells", I

Tunbridge Wells: The Pantiles

cannot but admire the operation of the gambling system. This little *toadstool* is a thing created entirely by the gamble.' And up, up went the houses: villas and hotels on Mount Ephraim, and elegant terraces on the Calverley Estate, designed by Decimus Burton from 1828.

'Dear Tunbridge Wells, I am so very fond of it,' enthused a young princess who was on holiday in Calverley House. The future Queen Victoria, like Macaulay and Meredith and many others, loved the town, and today 'Thackeray's House' (the novelist spent much of his childhood here) will offer you the best food for many miles around. Unfortunately, the rest of the town is not so impressive: office blocks, car parks, ugly modern buildings of all sorts, a giant supermarket right in the centre, and the Georgian Corn Exchange restyled into a shopping centre with fancy postmodern trimmings. Disgusted, Tunbridge Wells...

Following the trail of Burne-Jones church windows is not a bad way to see Kent and its art. In *Bishopsbourne*, a picturesque village on the North Downs, south-east of Canterbury, the west window of St Mary's shows Burne-Jones's allegorical figures of Faith, Hope, and Charity, while the tracery contains angels by Morris. In the choir is the memorial bust of an Elizabethan scholar between columns of books. This is Richard Hooker, author of the *Laws of Ecclesiastical Polity*, the strongest exposition of Anglican theology ever written, a major text for English political philosophy, and a foundation of the language to boot. He wanted to show that church and state were one single community, headed both by the monarch; but this monarch's authority was limited by the consent of the people and the tra-ditions of the law. Hooker spent the last five years of his life as rector of Bishopsbourne. Another to spend his last years here was Joseph Conrad, the sailor and English novelist born in the Polish Ukraine. He started to learn English in 1878 at the age of 21, and did not start writing for another 21 years, all spent at sea; by the time he was fifty he had already completed some of the great novels in the language. Can we hear the voice of a sailor, used to constant motion and change, in his description of 'my unconventional grouping and perspective... wherein all my art consists...it is fluid depending on grouping (sequence), which shifts, and on the changing lights giving varied effects of perspective.' From 1920 until his death in 1924 he lived near the church, at Oswald's, the present parsonage. (He is buried in the cemetery in Canterbury.)

Maidstone, a town of hops and apples, lies between Downs and Weald, and is the county town of Kent. Burne-Jones is here as well: *The Good Shepherd*, on the east window of the Congregational Church in King Street, is his first known design for a stained glass window (*c.* 1857). In Maidstone Wat Tyler, leader of the Peasants' Revolt of 1381, gathered together the men of Kent to march on London in protest against Richard II and his poll tax. The rallying cry was: 'When Adam delved, and Eve span, / Who was then the gentleman?' Serfdom was to be abol-ished and 'lordship divided between all men' – as well as the wealth of the church. Small wonder that he was assassinated as soon as possible; but governments heeded the warning and few have attempted to impose a poll tax since.

Satirist Among the Tories: Ralph Steadman

England's most biting satirist is a gentle man who likes to make music. Every morning at five he has a blow on the horn: 'It clears the head and is cheaper than keeping a cock.' Since 1980 Ralph Steadman (pictured on p. 7), his wife Anna, and their collie dog have lived in *Loose*, near Maidstone. In his studio stands a sheep, stuffed with chair legs. It's a wolf in sheep's clothing, akin to a socialist in a Tory environment. 'Here in Kent I'm one of the few landed socialists. My neighbours are all thoroughbred Conservatives, bloody terrible Tories. England is such a boring country, full of boring career people, football fans and dog-lovers. I can't imagine anything worse.'

He was born in a suburb of Liverpool in 1936, son of a sales rep. He left school at 16, and worked in an aircraft factory, at Woolworth's, as a rat-catcher, and as a swimming instructor, but then his mother suggested he should do a correspondence course in art. People in pubs were his first models – a cartoon for a pint of beer was how it all started. It turned out to be a seven-year course of evening classes at the bar. By day he earned his crust doing cartoons for newspapers for £10 a week. It was not until he got in with the satirical magazine *Private Eye* that he was able to develop his wit. Then at the end of the 1960s the angry young man found a new outlet in America – the magazine *Rolling Stone*. He also had a great deal of help from a reporter named Hunter S. Thompson, who showed him his 'real targets, the Nixons of this world. My best work came out of a sense of outrage.' (His drawings for Thompson's *Fear and Loathing in Las Vegas* are unforgettable evocations of hallucination, hysteria and hilarious rage – classics of illustration.)

With explosive strokes of the pen, and characteristic blots and scrawls, Steadman drew party delegates as voting cattle, a starving black man gnawing on a rifle butt, politicians shaking hands and squashing people between those hands. 'It's a sad fact that oppression, deceit, injustice, cruelty and violence are the mothers of satire.' As a moralist, Steadman stands firmly in the English tradition of satirical political art which began with Hogarth, and enjoyed its golden age around 1800 with James Gillray and George Cruikshank. Steadman's savagely critical 'Visages and Visions' appeared in the *New York Times*, the *Observer*, the *New Statesman*, *Punch* and *Penthouse*. But the old complaint that satire has no effect is echoed even by this master of the genre: 'The traditional cartoonist is looked upon as rather a court jester to be patted on the back. What you end up realizing is that you're not going to change anything.'

Nowadays Steadman rarely draws political cartoons for newspapers. Long before *Private Eye* became part of the Establishment, he viewed satirical magazines as being like 'old ladies drinking tea'. Instead he has concentrated on books. He wrote and illustrated a psycho-analytical satire *Sigmund Freud*, a biting book

Steadman's pirates

about dogs, and a fictional autobiography called *I, Leonardo*, a brilliant satire on the myth of the artist. His illustrations for *Alice in Wonderland* and Stevenson's *Treasure Island* are psychographical showpieces. His model for 'The Admiral Benbow' in *Treasure Island*, all pointed gables and crooked walls, was his local pub in Loose, 'Chequers Inn'. He also illustrated a calendar for the village, not entirely to the delight of the community. With the years he has discovered the more lucrative sides of satire. He wrote an oratorio for TV, and for advertising campaigns travelled through the vineyards of the world. The result was a book for epicureans, *The Grapes of Ralph*, and an heroic attempt to grow vines in his own garden. The biggest collection of his political drawings is at the Cartoon Centre of the Templeman Library, University of Kent.

In the Gardens of the Artists: Where Peter Greenaway Made his Film

The people wandering round the gardens of *Groombridge Place* are not all garden-lovers. Since Peter Greenaway filmed *The Draughtsman's Contract* here in 1982, cinema fans have flocked to the mysterious draughtsman's garden to look for his imaginary grave. The estate lies right on the Kent/Sussex border, south-west of Tunbridge Wells, and Peter Greenaway was not the first to recognize its charms. Sir Arthur Conan Doyle was a frequent guest at the house, which then belonged to two old sisters. Several of its features appear in *The Valley of Fear*, particularly the 'drunken' topiary garden. There is a little Conan Doyle Wendy house there now; and there are peacocks sitting on the walls, making shrill comments on the passers-by, a flock of white doves flies over the moat; and an oversized female head sometimes stares stiffly out of the bridge-house window, like a Magritte.

The little River Grom gave the village its name, and gave the manor house its water – more than enough for its moat, ponds and gardens. Philip Packer built it in 1660, on the site of an earlier house connected with the poet Waller. The new building was a modest one of red brick, with two storeys, high sash windows, hipped roof and dormers, while the working quarters and stables are at the rear. A note of luxury and Italian sophistication is given by the little classical loggia on the front, and the decorated bridge over the moat: it was not for nothing, presumably, that Packer was a friend of Sir Christopher Wren. In its straightforward simplicity, Groombridge Place is one of the most beautiful of all the small Restoration manor houses. Like many gentlemen of the time, when the Civil War ended and the monarchy was restored under Charles II, Philip Packer decided it was also time for a new garden. He sought the advice of his friend John Evelyn, the diarist who was also a gardening expert. The garden is enclosed on three sides by 15th-century grey rubble walls supported by buttresses. Outside this enclosure, a path leads through orchard and vineyard to a wooded hill, where an old garden was uncovered with ponds and waterfalls. It's still beautiful, but now it's called the Enchanted Forest; Ivan Hicks redesigned it, with exotic tree-ferns and exciting surprises. Historically, though, the most interesting area is the walled garden with its central avenue of yews and symmetrical lawns – one of the few laid-out gardens of the Restoration to have survived virtually unaltered after the landscape movement of the 18th century. This is a cosy, enchanting, and even mysterious place – a magic echo of times long gone. Round its borders stand ancient yew trees leaning on their crutches, and box and holly, like figures looming out of dark dreams.

This, then, is the garden that plays such a major role in Peter Greenaway's film – a social-historical-philosophical-mystery drama that takes place on a country estate in 1694: The Lady of the Manor employs a draughtsman to make twelve drawings of the house and garden during the twelve days while her husband is away. According to the contract, part of his fee is to be the lady's hospitality, with whatever that may imply. The orderliness of the Baroque garden is broken by disorder – passion breaks all rules. As he draws, the observer is himself drawn ever deeper into the sticky web of relationships, and what he sees and meticulously records leads on to strange and terrible truths behind the beautiful façade of the garden world: intrigues, jealousy, and maybe even murder. 'I like mysteries,' says Greenaway. 'Most things in life remain unexplained.'

The Draughtsman's Contract is funny, macabre, tense, and mannered, like all of Greenaway's films. It's an ironic costume drama which delves into the nature of æsthetics – a picture puzzle concerning the nature of perception. Within the artificial world of the garden, there unfolds a game of perspectives, viewing nature in a wide variety of different ways: as it is, as the gardener fashions it, as the draughts-man draws it, and as the camera sees it. 'I'm not a film-maker,' says Greenaway. 'I'm a painter in cinema.' Whether he is painting, writing, exhibiting, or directing films or opera, what interests him is the artificiality of art, the orgiastic language of pictures, and the enigmatic world of signs. He brilliantly cannibalizes art history. *The Draughtsman's Contract* was his first major film and his biggest success to date. In making it, he awoke Groombridge Place from its Sleeping Beauty sleep, and gave it a new fairytale role to play. The place has never been the same since.

Oast Houses and Apple Blossom: Villages in the Weald

'Kent, Sir – everybody knows Kent – apples, cherries, hops, and women.' Thus Jingle, the Rochester rogue of *Pickwick Papers*, describes his native county and that of Dickens his creator. It's the hops that have given Kent its most distinctive sight: the oast houses. It's almost as if the Martello Towers had become pacifists as they marched inland: they have stuck pointed caps on their heads, and given them-selves warm red coats of brick before taking up residence on the hills of the Weald. This is the heart of hopland, or 'the Mother of Hop Grounds in England', as Defoe described the area around Maidstone. That was where the first hop made its way from the Continent into British soil during the 16th century – an historic event encapsulated in Defoe's historic couplet: 'Hops, Reformation, bays, and beer,/Came into England all in a year.' (Before hops, beer was not beer but merely ale, unflavoured.) In the oast houses, the hops are dried, or 'cooked' as the natives say. A fire burns on the floor, the hops lie on a platform above, and the warm draught is pulled up through the conical cowls, which rotate while wind-driven dryers on the conical roofs draw off the smoke. The form and function of these round (but in Victorian times rectangular) towers are as inseparable as hops and malt. It is the simple, classical beauty of functionalism that we admire in these rural industrial landmarks, and their æsthetic appeal is even greater when, as is often the case, they are linked up like a series of sculptures imposing their own gentle rhythm on the landscape.

A monumental example of this is at *Beltring*, near Paddock Wood. The Whitbread Hop Farm, with 25 oast houses, is the biggest in England. It's open to the public, and is especially worth seeing at harvest time on a misty morning in September. 'That's hop-picking weather,' say the locals. But a conservative esti-mate suggests that altogether no more than five per cent of all Kent's oast houses are now used for their original purpose. The rest have been converted into barns or homes. Rape has become more profitable than hops, and so gradually the tall trellises of the hop fields have given way to the staring yellow of rape (previously unknown in Kent) and of sunflowers, and the blue of flax. The landscape is changing, and the prime agent of this change is the agricultural policy laid down in Brussels.

Anyone who values his beer must pay a visit to 'The Three Chimneys' (15th century) in Biddenden, and 'The Bell' in Smarden, in order to sample Fremlins and Goachers and Shepherd Neame, amongst other highly palatable local brews.

In the early Middle Ages, the *Weald* was nothing but impenetrable forest. Then came the iron industry (the iron railings round St Paul's Cathedral come from Lamberhurst), and the forests supplied the essential charcoal. From then on the gentle slopes became the setting for apple and cherry orchards. The beginning of May is apple-blossom time, and the countryside becomes a great splash of pink and green, interspersed with picturesque villages: Smarden and Biddenden, the single street of Headcorn, Goudhurst perched on its hill. The brick and half-timbered houses are picturebook material, with their hanging tiles or their equally characteristic black or white weatherboarding. To the north of the Weald there is also pebbled sandstone and, on the coast, flint. These natural materials determine the character of the landscape and the colour and structure of the houses, making the villages a harmonious and ravishingly beautiful feature of the countryside.

Biddenden is an inhabited, open-air museum, whose emblem is the Biddenden Maids. They were Eliza and Mary Chulkhurst, who lived here over 300 years ago and were literally inseparable, being Siamese twins. The restaurant named after them, 'Ye Maydes', is one of a row of half-timbered houses whose ground floors were linked to form a single weaving mill. The Old Cloth Hall (16th century), north of the village green, is one of many fine houses in and around Biddenden built by rich cloth-makers between 1400 and 1700. The centres of the cloth industry, which flourished in the Weald until the 19th century, were Tenterden and Cranbrook, small towns with the same comfortable feel of a hand-knitted pullover. *Tenterden's* main claim to fame is as one possible birthplace of William Caxton, the first English printer and publisher. 'In 1422 I was born and learned my English in Kent, in the Weald, where English is spoken broad and rude,' is the only clue he left. His books (from 1475 onwards) included editions of Chaucer, Gower and Langland, which gave a powerful boost

The Biddenden Maids

to the vernacular, by contrast with continental countries, where most printed books were devoted to classical literature in Latin. Caxton was also a notable

The Biddenden Dole: bread and cheese distributed in memory of the Biddenden twins, handed out at the workhouse by the churchwarden; why three policemen are needed is not clear. Photograph c. 1900 by Sir Benjamin Stone

translator, who 'englysshed' romances, saint's lives and Æsop's fables, though the most famous translation published by him was Malory's great *Morte Darthur*, still widely read today.

In *Smarden* stands another of those idyllic village churches, St Michael's (14th century), surrounded by weatherboarded houses topped off with pantiles. This is the only church in England with a rocking-horse for a monument. The Stevensons had it placed there in 1990 in memory of their daughter Daisy, and for all the 'free range children' of Marsden. Opposite the church is a cottage where the photographer George Rodger once lived – co-founder of the legendary Parisian agency Magnum. He made a pictorial record of the blitz in London and of the horrors of Bergen-Belsen. One photograph of his became world-famous: the *Nubian Wrestler,* a last triumphal icon of old Africa.

Swan Lake and Magic Battlements: Leeds Castle

Leeds Castle stands in the middle of a lake where black swans swim across the reflected battlements. This is the perfect English medieval castle, imported directly from Fairyland. Beyond this enchanted realm roars the M20, an anachronism not entirely unwelcome to the owners of Leeds. Such a link between the Middle Ages and their modern marketing could hardly be bettered. Long before the comforts of the Channel Tunnel, England's kings used to break their journey to the Continent by staying at Leeds Castle. It was perfectly situated, one day's ride from London and one day's ride from Dover. On 22 May 1520 Henry VIII, with an entourage of 3,997 people, stayed the night here on his way to a summit conference with the French king on the Field of the Cloth of Gold. Today's VIP's whirl down in helicopters, and advertisements drift up on coloured balloons, and hot air circulates all over Leeds Castle in the form of European Foreign Ministers' conferences, Middle East peace talks, congresses and banquets. The castle is regarded as virtually terrorist-proof.

Seen through sober eyes, Leeds Castle is crumbling a little. Architecturally it falls, so, to speak, into four sections: the D-shaped gloriette, linked by a two-storeyed bridge to the main building at the northern end of the island, the Maidens' Tower, and the gatehouse at the southern end. The history of the castle is also in sections. In 1280 Edward I had the gatehouse reinforced and replaced the Norman keep with the gloriette. There were Tudor modernisations, and then in the 19th century a completely new main block was built (1822-25, by William Baskett), a symmetrical building with towers and battlements. This early 19th-century medievalism is now the most striking feature of the castle.

This was Edward I's favourite home, and he set up a chantry for a daily requiem mass to be held in the chapel. He gave the castle to his wife, Queen Eleanor of Castile, whose flag still flies over the battlements, and from then onwards it belonged to royal widows: Margaret and Isabella of France, Anne of Bohemia, Joan of Navarre, and six English queens lived there as more or less merry widows. After the death of Henry V, the 21-year-old Catherine of Valois comforted herself with the master of her wardrobe, the Welsh nobleman Owen Tudor and the son born of this *liaison scandaleuse* became the father of Henry VII, and thus the founder of the Tudor dynasty.

From 1278 until 1552 'our queenliest castle' (*The Times*) belonged to the Crown – a place of royal romances, tears and glamour. Subsequently, three famous English families, St Leger, Culpeper, and Fairfax, lived here. In 1924, death duties forced the sale of Leeds Castle, and it was almost bought by William Randolph Hearst, the American press tycoon. 'Want buy castle in England' was the cable he sent to his agent. The latter, however, warned him about the enormous cost of restoration, as well as the fact that there were no bathrooms, the place was lit by oil lamps, and the servants' quarters were down in the dungeons. None of this, however, daunted another American, Olive, Lady Baillie, and she pipped Hearst to the post in 1926.

Lady Baillie, heiress to the Whitney fortune, restored Leeds Castle and is responsible for its present interior. What was left of the original furnishings and paintings had already been auctioned by Christie's in 1830. Lady Baillie filled her new home with antiques, just as Lord Astor had done in nearby Hever Castle (see p. 77). A 16th-century fireplace and spiral staircase were transplanted from France, there are X-framed chairs from Italy and tapestries from Brussels. Leeds is a bona fide European castle. The dove-tailed ebony floorboards and the superbly carved Tudor beams were all made after 1927. There is a meticulous reconstruction of the Queen's bathroom, with rush matting, washtub, and white linen towels. Next door is the bedroom: four-poster bed with ruby-red canopy, walls covered with green damask, and the royal monogram all over the place: HC lovingly inter-twined – Henry and Catherine together for ever.

Lady Baillie had a penchant for Australian long-tailed parrots, zebras in the park, and guests from Hollywood and High Society. The Spanish King Alfonso XIII, Errol Flynn, Douglas Fairbanks, James Stewart, the grande horizontale Pamela Digby, later Churchill, later Harriman – they all enjoyed themselves at Leeds Castle in the 1930's before the world went dark. Lady Baillie herself lived longer here than any of her royal predecessors, but in 1974 she bequeathed it to the Leeds Castle Foundation, as a centre for the arts and for international confer-ences. Leeds Castle Enterprises Ltd employs around 300 people, and has followed all the rules of history-marketing. There are medieval tournaments and banquets, falconry and archery, a golf course, wine-making and fireworks. Visitors come from far and wide – more than half a million a year, not far behind Hampton Court. Pavarotti has sung here, sometimes a band plays in the park, and at all times the birds twitter in the aviary. More than 100 exotic species, some rare, some endangered, have been bred beneath the lofty, pyramid-shaped roofs, with the ultimate purpose of returning them to their original places of origin.

Since 1988 Leeds has also enticed its visitors into a labyrinth – a topiary castle with its own battlements, made from 2,400 yews. The subterranean exit leads through a beautifully restored grotto full of strange sculptures and ornaments. There were conflicting views of grottos in the 18th century, when they were so fashionable: some said they were 'nice, neat, dry and splendid for shells'; others sided with Dr Johnson, who snorted that a grotto was 'a very fine place – for a toad.'

There is no argument, however, about one of the most sublime attractions at Leeds: Culpeper Garden, designed in 1980 by Russell Page: lined with low box hedges, its informal flowerbeds are full of roses, poppies, lupins and lavender. As well as the traditional flowers of English country gardens, herb specialists will find a remarkable collection of different mints.

Estates like Leeds have always had plenty of dogs running around them – mas-tiffs, greyhounds, lapdogs, bloodhounds, and hounds to hunt deer or duck. And they have always worn collars, for protection, decoration, or identification. A

1. Dover Castle

2. Canterbury Cathedral

3. Canterbury Cathedral: St Paul with the Snake of Malta, fresco in the Anselm Chapel

4. Canterbury Cathedral: Thomas Becket, window in the Trinity Chapel

5. Rochester Castle in the early 19th century

6. Downe House: Darwin's home

7. Eltham Palace, showing the medieval Great Hall, and, behind, the Art Deco house

8. Ramsgate Sands, *by William Powell Frith, 1851-54*

9 & 10. Prospect Cottage: Derek Jarman's refuge at Dungeness

11. The White Garden at Sissinghurst

12. Walmer Castle: Wellington's own Boots

13. Walmer Castle: Queen Elizabeth the Queen Mother, Lord Warden of the Cinque Ports, at her official residence

15: Groombridge Place

14 (opposite) Scotney Castle

15: Groombridge Place: miniature house

17: Great Maytham Hall, by Edwin Lutyens: the main façade

18: Great Maytham Hall: the stable block

19: Great Maytham Hall: the Secret Garden, which inspired Frances Hodgson Burnett

20. Tudeley: Window by Marc Chagall

collection of this neckwear was put together by an Irish scholar (a collar-scholar?) and is now on show in the gatehouse. A dog-collar museum. Could anything be more English? There are specimens from five centuries – leather, copper, even silver, some with metal spikes, and some richly decorated with baroque engravings and coats-of-arms. Dog collars even appear in anthologies of English poetry: Pope wrote a couplet for one that went 'I am His Highness' dog at Kew,/ Pray tell me, Sir, whose dog are you?'

From Sissinghurst to Chartwell: Vita's Garden and Churchill's Swans

If you call a landscape or building 'picturesque', the tourists will come flocking to see their picture postcard dream visions brought to life. There is no more picturesque country than England. This is where the term was first coined and the theory first put into practice, and *Scotney Castle* is a perfect illustration of the concept and its history. A sandstone tower remains from a 14th-century castle; a cypress stands nearby, and beside it are the ruins of a 17th-century brick house surrounded by a moat in which the reflections of trees and buildings merge together. You can look down on all this, across azaleas and rhododendrons, from a neo-Tudor house (1837-43) on the hill above – designed by Anthony Salvin, who may have been a pupil of John Nash. Edward Hussey had the house built so that he could gaze at the old one down below as if it were a ruin in some landscape by Claude. A dramatic foreground was formed by the stone quarry – now overgrown – which lay directly at the feet of the new house, like a faithful dog; the romantic background was enhanced by tearing down more of the ruins until they looked exactly like the workings of chance – Art made to look like Nature. This was the principle of the picturesque: wild, ruined, melancholic. The classic text is Uvedale Price's *Essay on the Picturesque* (1794), which recommended that landscape gardeners study the pictures of landscape painters like Claude, Poussin, or Salvator Rosa. Even before writing his *Enquiry into the Principles of Taste* (1805), Richard Payne Knight had exercised great influence through his own gardens at Downton Vale in Herefordshire (begun in 1774), a prototype of the picturesque country estate. And the standard history of the picturesque was written by none other than Edward Hussey's grandson Christopher, the architectural historian and *Country Life* writer, whose life was shaped by living here. A later famous tenant was not so æsthetically inspired: Margaret Thatcher.

Kent is the Garden of England, and no garden in Kent embodies this English horticultural passion more than that of *Sissinghurst Castle*. The White Garden, as its name implies, contains nothing but white flowers and plants – 150 different kinds; the rose garden is a rondel – a circular garden surrounded by a hedge of yew; the orchard is in the remains of the old castle moat; in the herb garden, the scents of thyme and saffron and sage will send you into olfactory raptures. There are ten gardens altogether, and they were created by the writer Vita Sackville-West and her husband Harold Nicolson. When they moved here in 1930, they found nothing but stinging nettles and a sadly neglected Tudor gatehouse. On their first evening, 'the tower sprang like a bewitched and rosy fountain towards the sky,' wrote their biographer Anne Scott-James. 'They climbed the steps of the tower and stood on the leaden flat, leaning their elbows on the parapet and looking out in silence over the fields, the woods, the hop-gardens and the lake down in the hollow from which a faint mist was rising.' This Sleeping Beauty the Nicolsons set

about restoring. Vita made the red-brick tower with its octagonal side turrets (1570) into the perfect retreat for a writer, where she spent many happily solitary hours working and writing. with the view of the Wealden hills for company. Her husband lived in South Cottage. This was very much a marriage of separate lives, since both were drawn to partners of their own sex. Their son Nigel Nicolson, himself a writer and former partner in the London publishing firm of Weidenfeld and Nicolson, was unaware of their histories until he discovered their letters in a trunk after their deaths. He described their life in *Portrait of a Marriage*, which shocked the English public in 1973 – especially its account of Vita's affairs with Violet Trefusis and Virginia Woolf.

Vita Sackville-West

'She is a grenadier; hard, handsome, manly,' was Virginia Woolf's description of the dynamic, aristocratic Vita after their first meeting in 1922. 'She is stag-like, or racehorse-like, save for the face, which pouts, & has no very sharp brain. But as a body hers is perfection.' Virginia Woolf also cottoned on very quickly to the fact that the diplomat and prolific writer Harold was 'simple down right bluff' and that Vita, though competent, wrote with a 'pen of brass'. Although Vita's novels and biographies were once very successful, her best prose is undoubtedly the gardening columns she wrote for the *Observer*, and her greatest masterpiece is the garden at Sissinghurst. With almost 200,000 visitors a year, it is a Mecca for this garden-worshipping nation. All the more wounding, then, the criticism levelled against the Nicolsons by the historian David Cannadine: 'They were both terrible snobs who "hated" the middle classes and the workers, generally disliked Jews and dismissed all people who were not their type as "bedint". They were out of sympathy with the twentieth century, and at Sissinghurst they created a refuge from the harsh contemporary world that never let them down.'

For Vita, it must certainly also have been a substitute for the house where she was born – *Knole*, which she could not inherit because she was not a son. Knole was her great love and her most bitter loss. It stands some 18 miles north-west of Sissinghurst, on the outskirts of Sevenoaks. 'Knole is a conglomeration of buildings as big as Cambridge I daresay; if you stuck Trinity, Clare and Kings together you might approximate,' wrote Virginia Woolf in 1924 after lunch 'alone with His Lordship' in the huge palace. 'Life has left them.' But the visitor felt the presence of the dead, Vita's forebears, indeed the whole of English history. 'This vast, yet ordered building, which could house a thousand man and perhaps two thousand horses, was built, Orlando thought, by workmen whose names are unknown. Here have lived, for more centuries than I can count, the obscure generations of my own obscure family. Not one of these Richards, Johns, Annes, Elizabeths has left a token of himself behind him, yet all, working together with their spades and their needles, their love-making and their child-bearing have left this.' Orlando was Vita, transmuted by Virginia in her most romantic novel, where the hero/heroine (for Orlando keeps changing sex) travels through the centuries, always returning to the great house, Knole. 'There it lay in the early sunshine of

Picnic at Sissinghurst Castle

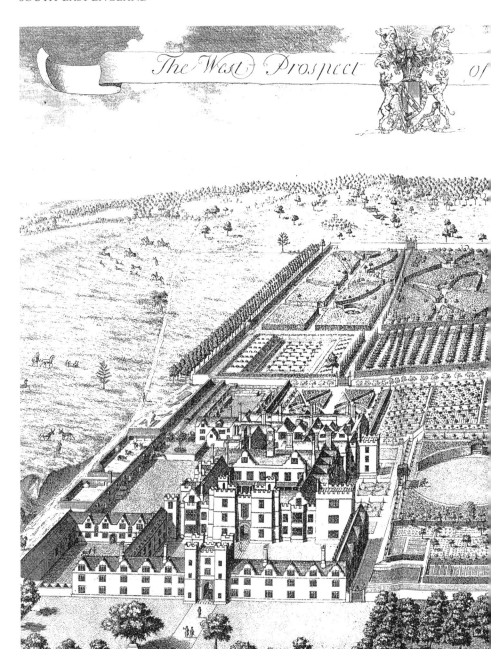

The West Prospect of

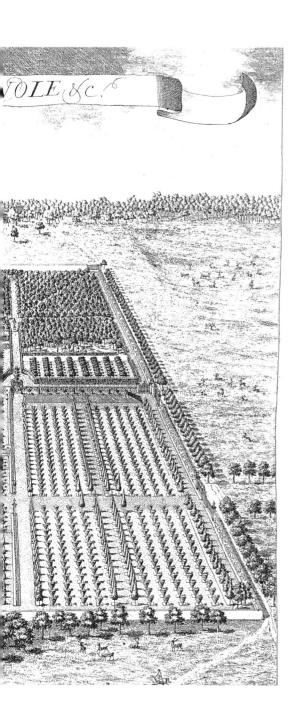

Knole in the 17th century

spring. It looked a town rather than a house, but a town built, not hither and thither, as this man wished or that, but circumspectly, by a single architect with one idea in his head. Courts and buildings, grey, red, plum colour, lay orderly and symmetrical; the courts were some of them oblong and some square; in this was a fountain; in that a statue; the spaces of the greenest grass lay in between and clumps of cedar trees and beds of bright flowers; all were clasped– yet so well set out was it that it seemed that every part had room to spread itself fittingly - by the roll of a massive wall; while smoke from innumerable chimneys circled perpetually in the air.'

Virginia gave the manuscript to Vita, and it is still at Knole. Vita herself also wrote an historical account *Knole and the Sackvilles* as well as a literary one in her novel *The Edwardians*. The present Lord Sackville lives in Knole as a tenant of the National Trust.

The first building here was a palace for the Archbishops of Canterbury, including the notorious Morton, he of the legendary Fork by which he extracted money from both those who looked rich – because they were – and those who lived meanly – because they must have plenty stashed away. Archbishop Morton invented the technique on behalf of the king, starting a long association between state finance and Knole, most of which over the centuries was built and furnished with the perks of office. But kings, once taught how to grasp, are apt pupils – and one of Morton's successors, Cranmer, had Knole gouged out of him by Henry

VIII. Elizabeth is said to have given Knole to her cousin, Thomas Sackville, but in fact he acquired the freehold by a combination of legal sleight of hand and lots of money (his father had done so well out of the dissolution of the monasteries that he was called 'Old Fillsack'). Thomas is remembered at Knole by his initials on the gutters in one of the courtyards, TD (Thomas Earl of Dorset); scholars know him as the probable author of the first English tragedy in blank verse, the 'otherwise unremarkable' *Gorboduc*; but he was also a statesman, and it was he who had to tell Mary Queen of Scots that she had been sentenced to death. He employed 300 Italian workers to extend and indeed transform the house. When it was finished, he died (1608). I'm afraid I didn't check, but the National Trust guide assured me that Knole has as many inner courtyards as there are days of the week, as many staircases as there are weeks in the year, and as many rooms as there are days in the year. Little wonder that in 1623 the Sackvilles employed 111 servants, so that from time to time at least one of their employees would find them. With its massive silver-grey stone, its countless gables and chimneys, Knole seems more like a medieval village than a private house. Like the oaks and beeches in the 1,000 acres of parkland, Knole grew and grew after Thomas Bourchier, Archbishop of

Thomas Sackville's initials at Knole

Canterbury, purchased it in 1456. But since the days of Charles I it has remained virtually unaltered. Here you have a rare opportunity to see a wide variety of outstanding early English furniture. In the Leicester Gallery are Jacobean chairs with their original silk covers, and the Knole Sofa with its adjustable armrests. In the Venetian Ambassador's Bedroom is the beautifully carved, gilded bed made for James II; in the King's Bedroom another magnificent four-poster with curtains royally worked in silver and gold; there is also a unique collection of silver furniture from the late 17th century. After the portrait gallery of the Sackvilles in the ballroom, and the many copies of old masters, one is surprised by a collection of genuine Reynolds, including his portraits of David Garrick, Oliver Goldsmith, and Samuel Johnson. The atmosphere of Knole cannot be conveyed by a list of its treasures, yet these are endless: the carved monsters in the wooden panelling, the plaster ceilings, the Flemish tapestries, the miles of solid oak floorboards. Every so often you come across one of its past inhabitants – but flattened; a dummy – one of those carved, painted wooden figures that one likes to chat to around the fireplace (or that help to keep the heat off). They were a Dutch import fashionable in the 17th and 18th centuries.

Estates and manor houses come thick and fast in this part of southern England. The fact that in Kent the landscape seems more parcelled out than elsewhere, and the parks and estates are smaller, is due to a particular law of inheritance unique to

Kent among southern counties since the 11th century. Land was not inherited by the eldest son, but was divided equally among all the sons. Thus just a few miles south of Knole, you can walk from the park of Hever Castle (see p 75) into the next park at Chiddingstone Castle – a neo-gothic delight with one of the great collections of the minor Japanese arts and even more minor Jacobite relics – and from there across a few fields and roads to *Penshurst Place*.

When Sir John de Pulteney, a London cloth merchant and mayor, built this house in the Medway Valley in 1340, he took a risk: instead of a fortified but uncomfortable castle, he built a turreted, crenellated manor-house. After all, there had been peace for decades, and this remarkable fact influenced the architecture of the time, with Penshurst Place a prime example. Its groundplan is typical of late medieval English manor-houses. The Great Hall is the dominant feature, as the centre of domestic life, and only some 200 years later did this shrink to a mere entrance hall. There is a living-room on one side of the hall, and on the other you go through a passage to the kitchen and other workrooms. This is the house where in 1554 Sir Philip Sidney, soldier and poet, was born. A man 'not only of an excellent witt, but extremely beautifull' (Aubrey) he was the perfect Renaissance gentleman. His *Astrophel and Stella* inspired the Elizabethan craze for sonnets, and he died at the same age as James Dean, fighting for the Protestant cause in the Dutch War of Independence against Spain. His funeral helmet can be seen in the Barons' Hall, from whose open chestnut trusses ten vast figures have gazed down for centuries at the feasts below. These were memorialized most famously by Ben Jonson, who wrote his greatest poem, *To Penshurst*, in honour of Philip Sidney's brother Robert – and, one might think, as a long dig at nearby Knole:

> Thou art not, *Penshurst*, built to envious show,
>   Of touch, or marble; nor canst boast a row
> Of polish'd pillars, or a roofe of gold:

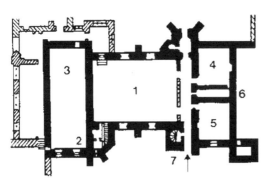

Penshurst: plan, showing
1. *Great Hall*
2. *Undercroft*
3. *Solar*
4. *Buttery*
5. *Pantry*
6. *Kitchens*
7. *Visitor's entrance*

Sir Philip Sidney

> Thou hast no lantherne whereof tales are told;
> Or stayre, or courts; but stand'st an ancient pile,
> And these grudg'd at, art reverenced the while.

The present owner, Viscount de L'Isle, former Governor-General of Australia, has planted a patriotic flowerbed at Penshurst: a Union flag of red and white roses and lavender-blue.

One of the greatest red, white and blue heroes of our time was, like Sir Philip Sidney, a writer and a knight-at-arms. As pugnacious in a polo match as in the Boer War, he was a painter, an historian, and an orator second-to-none. Winston Churchill's country house at *Chartwell* stands north of Penshurst, just 25 miles away from Westminster, and a favourite place of pilgrimage. Churchill found the house itself 'irredeemably ugly', but he loved the garden and the hills around. There he lived with his wife Clementine and his family from 1924 until shortly before his death in 1965, during which period he was twice Prime Minister, and it was to Chartwell that he would return after all his victories and all his defeats in order to write and to paint. 'A day away from Chartwell is a day wasted.' His study, under the roof, is a small room from where he had a panoramic view over the Weald, and a complete grasp of the History of the English-Speaking Peoples, the life of John Churchill, 1st Duke of Marlborough, and the Second World War. These were some of the works that he would dictate in bed or at his high desk – histories that earned him hundreds of thousand of pounds from the moment he wrote them. Chartwell is a shrine. Its relics include Churchill's *Boîte Nature*, the cigars of which he smoked three thousand a year; on the mahogany desk are busts of Nelson and Napoleon; the glass cabinets contain his Order of the Garter, his Nobel Prize for Literature, his hats, uniforms, and political souvenirs of his great contemporaries. All of this was purringly watched over until 1974 by Jock, his faithful cat. Churchill used to sign his paintings WSC, and his work (under a pseudonym) was even accepted by the Royal Academy in 1947. He was encouraged to paint by his friends Lavery and Orpen, some of whose own works are here, and he became a good amateur painter, as can be seen from his still lifes and landscapes in the house and in the garden studio. There is a bust of Kipling in the latter, with the inscription: 'One sang of Empire and the other saved it.' On the lake in the park there are black swans, which he loved. He also loved to sit by the pond behind the rose garden – his 'magic place' – and feed the goldfish.

Long before his death, a group of Churchill's friends clubbed together to buy the house for the National Trust. Churchill paid a nominal rent of £350 a year. Octavia Hill would have approved. She was joint-founder of the National Trust, and lived in the neighbouring village of Crockham Hill, where she died in 1912

Between Chartwell and Chevening (*c.* 1630, by Inigo Jones), the country house of the Foreign Secretary, lies the little town of *Westerham*, which is graced by Churchill in monumental bronze (Oscar Nemon, 1969) and just a few steps further, General Wolfe (Derwent Wood, 1910). Wolfe, famous for taking Quebec and for regretting the fact that he had not written Gray's *Elegy in a Country Churchyard* (which, as *1066 and all that* pointed out, had already been written, by Gray), was born here in 1727. The triple-gabled house is now a National Trust property. 'Wolfe's Inn', with a Janus-headed inn-sign of the young and old General, dominates one end of the town. At the other the 'Marquis of Montcalm' keeps up a culinary opposition - and all under the watchful eye of Pitt the Younger, whose country house is now a restaurant, 'Pitt's Cottage'. The road between Westerham and *Brasted* is known as the 'Portobello Road' of Kent, with nearly twenty antique shops in two miles of road.

Exotic Tudor with Electricity: The Astors of Hever Castle

Just a few miles south-east of Churchill's Chartwell lies one of the most popular showplaces of English history. When Henry VIII was courting Anne Boleyn, he rode out to see her at *Hever Castle*. This was where the beautiful Anne had spent her youth, and every Christmas Eve her ghost walks back across the bridge. On an ordinary weekday, the castle is under siege and the drawbridge is like a bus-stop: QUEUE HERE, PLEASE. Some 280,000 visitors do just that every year.

It all began as a royal romance, and ended with the English Reformation, and there are still visible traces (or reproductions) of these events to be found in this relatively small castle, which the Boleyns transformed into a Tudor home in 1462. There are sections of the four-poster bed in which Anne Boleyn slept; you can see the portable lock which Henry had placed on the door of whichever bedroom he chose to sleep in; there is also the papal bull that was meant to prevent his divorce from Catherine of Aragon. In a miniature National Portrait Gallery are assembled all the main characters of this romantic drama and its many sequels: Henry VIII himself in a copy of Holbein's famous portrait – a Renaissance prince, monarch of all he surveys, including the women; Elizabeth I, daughter of Henry and Anne, painted by Holbein's contemporary John Bettes – a queen gazing coolly, even severely from above her lace collar; and Anne Boleyn, half length, quarter profile – a woman with black eyes, sensuous lips, mercifully unaware that in three years' time she will lose her crowned head. When she failed to provide the King with the heir he so desperately wanted, he had her tried for adultery and high treason. In 1536, Anne of a Thousand Days was executed in the Tower. In Hever Castle you can see the book of hours she carried with her on her way to the scaffold. Her lady-in-waiting, Jane Seymour, was next to marry the King, and she

Anne Boleyn

was Queen for a year before dying in childbirth. The portrait of her son, Edward VI, is by another court painter, William Scrots. Jane Seymour's successor, the German Anne of Cleves, was soon divorced and packed off to Hever. Her portrait is by a pupil of Holbein's. In the same room as all these (plus Mary's husband Philip II, School of Titian) are Lucas Cranach's portraits of the Reformers Melanchthon and Luther, whose teachings Henry had rejected in 1521 with his book *Assertio Septem Sacramentorum*. As a reward for this, Pope Leo X gave him the title 'Defender of the Faith', which the monarch has retained right through to the present day. All these pictures are as much a part of the house as the story of Anne Boleyn, and as the Astor Suite on the top floor – the transatlantic continuation of the saga.

Hever Castle was the fulfilment of an American dream. This is the story of a

Henry's signature in a letter to Anne: H[enricus] aultre AB ne cherche R[ex] – *'seeks no other than AB', with Anne's initials enclosed within a heart*

romantic return, a restoration on the grand scale, and a crippling recession. It all began with Johann Jakob Astor, a butcher's son from Walldorf near Heidelberg. At the age of 15 he emigrated, made a fortune with fur and property in Manhattan, and died in 1848 as the richest man in America. His great-grandson, however, wanted to go 'home': 'America is not a fit place for a gentleman to live.' William Waldorf Astor, incidentally an admirer of Bismarck, came to England in 1890. Like many other Americans, he bought himself some status symbols of the Old World: castles, newspapers, and a title. Then in 1903 he found the love of his life: Hever Castle.

For the then unheard-of sum of £10 million, he restored the castle, collected old weapons, armour, furniture and paintings, and what he couldn't obtain in the original, he had copied: the carvings in the Library are in the style of Grinling Gibbons, and there are plaster ceilings à la Hampton Court, and stairs and a Long Gallery. Hever Castle is a vision of the English Middle Ages, a specimen of virtuoso Edwardian craftsmanship, a fully electrified piece of Tudor Exotica. Beside this knight's castle with Fifth Avenue comforts, Astor built a 400-year-old village. It took him just three years. As the founder of the Waldorf Astoria, then the biggest hotel in the world, William Waldorf Astor knew what to offer his guests at Hever Castle: a Tudor village with over 100 rooms. Subterranean passages link this feudal guest wing to the castle itself. He also employed 800 Irish navvies to dig out a lake. He adorned his Italian garden with Greek, Etruscan and Roman sculptures and sarcophagi, which he had collected when he was American ambassador in Rome.

One can imagine him majestically ordering the drawbridge to be raised once he had entered the castle. There he would sleep with two loaded revolvers on his bedside table. His obsession with security led him to surround Hever with high walls. William 'Walled-off' Astor acquired almost everything an American in England could wish for – even the *Observer*, Britain's oldest Sunday newspaper. Shortly before his death in 1919, he also gained the title he had coveted: Viscount Astor.

For David Cannadine, chronicler of the decline of the British aristocracy, the Astors are 'the most famous example of an alien and plutocratic dynasty establishing itself, largely by the power of the purse'. Between 1910 and 1945 four Astors sat in Parliament. The first woman to gain a seat in the House of Commons was an Astor, the beautiful Nancy from Virginia, who was the most vocal of the whole clan. Her father-in-law already had his hands full with Hever Castle, and so as a wedding present he gave her Cliveden, on the Thames. There, between the wars, Lady Nancy assembled all the political and intellectual élite of England in her salon, the notorious 'Cliveden Set'. And after the war too: it was at the Astors' swimming-pool in Cliveden that the 'Profumo Affair' began in 1961, when John Profumo, a government minister, was introduced to Christine Keeler, a call-girl. Would Christine Keeler ever have got into Hever Castle? Would Henry VIII ever have allowed such a pretty girl into his presence?

Hever Castle hit the headlines once again when Lord Astor announced that he was quitting the place and renting it out to holiday-makers for £220 a night. Even the super-rich found country houses like Hever a little beyond their grasp. In 1966 Astor had already had to sell *The Times*, which he found brought him a lot of prestige and no profit. In 1983, Hever Castle came under the hammer. After three generations, Gavin, 2nd Baron Astor of Hever, educated Eton and Oxford, married to a daughter of Field-Marshal Haig, was selling the family home. Too expensive, he said. The electricity bill alone in 1982 was around £60,000. None of his five children wanted to take on the burden. 'So that was that. Of course, it's very sad.' The rest was up to Sotheby's. In a series of auctions, the castle, its contents, and the estates were sold off. For some £9 million the castle passed to a property developer in 1983, but without its most valuable works of art. William Waldorf Astor's collection of old weapons and armour, together with his ivories, were sold separately, for another £6.5 million. The jewel of this collection was a Milanese suit of armour made in 1550 for the French King Henry II, which went to an American investment banker for around £1.9 million – a record price for a piece of applied art.

A year after the sale of Hever Castle, Gavin Astor died on his estate in Aberdeenshire. One of his sons, William Waldorf, 4th Viscount Astor, is director of a chain of hotels that include Cliveden. Today Hever Castle is available for conferences, parties, wedding receptions, or – somewhat cheaper – plain straightforward visits. If you don't get lost in the maze of a thousand yews, you can wander round Lord Astor's lake, or royally follow Anne of Cleves' Walk or Anne Boleyn's Walk. But watch your head.

Godinton Park: The English Art of Sitting

In Kent alone there are more than 80 castles and country houses open to the public. We might take a brief look at just a few of these. *Mereworth Castle* (*c.*1720–25) was designed by Colen Campbell, author of *Vitruvius Britannicus*, and is a version (without pediment sculptures, but with a stronger dome) of the Villa Rotonda near Vicenza, an authentic example of English Palladianism as first introduced into England by Inigo Jones – a style marked by harmonious proportions, arcades and porticoes. A minor practical disadvantage of copying a Venetian summer house in England was the lack of chimneys; Campbell solved this by leading the smoke from every fire in the house out through the dome, using the space between outer and inner shells to house an original system of flues. Part of the James Bond film *Casino Royale* was shot here, and Mereworth is now the weekend residence of one of the richest men in the world, Sheikh Mohammed Al-Tajir from Bahrain. As ambassador for the United Arab Emirates he was one of many Arabs in the 1970's to take advantage of the weak pound and the oil boom to buy up large chunks of England and English silver. *Brasted Place* – from where Prince Louis Napoleon set out in 1840 to Boulogne, in a failed attempt to seize power in France – and *Mersham le Hatch* near Ashford (1762-65) are both neoclassical country houses by Robert Adam. Brasted Place, with its plaster decorations in Etruscan style, was built for George III's court physician in a park on the North Downs, and today is a theological college. Another religious institution is *Allington Castle* (13th century, restored in 1930) which lies in the Medway Valley near Maidstone, and is owned by the Carmelites. It is the birthplace of the poet and diplomat Sir Thomas Wyatt, 'Father of the English Sonnet' and lover of Anne Boleyn. In 1557 he had something to say worth remembering for every writer:

> Throughout the world, if it were sought,
> Fair words enough a man shall find.
> They be good cheap; they cost right naught;
> Their substance is but only wind.
> But well to say and so to mean–
> That sweet accord is seldom seen.

Not far away, towards Sevenoaks, and in glorious rural isolation despite its proximity to London, is *Ightham Mote*. Hidden in its little valley, this is one of the best-preserved 14th-century moated manor houses in England. Its air of modesty is reflected in the history of minor gentry who lived here and lovingly changed so little. That it survived at all, though, is again due to an American – Charles Henry Robinson of Maine, who had fallen in love with a picture of the house as a young man and was flush with a fortnune he had made in the paper

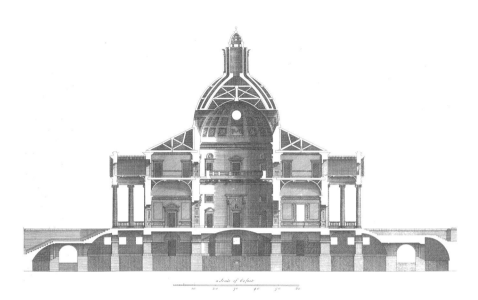

Mereworth by Colen Campbell, from Vitruvius Britannicus. *All the 24 chimneys in the house debouch into the lantern.*

industry when he chanced on another photograph, this time a sale advertisement in *Country Life*. He lost no time in buying the house and pouring his fortune into its preservation.

Full of charm and hidden delights are some of the smaller country houses like *Godinton Park*, near Ashford (14-17th century), where the owner himself sometimes acts as guide. The pride of Godinton is the Great Chamber, with its Jacobean panelling (1632–38) and a frieze which in great detail depicts the various pike and musket drills still used today in certain court ceremonies. This was probably the work of a Huguenot craftsman. Yet even more striking, at least to foreign eyes, is the joy of seeing here, in its original form and setting, the work of the great furniture designers of Georgian England, Thomas Chippendale, whose neo-Gothic and Chinese motifs, with scrolls and curves, created a sort of English Rococo fashion in the second half of the century; George Hepplewhite, whose use of shield or heart-shaped chair backs was very influential between 1775 and 1790; and finally, Thomas Sheraton, who returned to a stricter, more functional neoclassical style, and whose influence was certainly the most lasting. 'To unite elegance and utility, and blend the useful with the agreeable, has ever been considered a difficult, but an honourable task,' wrote Hepplewhite in his introduction to the

Cabinet-Maker and Upholsterer's Guide of 1788. Such chairs roused the enthusiasm of the great German traveller and gardener Prince Pückler-Muskau, who travelled to Britain in 1826 and reported back to his wife on the truly magnificent British art of sitting: 'To begin with, the stranger must admire the refined comfort in which the Englishman knows how to sit, and one must also confess that anyone who does not know the ingenious English chairs of all forms and for all degrees of fatigue, sickness and constitutional particularity, is really missing a large proportion of earthly pleasure.' We can think of Jane Austen, enjoying her most relaxed and productive times at nearby Godmersham: 'at the present time I have 5 tables, 8 and 20 chairs and 2 fires all to myself,' she wrote in an admiring letter to her sister.

If you want to have a picnic in the large park at Godinton, what more English spot could you choose than the remains of the Domesday Oak? This mighty tree, unshaken by all events since the Norman invasion, is said to have burst asunder at 11 am on 3 September 1939, as Chamberlain informed the nation that it was at war with Germany.

Chair designs : This page, armchair from Knole. Opposite, Chippendale above, showing his mastery of Gothic and Chinese inspired forms; Hepplewhite below, with his more delicate and chaste neoclassical design

Sussex

That part of England which is very properly called her
Eden, that centre of all good things and home of
happy men, the county of Sussex
Hilaire Belloc, Hills and the Sea, 1906

The waves walk dry foot on the land, and the land rolls on in waves, and the foam stiffens into chalk, and the chalk foams over the sea – these are the Downs, on the coast of Sussex, and it is the perfect image of England's island mixture of earth and water. Could it really be true that this interplay of the elements has been created solely by ice ages and movements of the earth? The geologists think so, but the people of Sussex have never really believed the geologists. After all, there are places that have clearly been touched by some force that is beyond nature – mysterious prehistoric remnants from the days of the megaliths: 'Devil's Humps' and 'Devil's Jumps'. Even the hardened and sceptical tourist must beware of *Devil's Dyke*, five miles north-west of Brighton, for the gorge at his feet is part of a canal that the Devil himself dug one night in order to let the sea invade the land and swallow up the many churches in the Weald. Fortunately, one old lady was woken up by the noise, lit a candle, and looked out of her window, and Satan thought it was the sunrise, so he abandoned his devilish plan before the work was done.

From the hill above Devil's Dyke, in clear weather you can see the whale's back of the South Downs. 'The hill', as local villagers call it, stretches parallel to the coast from *Beachy Head* across 60 miles or more to Winchester. Beachy Head, the Norman *Beau Chef*, is the highest cliff on the whole Channel coast (600 feet). Friedrich Engels did not wish to be buried next to Karl Marx in London; he had his ashes thrown into the sea near Beachy Head. Now there are hang-gliders taking off from the top – exotic birds with bright wings and crash helmets, floating along the sheer rockface, past the somewhat surprised terns as they sit minding their own business in their nests, then hovering out across the water, doing a lap of honour for Engels, and coming in to land on the pebbled beach.

Inland, towards Kent, are the North Downs, with the broad woods and heaths of the Weald. 'Green Sussex fading into blue, with one gray glimpse of sea': Tennyson's landscape has retained its own character and atmosphere, even if the

The Arun at Stoke

Paul Nash: Wood on the Downs, *1929*

coast has been largely built on to meet the wishes of Londoners wanting to live by the sea. From *Cissbury Ring* you can see far across the rolling hills towards the sea and Worthing. Up here, nobody could approach unseen from any direction, and so – like the beech-crowned Chanctonbury Ring – this prehistoric plateau, with double earthworks and trenches, was a natural refuge for man and beast in the early Bronze Age, and was one of the defensive rings against the Belgi who invaded in 50 BC. Over 200 shafts bear witness to the fact that flint was quarried in Cissbury during the Stone Age. There are only a few isolated trees here, whereas further west the Downs are flatter and more forested. Sheep graze on the grassy limestone hills, cows and horses are down below in the valleys. The slopes glow beneath the swift changes of the clouds, which throw their broad shadows over the fields and into the hollows, as if the Downs were one gigantic golf course for a game between wind and light. (Indeed there are golf courses everywhere, rising from all the coastal towns and forming wide, curving terraces on the hillsides. The finest is near *Seaford*, with a view down over the chalk cliffs of the *Seven Sisters*.)

The Italian writer Ennio Flaiano noted in his *Nocturnal Diary*: 'God is a gentleman; as such, he speaks fluent English. He is present in all places, but I believe his favourite residence is the sky above Sussex.'

The gods of English pop music also love this area. Led Zeppelin bought themselves noble Hammerwood Park as a recording studio (and quickly abandoned it to rot), and the Rolling Stone Brian Jones met his end in his swimming-pool at Cotchford Farm – once paradise for none other than Winnie the Pooh (see page 121). On his estate in Peasmarsh near Rye, the vegetarian Paul McCartney and his family grow organic foods, and he also has his own recording studio in an old mill. There is another singer living in Sussex who was once even more popular than the Beatles: Dame Vera Lynn. When the Forces' Sweetheart sang 'We'll Meet Again' to the boys on the Front, she gave them more courage than half a dozen generals.

Sussex has attracted many artists. 'If you have been a little child brought up in those hills and in those days,' wrote the great sculptor and letterer Eric Gill,' you will understand their immortal loveliness.' Gill moved to Ditchling in 1907 to immerse himself in rural life, but a commune of painters and craftsmen, including David Jones, soon gathered around him, and their successors have their workshops in Folders Lane. Frank Brangwyn lived there at the same time, while not far off at Petworth the abstract landscape painter Ivon Hitchens set up home after his London house was bombed in 1940. Rural tranquillity and new ideas were what brought the American photographer Lee Miller to Farley Farm in Chiddingly, and there she lived with the writer and artist Roland Penrose until she died in 1977. And a converted oast house in Northiam was the home of the film director John Schlesinger (*Sunday, Bloody Sunday*). He shot *Cold Comfort Farm* (1994) here in Sussex, where Stella Gibbons had set her coruscating satire on the elemental squalor of country life and the rural muse.

As for writers, Percy Bysshe Shelley was born at Field Place near Horsham, though of course that was not by choice. Others, however, such as Hilaire Belloc, Edward Thomas, Rudyard Kipling, Virginia Woolf, Henry James, H. G. Wells, John Galsworthy, Malcolm Lowry and Alan Sillitoe all made their homes in Sussex, and indeed many of their works were profoundly influenced by the countryside and its people. In 1930, Sir Arthur Conan Doyle died in Crowborough, and his grave in Minstead bears the following pithy inscription: 'Steel true/Blade straight/ Arthur Conan Doyle/ Knight, Patriot, Physician & Man of Letters.' It must have been a comfortable grave, since he failed to rise from it to attend the famous séance held in his posthumous honour in the Albert Hall. Another unlikely local revenant claimed to have been buried for much longer. Piltdown Man was one of the most famous fakes in scientific history. The 'bare bones' of the case are as follows: in a gravel pit near *Piltdown* – some twelve miles away from Conan Doyle's home – a skull, jaw and canine tooth were found in 1912, henceforth to be known as 'Piltdown Man', the missing link between ape and man.

Over the decades the discovery became more and more anomalous as the early history of man became clearer, yet it was not until 1953 that it was definitively proved to be a fake. The jaw was that of an orang-utan, the skull was no more than 50,000 years old, and the whole lot had been aged with brown paint. The jury is still out on the identity of the hoaxer: was it the pompous leader of the local archæological society, consumed with the need to make a great discovery – or his assistant, the quick-witted French priest and later famous mystic, Teilhard de Chardin?

Piltdown notwithstanding, Sussex can still claim to be the scene of England's most significant archæological find. Down below the southernmost regions of the South Downs near Chichester, in the gravel pit of Boxgrove, more old bones were found in 1993: the fossilised shinbone of the oldest hominid in Europe, who lived there some 500,000 years ago when Great Britain was still a peninsula. Boxgrove Man has so far passed all his tests, even by the experts at Sussex University, who have no doubts as to his authenticity. Conan Doyle style Ouija boards not required.

The county's university is in *Falmer*, between Lewes and Brighton, directly on the A27, but sheltered from the traffic by the trees of its extensive park. With its

Sussex University: the forms echo the nearby Downs, but also recall the Colosseum, epitome of classical urban architecture

various layers of buildings and inner courtyards, this modern university (1960) has continued the tradition of English collegiate architecture, and yet at the same time it is unmistakably a creation of the 20th century. Following on from Le Corbusier, Sir Basil Spence – the architect who rebuilt Coventry Cathedral – here translated landscape into architecture. The high and low arches of the inner courtyards and the passages, and the wide, flat windows echo the forms of the Downs, with all their different curves and rhythms.

'Thank God for Brighton!'

As you enter Brighton, you can feel the ` curving below the asphalt. Down you go to the broad and impressive Promenade, with its gleaming white façades, and its turquoise, cast-iron railings full of dolphins, the town's emblem. The miles and miles of green along Marine Parade and King's Road are just a foretaste of the copper green domes, minarets and pagoda roofs of the Royal Pavilion – the greatest *folie de grandeur* that royalty ever plonked onto an English lawn. 'That folly of all follies that it is now,' to quote Sir Nikolaus Pevsner. An Indian Kremlin in England – not hidden modestly away in the countryside, where most people put their follies, but placed slap bang in the middle of the town. William Hazlitt, the great essayist, described it as 'like a collection of stone pumpkins and pepper boxes'.

And yet it all began very seriously, with Dr Richard Russell's *Dissertation concerning the Use of Sea Water in Diseases of the Glands*. That was in 1753, and when the 21-year-old Prince of Wales, later George IV, first visited the town in 1783, the old fishing village of Brighthelmstone was already a fashionable spa for the upper classes. 'Prinny' had two passions: chinoiserie, and the beautiful Maria Anne Fitzherbert. In order to get both of them under one roof, the Prince Regent spared neither cost nor reputation. His head chef, a German named Louis Weltje, had found him a summer residence in Brighton – a farmhouse with sea view, where the Prince wished to live like shepherd and shepherdess with the woman he had secretly married in 1785. But Prinny soon tired of the simple life, sent for the architect Henry Holland, and they got to work. The result was the Marine Pavilion (1786/87), a villa with round bays and wrought-iron railings, such as were to become typical of so-called Regency architecture in Brighton and elsewhere. But for George, fashion king and 'First Gentleman of Europe', even this was too stiff and dull. He therefore gave free rein to his love of chinoiserie, and as time went by, this eastern exoticism finally burst its classical banks and flooded the whole façade with Hindu Gothic.

The Regency Romantics loved India. Lord Byron wrote an *Indian Serenade*, and Coleridge's famous *Kubla Khan* sounds like an introduction to the Royal

Pavilion: 'In Xanadu did Kubla Khan/A stately pleasure-dome decree.' Already in 1805 George had commissioned the landscape architect Humphrey Repton to design an Indian pavilion, but it was Repton's one-time associate and George's pet architect John Nash (who also built Regent's Park and Regent Street for him) who finally came up with the *Royal Pavilion* (1815–22) in its present anything-but-classical form. In the meantime, George's domestic circumstances had somewhat changed. He had had to separate from his Catholic/commoner mistress/wife Mrs Fitzherbert – the marriage being deemed invalid – in order, against his will, to marry the stout and smelly Caroline of Brunswick. The marriage took place in 1795, and in exchange Parliament agreed to pay his debts of £650,000. A year later he tried to divorce her, but times had changed since Henry VIII's day. George's extravagant lifestyle made him increasingly unpopular, and there was even an attempt to assassinate him. In 1820 he succeeded his father George III to the throne but, tormented by ill health and the satirists, he withdrew more and more to London. Ten years later he died more or less respectably in Windsor Castle. Francis Chantrey's bronze statue of him (1828) stands at the northern end of the Pavilion garden, not far from the domed former stable block, which is now a concert hall.

Brighton Pavilion is one of those buildings you either love or hate. 'Kitsch' would be an over-simplification for its sophisticated, vulgar splendour. It's a hot-house of ornaments and exotic styles: lotus chandeliers, water-lily gas lanterns, sphinx and dolphin furniture, clock pagodas, liana wallpaper, palm and snake columns, and a couch that is an Egyptian barque on crocodile feet. There are dragons everywhere, and bamboo, but the bamboo banisters are of cast iron, and much of the bamboo furniture is made from different, far more expensive woods, such as mahogany, palisander or satinwood – wonderful imitations created by the firm of Frederick Crace. This is eclecticism run riot, a masked ball of styles. Even Chippendale had been here with his furniture designs. The taste for the Oriental had been started by William Chambers, George III's court architect, who had himself been to China and India. In 1757 he wrote a book about Chinese architecture, and later built the pagoda in Kew Gardens (1761–2). By the time of the Regency, and particularly at the Royal Pavilion, the calm elegance of the Georgian style is overloaded with ornament, and the lightness of line weighed down with historical paraphernalia. The Banqueting Room, with its gold and paint, is at one and the same time oppressive yet amusing – perhaps the high point of George's Far-Eastern phantasmagoria: above the Chinese wall-paintings is a sky-blue dome filled with luxuriant banana leaves of painted copper, held up by a mighty silver dragon, in the claws of which is a chandelier of 2,200 crystals, weighing a ton and costing £5,613. Such exotica out-Hollywood Hollywood. Even the kitchen is resplendent with palm trees of cast-iron, the decorative material that emerged most productively from the Industrial Revolution. This was what most

Nineteenth century tradesman's card featuring the Brighton Pavilion.

In 1822 William Cobbett gave a recipe for a Brighton Pavilion: Take a square box, the sides of which are three feet and a half, and the height a foot and a half. Take a large Norfolk-turnip, cut off the green of the leaves, leave the stalks 9 inches long, tie these round with a string three inches from the top, and put the turnip on the middle of the top of the box. Then take four turnips of half the size, treat them in the same way, and put them on the corners of the box. Then take a consider-able number of bulbs of the crown-imperial, the narcissus, the hyacinth, the tulip, the crocus and others; let the leaves of each have sprouted to about an inch, more or less according to the size of the bulb; put all these, pretty promiscuously but pretty thickly on the top of the box. Then stand off and look at your architecture. There! That's a 'Kremlin!' Only you must cut some church-looking windows in the sides of the box. As to what you ought to put into *the box, that is a subject far above my cut.*

interested the visiting head of the Prussian Planning Department in 1826: 'First of all, the kitchen,' wrote Karl Friedrich Schinkel in his diary entry of June 10, 'every item is steamed – very fine; tables with iron hotplates into which the steam can be directed so that everything stays hot.' Mrs Fitzherbert's salon is here, but she never used the kitchen, for George's true love did not live in the palace of her

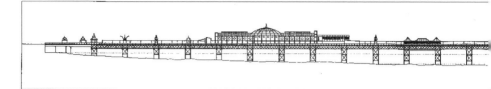

Great Mogul; her home was opposite, at No. 55 Old Steine. Queen Victoria came to Brighton for a summer break, but was ill at ease in the overcrowded seaside resort and the strange, much-gawped-at grand saloons her uncle had built. 'The people are very indiscreet and troublesome here really,' she complained, packing her bags – all 143 carriage-loads of them – and retreating to Windsor Castle. She was neither impressed nor amused, and sold the Royal Pavilion, which had cost George half a million pounds, to the town council for a laughable £50,000. They have been responsible for the administration ever since, and have profited considerably, not only thanks to the millions of tourists, but also because this ex-royal palace has been able since 1995 to stage royal registry office weddings in the Red Drawing Room for around £300 per I-do.

'Thank God for Brighton!' Sir Laurence Olivier, who lived here, once prophesied the fall of the Empire if ever British Rail ceased to serve kippers on the London to Brighton line. Both kippers and Empire have duly disappeared. Now there is only a wilting Commonwealth and pre-wrapped sandwiches. But for all that, Brighton continues to flourish, though with the somewhat faded charms of a mature prima donna. London-by-the-Sea is just 50 minutes away from Victoria Station, but the vintage cars that have tackled the yearly London to Brighton Rally since 1896 tend to take a little longer. Take Brighton at a vintage pace as you wander along the prom; admire the terraces, squares and crescents, and the comfortable English homes that constitute the tasteful examples of Regency architecture here.

Then there are the piers. Freshly painted to protect against the rust that comes from the waves below and the rain above, they are wondrous products of the English delight in going out to sea with dry land under your feet. The *Palace Pier* stalks out 1,710 feet on its spider legs, and at ebb-tide stands 39 feet above the sur-

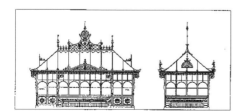

The Palace Pier, Brighton:
Above: side elevation
Left: Toilet block elevations
Right: Decorative iron work elements
Overleaf: Tea Party at Brighton

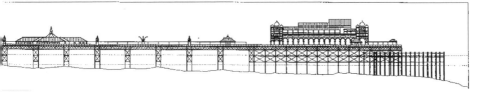

face of the water. It is a marvellously eccentric child of the cast-iron age, held up by 369 pillars and an irresistible urge to enjoy itself. Its shipless deck is a permanent invitation to walk and to spend: little shops, shooting galleries, fortune-telling machines, restaurant, big wheel, casino, and a theatre crowned with two onion domes where Pavlova once danced. The Palace Pier (1891–99) is a prime example of this peculiarly British form of seaside architecture, which is the maritime equivalent of 19th-century covered arcades.

Not far from the Palace Pier stood another, grander crystal palace on the water, but this one, closed since 1975, its dilapidation perhaps symbolic of the fading of Brighton's beauty, was finally claimed by the sea in the winter storms of 2002, and then given the *coup de grâce* by an arsonist. *West Pier* (1866) made literary and cinema history, in Graham Greene's *Brighton Rock* (1938), filmed with the young Richard Attenborough, who returned to make the film version of *Oh! What a Lovely War!* in 1968. It was listed, of course, and its long overdue restoration was one of the prestige projects to be undertaken as part of the millennium celebrations, with piles of lottery money. Enough money in fact, to arouse the jealous ire of the Palace Pier, which has managed to put a spoke in the wheels of all the projects. The West Pier was designed by Eugenius Birch, a former railway engineer, who rose to be the most successful pier-builder of his time. When Napoleon III, another crowned paragon of taste, landed here at the beginning of his exile in 1870, he praised the West Pier as 'the most beautiful building in Britain'. He and Empress Eugénie stayed diagonally opposite in the Grand Hotel, where in 1984 an IRA bomb was meant to send Margaret Thatcher and the entire Cabinet to kingdom come. The damage was immense, but no one even talks about it now, and the hotel guests are far more concerned with their legendary three-course afternoon tea.

From the Palace Pier you can take Magnus Volk's electric railway (1883, the first in England) along the shore, past the magnificent villas of Kemp Town, as far as the textile-free beach, where naturists lie sunbathing on the pebbles with the equanimity of Indian fakirs. Nearby is Europe's largest marina (1978), which seen from inland is a concrete eyesore. The Georgian Group protested, but failed to prevent its construction, to the dismay of Sir John Betjeman, who called it 'a garish pleasure slum built on the water'. The conference centre that was opened a year earlier is an even greater disaster. The planners simply dumped this and another kindred monstrosity right in the middle of Brighton's most beautiful, most sensitive area – the Regency houses along the promenade. For decades the council shamelessly neglected its rich historical heritage, and it has failed dismally to provide any good examples of modern architecture. Now it even faces being outshone by its tiny, genteel neighbour, *Hove*, which plans to erect four vast twisted, turning towers by Frank Gehry, supposedly 'reflecting the hedonistic nature of Brighton and Hove' – a nature which does indeed have quite a history.

'Brighton is the receptacle of the fashion and off-scouring of London – and the beach is only Piccadilly by the sea-side,' wrote John Constable in a censorious mood; but it has never been any different. In the early sixties Brighton was a Mecca for mods and rockers from all over England. There were the wildest beach parties on record. More recently Fat Boy Slim, the world's favourite DJ, has hosted open air parties here; the last (2002) more savage than wild, left one man dead and so much glass on the beach that it may take seven years to clear. Over these decades, too, holiday-makers began to make their way to warmer coasts, and the cold winds of recession hit Brighton. They even blew as far as the narrow alleyways of the former fishing quarter, The Lanes, where Queen Mary had wandered looking for antiques. (She was notorious for admiring pieces pointedly until they were presented to her, so shops were said to close up their shutters if they heard that she was in the neighbourhood.) Brighton's new attractions like the marina and the conference centre are attempts by the Queen of the English Riviera to regain her throne. But unemployment remains high, and there are more homeless people here than anywhere else in Britain. There is also a very high proportion of retired people. One new attraction that has really caught on is the language business, with students from all over the world coming to learn English and thus bringing young blood to this part of the Costa Geriatrica. You will also find the supermarkets teeming with gay couples pushing their trolleys like prams. Brighton is England's Gay Capital, relaxed and tolerant as in the days of dear Prinny. 'Kind, cheerful, merry Doctor Brighton,' enthused Thackeray. Pückler-Muskau, 'the most fashionable of all eccentrics' (Heine), driven to the verge of bankruptcy by his passion for English parks, came to Brighton in 1827 in the hope of finding a rich English bride to save him and his former wife – whom he had divorced for the very purpose! A constant stream of loving letters to her reveals his growing unhappiness with the project. 'Already I am tired of balls and dinners and am flirting with the sea, the only poetic thing in this otherwise prosaic world. I was at its edge just as night was departing, returning from a rout at the furthest end of town, and stood for a good half hour under the foam and thunder of the incoming tide. The stars were still and sparkling and everlasting peace ruled above while wild roaring and tumbling raged here below – Heaven and earth in their truest likeness!' Few travellers, it has to be admitted, have enjoyed such an awe-inspiring experience on Brighton beach.

Another great dandy was born in 1872 at an olive-green terraced house, 31 Buckingham Road. This was the illustrator Aubrey Beardsley. He lived there until 1887, when he went to London to work for an insurance company; just nine years later he was dead. 'The history of art has no stranger episode,' wrote one biographer, 'than the violent impact upon an entire generation of the impeccable art of this young dandy who knew he was dying, and whose working hours were interrupted by choking and haemorrhage.' More than anyone, even his friend Oscar Wilde, Beardsley ensured that the decadence of the Naughty Nineties would achieve some measure of immortality; and it has to be doubted whether a more accomplished eye for the possibilities of black and white ever lived. Picasso, Kandinsky, Klee and Mackintosh were but a few of his immediate successors who acknowledged his influence. The inscription on the house is short and to the point: 'Master of Line'.

Aubrey Beardsley, a pagan self-portrait, showing him with faun-like ears and tethered to the god Pan. 'Our utilitarianism was never rebuked in stronger or haughtier terms,' wrote the formidable critic Meier-Graefe

Beardsley's first step in his meteoric career came when he and his sister visited another master of line, the Pre-Raphaelite painter Edward Burne-Jones, who lies buried with his wife Georgiana in the graveyard at nearby *Rottingdean*. A laurel wreath marks the spot in the south-west corner of the little flint church of St Margaret's. Here Burne-Jones's only daughter, Margaret, was married, and for this occasion the painter designed a shining east window (1893) with the large figures of the archangels Gabriel, Michael and Raphael; in the smaller sections below are three biblical scenes. Burne-Jones and Morris surpassed even themselves with the colours and composition of the two lancet windows in the tower: *Jacob's Ladder* and the *Tree of Jesse* (1897).

Rottingdean had another claim to fame: Burne-Jones's nephew Rudyard Kipling lived here after 1897 at The Elms, diagonally opposite his uncle at North End House. But when the number of visitors became excessive, the Bard of the Empire moved back to the Weald. Kipling was born in Bombay, and spent his early years travelling through India and the Far East. He never really wanted to go to England ('stuffy little place'), and only when he acquired *Bateman's* in 1902 did he discover a new home: 'England is the most marvellous of all foreign countries that I have ever been in. It is made up of trees and green fields and mud and the gentry, and at last I'm one of the gentry.'

Bateman's originally belonged to the owner of an ironworks – it was a grey, Jacobean stone house built in 1634. Later it was extended, with 'two fat-headed oast houses with red brick stomachs and an aged silver-gray dovecote on top'. Kipling fell in love at first sight. 'That's her!' he cried to his wife, 'The Only She! Make an honest woman of her – quick!' Inside, Bateman's is dark and angular, full of black oak. 'Stiff furniture and lack of comfort,' as his daughter Elsie complained. But the view was incomparable: 'one of my oldest hills in England. Puck pointed to the bare, fern-covered slope of Pook's Hill that runs up from the far side of the mill stream to a dark wood. Beyond that wood the ground rises and rises for five hundred feet, till at last you climb out on the bare top of Beacon Hill, to look over the Pevensey Levels and the Channel and half the naked South Downs.'

Rudyard Kipling

And so Sussex was immoralised in a children's book that T. S. Eliot, no less, recognised as a whole new form of writing, seamlessly mixing prose and verse. More simply *Puck of Pook's Hill* is as great a celebration of the English countryside as any book written. Other books born at Batemans include the Empire and Jungle books, as well as parts of Kipling's last, autobiographical work, *Something of Myself*. Kipling was the first Englishman to be awarded the Nobel Prize for Literature (1907), and he invested the money in a pond for his garden. He also bought a lot of land all around, in order to ensure that it was not built on – much to the approval of the present owners, the National Trust. The Nobel collar can still be seen in the library, together with the original drawings for the *Just So Stories*.

Kipling's reputation today is occasionally controversial, because of his association with Empire. Yet he was also a man of broad imagination and compassion – it was he, for instance, in the aftermath of the First World War (in which he lost his only son) who insisted that all soldiers, irrespective of rank, should be commemorated with the same size and design of headstone. He died in 1936 at Bateman's, a somewhat reclusive and saddened man. On his desk are his pen and his pipe-cleaner, the essential requisites of any author's house. On the wall is his creed, the garden, in watercolours and in verse. Next to *If*, *The Glory of the Garden* is Kipling's most popular poem, which ought to be a second national anthem: 'Our England is a garden,' he proclaims. Anyone can garden, and indeed 'Adam was a gardener.' No doubt Adam was an Englishman as well.

If you want to visit a garden in Sussex, you can choose from well over a hundred. I should like to take you very briefly just to two. In the garden at *Nymans*, thousands of fritillaria bloom in spring, purple and white, while in October the nearby woods glow with all the colours of autumn. After the turn of the century, three generations of the Messel family worked on this garden in the Sussex Weald, south of Crawley. Its variety is enchanting, from the old roses to the Golden Milkboy from the Ilex Collection. Connoisseurs will enthuse especially over the trees and shrubs from North and South America and from the Pacific and Eastern Asia. After the hurricane of 1987, the National Trust has planted many new trees, including the Chilean *Araucaria araucana*, to replace what had been the biggest monkey-puzzle in the country. This stands in front of the ruined house, whose walls are covered with roses and wisteria, honeysuckle and magnolia. Evergreen birds and tortoises and other topiary figures make the scene even more colourful.

Nymans is the ruin of a family dream. It was a country house of the twenties, with Charles II oak furniture and tapestries to give a medieval atmosphere. It was Maud Messel who created this nostalgic illusion, and her grandson, the photographer Lord Snowdon, actually believed for a long time that it was a genuine country house and not 'a complete fake'. In 1947 it burnt down, although recently a section has been reopened to the public.

A few miles east of Nymans is *Sheffield Park*, most of which was designed by Capability Brown in 1776 and Humphrey Repton in 1789. Rare plants and wonderful autumn colours guarantee the lasting popularity of this park. Five artificial lakes rise in terraces towards the grey, neo-Gothic country house which James Wyatt remodelled for the Earl of Sheffield between 1775 and 1790. Here the Earl's friend Edward Gibbon, the great 18th-century historian, wrote the first volumes of the work that so impressed Churchill when he was a 22-year-old officer in the

Hussars in India. 'I set out upon Gibbon's *Decline and Fall of the Roman Empire* [and] was immediately dominated by both the story and the style. I devoured Gibbon. I rode triumphantly through it from end to end and enjoyed it all.... I was not even estranged by his naughty footnotes.' *The Decline and Fall* (1776-88) is famous for these footnotes, where Gibbon could expand on the gory, lubricious or simply irreligious details of history, 'which is little more,' as he put it 'than the register of the crimes, follies and misfortunes of mankind.' But even at his most controversial – his opinions of Christianity were shockingly relativistic – Gibbon's authority was accepted from the first, and continues to be. 'Gibbon is a great navigator of the sea of history – the greatest whom this country, or perhaps any has produced – and his work has the majesty, the precision and the reliability of a well-built ship,' wrote E. M. Forster. 'Although the *Decline and Fall* came out [some] two hundred years ago, it is still the leading authority on its period. Macaulay and Carlyle need correcting and supplementing, but the history of Gibbon stands firm.' Gibbon was buried in 1794 in the Sheffield mausoleum at the village church in nearby Fletching.

The Picturesque Landscape: J. M. W. Turner at Petworth House

I found the typical English landscape garden where I least expected it: behind a very untypically situated country house, which one enters in the middle of a town and leaves in the middle of the countryside. This is Petworth House, on the northern edge of the Downs. *Petworth* has about 2,000 inhabitants and a lot of beautiful 17th to 19th-century houses, antique shops, and a Flaxman relief in the chancel of its parish church. But the big attraction in this little market town is the mansion. The history and foundations of *Petworth House* go right back to the 13th century, when the estate was owned by the Percys, Earls of Northumberland. The present form of the house dates mainly from the time of Charles Seymour, the 'Proud Duke' of Somerset (1688–96). It is a narrow building, almost 320 foot long, with two main storeys. The façade is punctuated by 42 tall windows, but otherwise is almost completely without decoration. Even Anthony Salvin's reconstruction in the 19th century made no effort to transform Petworth into an architectural gem. The interiors and the park therefore seem all the more magnificent.

From Petworth House you can see over broad green hills with clusters of trees, and a serpentine lake. It all looks as if it has come about by chance and grown up haphazardly. You would certainly not say that it has been planned like the geometrical Baroque garden which was already there before 1751, when Lancelot Brown arrived and spied 'great capabilities' of improvement – a turn of phrase which gave this future royal gardener of Hampton Court his nickname of Capability Brown.

Village house in Petworth

In 1711 Alexander Pope had already satirised the geometrical hedges of the formal style of garden; from 1719 he even began to landscape his own garden in Twickenham. 'The beautiful wildness of nature' was also what Joseph Addison endorsed in his literary and political magazine *The Spectator*. The 18th century dreamed that it could regain Paradise in the ideal form of the landscape garden.

The very term indicates that, unlike French and Italian gardens, the English concept was not mastery of the landscape but integration with it. William Kent, who called himself the first landscape gardener, and his successors went back to nature but also went beyond it. If hills or lakes were not in the right place or were not there at all, they would be set where they offered the most surprising but also the most 'natural' view. Kent, originally a painter, even planted dead trees if he felt they fitted in with the landscape 'image'. Eighteenth-century English travellers, returning from their Grand Tour of the Roman Campagna, now wanted to live in idealised Poussin landscapes, with temples, grottos and ruins. The idea that, if you didn't actually want to create them, you could paint them on canvas and exhibit them like stage sets in the open air (as one horticultural theorist suggested), shows both the love of illusion and the artistic sensibility of the time. The French garden was geometrically bordered and enclosed, with its paths systematically directed towards central perspectives, whereas the English garden revelled in its fluidity and lack of boundaries. Instead of walls and hedges, it uses hidden ditches called ha-has to keep the grazing cattle away from the house, thus unobtrusively maintaining the continuity between park and landscape.

At its peak, the English art of gardening is pure nature. It's a landscape like a painting, and in turn the painters made paintings out of the landscape. Turner, for instance, painted the park and lake at Petworth with deer grazing against the swirling colours of the sunset. Landscape pictures and a picturesque landscape – these twin arts provide one of the most astonishing experiences at Petworth House. The continuity is very English: where Turner once stood gazing at the landscape and painting it, we can stand today and see both the painting and the landscape, which is exactly as it was then apart from a single missing tree. The house and park now belong to the National Trust, the deer to the Egremonts, and the Turner collection – the biggest outside the major galleries – to each in equal shares.

Turner painted twenty oils and about a hundred water-colours at Petworth House between 1827 and 1837. His friend and patron Lord Egremont had given him his own studio on the first floor of the house. The 3rd Earl of Egremont was one of the greatest land-owners and art collectors of his time, and his doors were always open to London's artists. 'I really never saw such a character as Lord Egremont!', wrote Benjamin Robert Haydon. 'He has placed me in one of the most magnificent bedrooms I ever saw! It speaks more for what he thinks of my talents than any thing that ever happened to me!... a Nobleman has taken me by the hand, whose Friendship generally increases in proportion to the necessity of is being continued. Such is Lord Egremont, literally like the sun. The very flies at Petworth seem to know there is room for their existence, that the windows are theirs. The dogs, the horses, the cows, the deer & pigs, the Peasantry & the Servants, the guests and the family, the children & the Parents, all share alike his bounty & opulence & luxuries.' Constable and Flaxman also came here frequently, but no one left such an extensive body of work as Turner, or such a valuable record of the history of the house. There are views of the park and lake, where he often went fishing, and pictures of Brighton's Chain Pier and the Chichester Canal, both of which were particularly close to Lord Egremont's heart as he had invested heavily in them. Turner also painted a series of Petworth interiors – a somewhat unusual subject for him, but still showing his typical concern for colour and light, and for the way objects and spaces merge in glowing forms. Nevertheless Turner's sketches from around 1827 were used as a historical record when the pictures in the Square Dining Room were rehung in the early 1990's. They were placed in their original positions, i.e. symmetrically, with Reynolds' *Macbeth and the Witches* in the centre, thus creating the optimum decorative effect in accordance with the way Lord Egremont, on Turner's advice, had wished to view his pictures.

More of these historical rehangs in recent years have given a special freshness to the art at Petworth. The Turner Room is certainly one of the highlights, but it is by no means the only one. Eight miniatures by Adam Elsheimer painted around 1605 on copper are among the treasures, and there are paintings by Rogier van der Weyden, Titian, Hobbema, Claude, Teniers, Gainsborough, Blake, Fuseli, and Angelica Kauffmann, plus a dozen portraits by Anthony van Dyck, Charles I's court painter, and a dozen more by Reynolds. This is a private collection that most museums would be proud to own. The glory of Petsworth House is enhanced by the work of yet another great artist – a man who began by decorating ships and ended up as Charles II's master carver: Grinling Gibbons. While he was still at work in Hampton Court and in the Library at Trinity College, Cambridge, he came to Petworth in 1692 and created a masterpiece: the Carved Room. This is still life in limewood: a wooden trompe l'œil of fruit and fish, musical instruments, putti, animals and flowers. It is almost uncanny how Gibbons was able to breathe life into the wood, creating tangible feathers and flesh, and endowing every surface with a reality of its own. The panelling behind the carvings was originally painted white – a bright background which emphasized the relief work but it was later stained dark. Together with his pupil John Selden, Grinling Gibbons created magnificent frames for magnificent pictures: Henry VIII after Holbein, Charles I on horseback after Van Dyck, and Kitty Fisher, the famous 18th-century courtesan, by Reynolds. In the Beauty Room, named after the portraits of Queen Anne's ladies-in-waiting, the 'Head of Aphrodite' stands on a table. It is attributed to none other than Praxiteles (4th century BC). This 'Leconfield Aphrodite' and the 'Egremont Apollo' are part of an extraordinary collection of ancient, Renaissance and neoclassical sculptures (including works by Flaxman and Chantrey among others). The Grand Staircase was painted by Louis Laguerre around 1720, with allegorical scenes and plans of the house on which one can see the central dome which was destroyed by a fire in 1714.

I had the good fortune to be allowed into one of the most beautiful rooms of all, the White and Gold Room in the private wing. The panelling is ivory coloured, with delicate ribs and tendrils of gilded wood – a rococo echo from the middle of the 18th century. The carpet is pink, the curtains and chair coverings pale blue. It is a room full of subtle shades (and is probably the room painted by Turner in his *Drawing Room at Petworth* now in the National Gallery). This is one of the rooms where Lord Egremont's heirs now live, as tenants of the National Trust.

The long decline in the agricultural economy had been steadily undermining the financial basis of the great estates since the late 19th century. When death duties rose from 15 per cent in 1914 to 90 per cent in 1945, the destruction of the landed classes and their houses seemed inevitable. 'After the war it looked as if there was no future for estates like ours,'says Max Egremont, the present head of the family. 'Petworth is a very big house, and we could no longer have maintained it on our own. In order to ensure that everything was kept intact for ever, and none of the works of art would have to be sold, my father gave Petworth to the National Trust in 1947 – a year before I was born.'

The real gentry never know how many rooms their houses have, or how much rent they have to pay the National Trust. Perhaps one shouldn't ask such vulgar questions. Lord Egremont certainly doesn't remember. He and his wife and four children (but no butler) live in one third of the house, and the rest is viewed by some 70,000 visitors a year. 'Occasionally one of them wanders through the double doors – our Berlin Wall,' he says, but such intrusions do not disturb him any more than does the National Trust. Lord Egremont – Oxford graduate, novelist, historical biographer, still lord of some 13,000 acres of land – is mindful and greatly appreciative of the fact that the National Trust has relieved him of the responsibility for this vast estate, while allowing him to enjoy it as if it still belonged to him.

When I left Petworth House, I understood just what Haydon meant when he said that even the animals here seemed 'happier than anywhere else in the world'. And I knew that what Prince Pückler-Muskau had said was not just a story: 'There is a house in England where for half a century a well-dressed corpse has been standing at the window and gazing undisturbed at what used to be his property. How this man must have loved domesticity!'

Parham House (1577) is built on a typical Elizabethan E-plan, and has a gabled façade. Its architecture, Downs setting, subtle garden and fine collection of paintings (Bellotto, Gainsborough, Romney) make it another extremely attractive house. The portraits offer a cross-section of English history, by way of the faces and the clothes worn by the top people of the age. In the Green Saloon is Reynolds' portrait of Omaih, the first South-Sea Islander to visit Europe – a trophy from the Banks collection, like the kangaroo skin from which George Stubbs painted an animal which at the time was still unknown in Europe. Sir Joseph Banks, Cook's companion on the *Endeavour*, was one of the greatest naturalists of his time, remembered not only for his travels and collecting, but for contributions to the general happiness of mankind, such as the introduction to cultivation of the mango.

The women of Parham must have spent half their lives embroidering. Generation after generation, century after century, they produced flowers and biblical scenes. The masterpiece of this astonishing collection of naïve needlework art, particularly rich in Stuart pieces generally, is a bedcover which is said to have been embroidered by Mary Queen of Scots while she was in prison.

The wood-panelled Long Gallery, which is almost 158 feet long, was virtually unfurnished during the 16th century. With a view of the Downs on both sides, this was where people went for a walk when it was raining, or played with the children, or got into training for the sporting or military demands of the Tudor Age.

Trees and Dreams: Edward James in West Dean

If you want to do a summer course in herbal medicine, calligraphy or rose-growing, there is no more beautiful setting for it than *West Dean*, north of Chichester. The students sit painting their watercolours among the sheep that are peacefully grazing in front of the College. Flint walls glitter in the sun, the mortar having been dotted with splinters of flint – a medieval technique which is both a stabiliser and a decoration. James Wyatt gave the house its Gothic style turrets and battlements in 1804 (it was rebuilt in 1893). Originally a country house, the College stands surrounded by gardens and a park whose meadows climb up the gentle slopes into the woods and onto the South Downs. This is the pastoral, patriarchal world in which Edward James grew up – a patron of modernity, whom Dalí once called 'the most surrealist of us all'.

Edward James was a godson, and probably even the illegitimate son, of Edward VII, who was always appreciative of the hunting parties at West Dean and the house's beautiful hostess. Edward's family made a fortune in America, but unlike most heirs to historic houses, Edward James not only took over a collection of Old Masters; he also collected contemporary art himself. He did this to an extent that has perhaps only been matched in 20th-century England by Charles Saatchi.

In the early 1930's, Edward James got to know two artists who at the time were not particularly successful: Salvador Dalí and René Magritte. He supported them by commissions and purchases, and also bought pictures by Paul Delvaux, Dorothea Tanning, and Leonora Carrington, and he financed the Parisian surrealist magazine *Minotaure*, to which he himself contributed essays and verses. In 1936 he organized Dalí's legendary 'Happening' in a diving suit. "I almost died of asphyxia,' the painter said afterwards. All this during a period

Edward James

when Surrealism was still extremely unpopular, especially in England. Edward James also helped Darius Milhaud and other modern composers, and he was the first to give George Balanchine a ballet company of his own. Art was his true element; it was life that caused him a few problems.

His disastrous marriage to the dancer Tilly Losch lasted only two years. You can still track her down in West Dean: her footprints are woven into a stair carpet, as if she had just run upstairs with wet feet. Edward James travelled around a great deal, between Paris and Malibu, and when he was in West Dean he lived most of the time in *Monkton*. This house is situated amid beech trees on the edge of the estate. It was designed by Edwin Lutyens in 1902 as a hunting lodge for James's parents. In the mid-1930s he had it rebuilt by Kit Nicholson and Hugh Casson, but Dalí was the consultant and the result was in strict accordance with the rules of the paranoiac-critical method: the external walls were purple, the drainpipes were bamboo, there were bronze palm-tree columns, padded walls in the dining-room, transparent alabaster walls in the bathroom. The lord of the manor's bed was draped in black, like Nelson's bier, and if he pressed a button, he could have the moon and stars shining from the night-blue glass ceiling above him. To sit, he had the lips of Mae West – Dalí's trademark red sofa icon; to speak to the outside world, the lobster telephone (now dead in the Tate Gallery).

Monkton was a surrealistic dream-house. Like all true dreamers, Edward James knew no limits in his quest for new forms of paradise. He found one in Xilitla, deep in the Mexican rain forest. There he decided to build a complete dream city, in the style of 'Jungle Regency'. This last, exotic passion did not stop him, however, from promoting historical projects back in West Dean. On the eastern borders of the park he gave some 50 acres of land over to the open-air museum of *Singleton* – a collection of different farmhouses and rural crafts from the Middle Ages through to the early 20th century. He eventually turned the family estate into a Foundation, and in 1971 he opened the College. West Dean was to be a creative centre, a community of artists, craftsmen, craftswomen, and musicians. It all cost more than even a millionaire could afford, and so in 1981 he had 28 masterpieces from his collection auctioned by Christie's, including Dalí's *Dream* of 1937. It was the beginning of the end for a collection which had included more than 100 of Dalí's pictures, 22 by Magritte, eight by de Chirico – altogether some 300 works making up the most important private collection of Surrealism in England.

Edward James died in 1984. There were two auctions held to dispose of the entire collection, and the first alone took five days. Since the Foundation never had sufficient funds, some sales were inevitable, but the fact that the so-called trustees even sold Monkton became a national scandal. With its bizarre juxtaposition of the Surrealist and the Victorian, Monkton was unique. It was the only modernist 1930's house in England to have remained completely unaltered until 1986. The break-up of such a place, while next door in Singleton old farmhouses were still being lovingly restored, was nothing short of grotesque, and a miserable reflection of the cultural philistinism of the Thatcher period.

Edward James's executors have paid a high price for preserving the estate and the College. With a highly reputed course for restorers, and workshops for carpet-weavers and musical instrument-makers, West Dean College certainly fulfils the tasks intended by the Foundation, but there are also courses for hobbies and leisure-time pursuits which were not part of Edward James's dream. 'I didn't sign away a fortune so that middle-class couples could enjoy a rather cheaper holiday than if they went to a hotel in Torquay,' he was heard to growl.

West Dean: sparkling flint, family portraits, Flemish tapestries, Whistlers, pictures by Leonor Fini, fragments, Edwardian, surreal, strangers in a place that was once a family home... What next for Edward James? Let us leave the house and go into the gardens – through Harold Peto's long pergola, into the kitchen garden with its thirteen large Victorian glasshouses, and from there to the water garden on the River Lavant, where maidenhair fern and a tulip tree stand near the grey stump of a beech tree, which Edward had dipped in synthetic resin, along with all its roots, like a gigantic fossil in amber. Gardens are dreams, and Edward James loved gardens. *The Gardener Who Saw God* was the title of his only novel, the tale of an art-loving gardener just like himself. His head gardener was Ivan Hicks, who moved a few miles to the west to Stansted Park. There he created his own esoteric and eccentric 'Garden in Mind'. To go in, you had to pay £1.01, or a lobster, or a giant shell, or a mirror, or any object so long as it was spherical or surreal. Dear Edward James would have heartily approved. Sadly, the landlords did not, and Hicks garden of delights was bulldozed.

Edward James' chosen burial place was not San Remo, where he died, nor the Mexican rain forest where his last dream lies crumbling. He wanted to lie beneath the trees of West Dean, and so his grave is situated in a clearing in the arboretum, among old *arbor vitæ*, Atlas cedars, and Himalayan pines. The spot is marked by a solid, greenish-blue slab of Cumbrian slate, with the inscription: *Edward James, Poet*.

Sculptures in the Woods: Heading for Goodwood

There are strange goings-on in the woods near *Hat Hill*, a few miles east of West Dean. Two hares are boxing in a clearing, an aluminium spiral swings from the branches of a beech tree, and a giant steel shooting star is sparkling in a meadow. The path is lined with magic stelæ and arches of limestone and flint, and at the edge of the forest, on a sea of white granite columns, two black catamarans head south, towards the shimmering coast of the English Channel. We are in an enchanted wood of contemporary art such as you will find nowhere else in England. This is the avant-garde dream of Wilfred Cass, who in 1994, at the age of 70, opened the sculpture park at *Goodwood*.

Mr Cass came from Berlin, and his real name is Cassirer. Bruno and Paul Cassirer, the Berlin publishers, art collectors and gallery-owners were his great-uncles and the inspiration for his own collector's zeal. As Jews and active

Socialists, his parents emigrated to England in 1935. Wilfred went to a boarding-school in Farnham, and when he joined the British Army he changed his name to Cass. Ernst Barlach's sculpture *Bäuerin* ('Farmer's Wife') in Hat Hill House is one of the few reminders of his childhood in Berlin. As an electronics expert, inventor, manager and entrepreneur, Wilfred Cass amassed a fortune. With his son Mark he founded Image Bank UK, the British branch of the biggest advertising photo and film agency in the world. In 1989 he acquired Hat Hill, but what should have been his retirement home was at once transformed by this restless spirit into a brand new enterprise.

All his life, Wilfred Cass had collected works of art – by David Hockney, Ronald Kitaj, Michael Ayrton and countless others. Now he saw an opportunity to put into practice the credo of his friend Henry Moore: 'Sculpture is an art of the open air'. The site was perfect: 22 acres of sparsely wooded country on the southern slopes of the Downs. There Wilfred and his wife Jeanette created a sculpture park which is quite different from any that they had seen on their travels. Even the much-vaunted Louisiana on the Öresund near Copenhagen seemed to them 'too packed with objects, too static and dominated by history'. In the wood at Hat Hill there are only about 40 sculptures to be seen, but every one is of outstanding quality. 'We don't want people to get mental indigestion,' says Jeanette. 'They should be able to look at a piece and think about it, then enjoy a walk through the beautiful grounds before they get to the next piece.' Thus each sculpture can create its own effect in its own ideal environment, with plenty of distance between itself and its neighbour.

About a quarter of the works are replaced every year by new ones. Wilfred Cass fears nothing more than ossification. I have never met a collector who was so willing to part with his finest items, but for him movement is more important than possession. 'If you keep a collection static, you stop seeing it. Contemporary art is what is happening now. Things change very quickly.' Nowhere else in England will you find such a broad overview of present-day British sculpture, regardless of current artistic trends. There are works of wood, stone, steel and many other materials and techniques – figurative and abstract, minimalist and mystical, constructivist and deconstructivist. Anthony Caro, Tony Cragg, Ian Hamilton Finlay, Elisabeth Frink, Andy Goldsworthy, Nigel Hall, Shirazeh Houshiary, Richard Long, David Nash, Bill Woodrow – these names bear testimony to the extraordinary flowering of modern British sculpture. Wilfred Cass does not, however, regard his park as a nationalist, insular concept; it is merely a beginning and a challenge, 'before we all become Europeans'.

The main aim of the Hat Hill Sculpture Foundation is to create a forum for young artists and designers. Works are commissioned, and their production is financed in exchange for the right to exhibit them for three years. Most of the sculptures are for sale, and the proceeds go to the artists after deduction of the

Wilfred and Jeannette Cass

original advance, which then goes towards financing new projects. The combination of art gallery, agency and patronage is as exemplary as Wilfred Cass's insistence that he remain independent of all public subsidy. What about the running costs? 'I take it out of Jeanette's housekeeping!' He invests about £180,000 a year in his park – eight times as much as the Turner Prize.

The gallery in the woods is as simple and as beautiful as a Japanese teahouse: White steel frame, end walls of glass, with the light and the surroundings integrated into the architecture. The birchwood side walls seem like a continuation of the trees outside. This is a piece of minimalist architecture in the Californian post-Bauhaus style of the fifties, designed by Craig Downie and built in just seven days at a cost of less than £100,000. It is itself a brilliant example of the work of the young designers who display their furniture and their objets d'art in Hat Hill (e.g. Ben Brooks, and Thomas Heatherwick). The gallery also serves as an electronic archive and the starting point of an educational programme that is available for schools and other institutions. This is a Foundation that makes a major contribution to æsthetic training and sets the highest standards for art in the public domain.

The official name of the park is *Sculpture at Goodwood*, as it is actually situated on the 12,000-acre Goodwood estate of the Dukes of Richmond and Gordon. These British aristocrats enjoy the rare addition of a French title: Duc de

Daubigny, bestowed on them when a forebear served the French King as a mercenary during the 12th century. Goodwood was originally nothing more than a hunting lodge, until William Chambers extended it (1757–60) with a stable the size of a country house. In order that the Dukes should be able to live as feudally as their horses, James Wyatt was summoned in 1771. He was eventually to build *Goodwood House* as a grand three-sided belvedere, using the flint typical of Sussex, but owing to money troubles the work was not finished until 1806. His patron, the 3rd Duke of Richmond, subject of a Reynolds portrait, was a man of many parts. As ambassador to the court of Louis XV in Versailles, he collected French furniture, tapestries, and Sèvres porcelain; as a military commander, he was responsible for building the Martello Towers; and as a riding fanatic, he started horse-racing at Goodwood in 1802.

After Epsom and Ascot, the Goodwood races are the most famous in the country. 'Glorious Goodwood' takes place every May in a setting full of contrasts, not to mention fashions. At the foot of the prehistoric hill fortress of *Trundle* are the high-tech stands built by Arup Associates (1990) – a white steel construction with a transparent tent roof, light and festive; behind the broad curves of the course itself are the green hills of the Downs. And in the salons of Goodwood you can see the 3rd Duke's own horses in training, painted by George Stubbs. Other

Bodiam Castle

treasures include paintings by Hogarth, van Dyck, Gainsborough and – especially – Canaletto. The latter were commissioned by the 2nd Duke of Richmond, and these were the first pictures Canaletto painted after his arrival in London in 1746.

Racing is in the Richmonds' blood, and for those who prefer more horsepower, there has been another racecourse in Goodwood since 1936. Stirling Moss, Jackie Stewart, Graham Hill and many others raced there against the 9th Duke. In 1993 his grandson Charles, the present Earl of March, inaugurated a yearly Festival of Speed at his own Mini-Ring – a course measuring 1.1 miles. 'Charley is wonderful,' says Wilfred Cass. 'He's one of the directors of our Foundation, and he's certainly got eyes in his head.' This is in marked contrast to his father, the 11th Duke, of whom it was said that he never even saw the pictures in his own house.

In the park at Goodwood there is a folly such as only the English can create. Over seven long years, the wife of the 2nd Duke of Richmond and her daughters decked out the walls of a grotto with coloured shells, and covered the floor with a design made from horses' teeth (c. 1740). Well worth making a detour for – but it is not normally open to the public. Not to worry: Sussex has many other eccentricities worth hunting out. One such is the pyramid at *Brightling* near Bateman's, a symbol of Britain's Egyptomania following the defeat of Napoleon in the Battle of the Nile. The Honourable John Fuller, later known simply as Mad Jack, had the pyramid built in 1810, during his own lifetime, as a shock-horror mausoleum. The story that he had himself buried there in an armchair with a top-hat and a bottle of red wine has proved to be apocryphal. Fuller was an MP, an early champion and collector of Turner, saved *Bodiam Castle* (1385) from becoming a ruin, and left behind an eccentric masterpiece called the Sugar Loaf – a church tower without a church. He had laid a bet that the church tower at *Dallington* could be seen from his house. It couldn't, and so he had a copy of the tower built where it could be seen. Mad Jack won his bet, and the world gained a folly.

Uppark: An Orgy of Restoration

There is a country house on the South Downs with a view over forests and hills and, in the distance, the sea. No house in Southern England has a more spectacular setting than *Uppark*, north-west of Chichester. The architecture is discreet and restrained: brick, two storeys, hipped roof and attic, tall windows, neat proportions. The combination of strength and grace makes Uppark a perfect example of a William and Mary house, built around 1690 for a political trickster, Lord Grey of Werke.

The rooms are 18th century, full of furniture from the Age of Elegance. Here the beautiful Emma Lyon is said to have delighted the guests by dancing naked on the table; this was before she married the collector Sir William Hamilton and achieved immortality as Nelson's mistress. The owner of the house, Sir Harry Fetherstonhaugh, loved art and women, and when he was over 70 married his kitchen maid, the 20-year-old Mary Ann Bullock. Romances and scandals – this was a great house for them. But its greatest moment came on 30 August 1989, when it burnt down. 'Down' is the operative word, as the fire was started by workmen on the roof. This meant that nearly all the furniture and paintings could be hauled out in time; but there was not enough water on this isolated hill top to save the filigree stucco garlands and ceiling medallions and gilded wood carvings and crimson velvet wall-coverings and ivory-coloured panelling and doorframes. What happened to all this glory?

For six years, in a positive orgy of restoration, the National Trust set about reconstructing the interiors of Uppark. They sieved through 4,000 tons of debris and rubble, identified 750,000 fragments of plaster, wood and metal, recorded them on computer, replaced them in their original positions, and made exact copies of whatever items had been destroyed. Only a nation with a passion for jigsaw puzzles and its own history could have pulled it off. Uppark became a high school for National Trust restorers, who had to learn anew all the old techniques of plastering and painting. This was traditional craftsmanship married to ultra-modern computer technology. The most difficult thing of all to restore was the ancient patina of past splendours. 'Uppark White' contains a special mixture of walnut oil and lead sulphide, so that instead of yellowing, it fades into a sort of silver-grey. The wallpaper was restored (or newly made) to its faded condition of 1989, and even the darker patches behind the pictures, where the light could not penetrate, have been artificially recreated, so that everything is just as it was the day before the fire. Crazy? Maybe, but that's the sort of craziness for which we love this country and its National Trust. This is the most expensive restoration project ever undertaken by the Trust, and has so far cost upwards of £20 million. It gives a new dimension to historical correctness, and it trained a whole generation of craftsmen in skills that had been lost, skills which have now been put to good use all over the country.

'The desire to preserve the past, or to recreate an illusion of it, is deeply ingrained in our national psyche,' wrote the architecture critic Jonathan Glancey, commenting on the restoration of Uppark. 'To question such activities, however, is to fail to understand the magic of the past. The more our daily lives become uncertain in a world where no job, no personal or professional relationship can be a fixed point of reference, the more we cling to the imagined certainties of history.'

After the reopening in 1995, Humphry Repton's park (1810–15) was also restored, and one of the rarities of the house was opened to the public for the first time: the Print Room is a miniature gallery, wallpapered with etchings of Old Masters simply stuck on the walls as was the fashion during the Regency. Sir Harry used to be shaved here. Down in the basement is the table at which the fourteen-year-old H. G. Wells sat and produced his first writings in the winter of

1880 – *The Uppark Alarmist*, a newspaper of domestic gossip. His mother was housekeeper here, and holidays at Uppark were among the few joys of his childhood. In his novel *Tono-Bungay* (1909), Wells described this house in some detail, under the pseudonym of Bladesover House. With its wealth of books and pictures, and a social hierarchy that was still intact, Uppark – perhaps transfigured by nostalgia – seemed to Wells like a model society of civilization and culture. But he also found his radical roots here, devouring Tom Paine and Voltaire in the attic; and he saw how the downstairs folk were kept down in their hidden quarters, though not, if truth be told, as violently as the underground Morlocks were to be in *The Time Machine*. At Uppark, downstairs 'retained a vitality that altogether overshadowed the insignificant ebbing trickle of upstairs life, the two elderly ladies in the parlour following their shrunken routine.' But the impressions of both culture and its discontents were indelible, and the future Utopias – and dystopias – that Wells created in his books had their roots firmly in the past.

Art in the Cathedral: Chichester

Chichester Canal: Turner's painting in Petworth stays in the mind, and a sailing paradise unfolds before the eyes. Chichester Cathedral must be the one cathedral tower in England that can actually be seen from the sea. The first thing and the last thing that meets your eye in *Chichester* is this cathedral, unimpeded by highrise blocks or factory chimneys. Eric Gill, who grew up here, called it 'the human city, the city of God, the place where life and work and things were all in one and all in harmony.' Such harmony between architecture, town and landscape has become rare, even in Britain. Chichester is one of the ancient towns; its present name derives from *Cissas castrum* (Cissa's castle), Cissa being one of the sons of the 5th-century Anglo-Saxon conqueror Ælla, who captured the town of *Noviomagus Regnensium*, which had previously been occupied by the Celts and the Romans. The four main roads (with the Late Gothic Market Cross of 1501 forming their centre point) branch off at right-angles from each other; they and the foundations of an amphitheatre excavated outside the eastern city walls bear witness to the Roman occupation. The pretext for a later invasion was King Harold's unwise promise to Duke William that he would not claim the throne of England; it was from just outside Chichester, at the little fishing village of *Bosham* that Harold left on his fateful journey to Normandy in 1064. The grand Anglo-Saxon church can be seen in the Bayeux Tapestry, with Harold and his entourage praying for safe passage.

Anyone who fell ill in Chichester after 1158 would find help at St Mary's Hospital in St Martin's Street. Since the closure of the Heilig-Geist-Hospital in Lübeck, this is the last great medieval hospital still functioning in north-west

Europe. In the 14th and 15th centuries, Chichester was an important harbour for the export of wool and later wheat. Today, although it is the county town of West Sussex and an agricultural centre, Chichester is simply a delightful little town with just 26,000 inhabitants. The Festival Theatre in Oaklands Park, designed by Powell & Moya in 1961, was directed for many years by Sir Laurence Olivier, under whom it built up an international reputation.

The slender central spire of Chichester Cathedral is what one sees from every angle of approach, but it is the bell tower (1436) that is unique, as it is the only one in England that still stands detached from the cathedral itself, though this was originally the case at Salisbury and old St Paul's, and indeed Westminster Abbey. More unusual than the aisles with their side-chapels is the arrangement of the cloister (*c.* 1400), which extends asymmetrically round the south transept. The interior is curiously satisfying, though in fact it is a combination of the normally conflicting Norman and Early English styles: the upper levels had to be rebuilt following a fire in 1187, only three years after the building was completed. The retrochoir, the area behind the partially preserved presbytery (14th century), is a fine example of the Norman Transitional style, with its harmonious mixture of round and pointed arches, combining the Romanesque and the Gothic. There are two Romanesque sandstone reliefs – probably part of a 12th-century choir screen – which are strikingly expressive, combining homeliness with monumentality: *Christ at the House of Mary of Bethany*, and *The Raising of Lazarus*. Originally these were brightly painted, and the eyes were inlaid with semi-precious stones. The composer Gustav Holst lies buried in the north transept, and when I visited the Cathedral at evensong, there were fresh freesias on his grave.

In the choir, behind the high altar, hangs John Piper's tapestry of the Holy Trinity, the Creation, and nuclear disaster – just one of the many pieces of modern art in the Cathedral. (Another long vista in English history: the workshop that made this tapestry has a direct link with the family that 'put together' the Bayeux Tapestry.) In the northern aisle of the choir is a glowing red stained glass window by Marc Chagall, based on Psalm 150 (1978), and Graham Sutherland's altarpiece *Noli me tangere* (1962) is in the south-east chapel. These and other works were commissioned by Walter Hussey, Dean of the Cathedral from 1955 until 1977. Dean Hussey's influence spread far beyond Chichester, for he was England's most committed champion of modern art in churches generally. Nor did he confine his love of God and the arts to an ecclesiastical context, for he also collected privately whatever works he liked and could afford: Henry Moore, Graham Sutherland, Paul Nash, Christopher Wood, Ivon Hitchens and Frank Auerbach, pottery by Lucie Rie and Hans Coper, drawings by Watteau and Tiepolo. The collection

The cross at Chichester, 'a very faire Cross of Stone like a Church or great arch, its pretty large and pirramydy form with several Carvings' Celia Fiennes, Journeys, c. 1685-96

F.L. GRIGGS — 1905

113

Blake's cottage: an illustration from his poem Milton

includes about 160 works, all of which this art-loving clergyman gave to the city of Chichester before he died. The collection has been housed in noble surroundings: *Pallant House*, the Queen Anne residence of a wine merchant (1712). In the beautifully restored interiors there is a fascinating mixture of ancient and modern art.

Chichester played an important role in the lives of two English writers. The early Romantic poet William Collins was born in East Street; he is most famous for his *Ode to Evening*:

> Now air is hushed, save where the weak-eyed bat
> With short, shrill shriek, flits by on leathern wing;
> > Or where the beetle winds
> His small but sullen horn...

When Collins was thirty he went mad, and died eight years later in 1759, in a house near the cloister. 'He pass'd in madd'ning pain life's feverish dream' are the words on his marble monument, which shows him leaning over the New Testament. This is one of six Flaxman monuments in the Cathedral. In what is now the Guildhall Museum, the visionary painter-poet William Blake was once tried for 'high treason'. He had thrown an obstreperously drunken soldier out of his garden at nearby *Felpham* – reason enough for him to be put on trial, since he was already under suspicion of being an anarchist for defending the French Revolution and the American War of Independence. But his neighbours spoke up on his behalf, and he was acquitted, though he was so unnerved he returned at once to London and never lived in the country again. Blake and his wife Catherine had come to Felpham from London in September 1800. At that time, Felpham was still a separate village, though today it is part of Bognor Regis. Flaxman had arranged for Blake to work as an illustrator for the poet William Hayley, and to help him on his edition of Milton. Aside from the fact that his patron forced him to spend evening after evening reading aloud the works of the German writer Klopstock, which Blake disliked intensely, he spent three happy years here, free of care and writing copiously. 'Felpham is a sweet place for study, because it is more spiritual than London. Heaven opens here on all sides its golden gates; the windows are not obstructed by vapours; voices of celestial inhabitants are more distinctly heard, their forms more distinctly seen,' he wrote to a friend, and, inspired by his work, began his visionary epic poem, *Milton* which includes England's great hymn *Jerusalem*.

> Away to sweet Felpham for heaven is there:
> The ladder of Angels descends through the air.
> On the turret its spiral does softly descend,
> Through the village it winds, at my cot it does end.

'The Turret' was Hayley's house; Blake's flintstone cottage, chalk-white and thatched, stands unaltered by time near the church in Blake's Lane.

The Roman villa at *Fishbourne* near Chichester, whose south wing once looked out on the sea but now lies buried beneath the A27, was discovered in 1960. Only a very rich man or the English King and Roman confederate Tiberius Cogidubnus

Mosaic, Fishbourne

115

himself could have afforded a palace of this size in 75 AD. It was big even by the standards of Rome itself: it covers an area of 16,145 square feet with four wings grouped round an inner courtyard with fountains and garden. The west and east wings were excavated but for reasons of conservation provisionally covered over again. Almost all the hundred rooms were extravagantly decorated with mosaic floors, of which those in the bath-house are reckoned to be the earliest surviving ones in England. The geometrical patterns and perspective illusions suggest a Roman Vasarely. A fire in the 3rd century destroyed this great villa by the Channel.

The mosaics in the Roman villa of *Bignor* were perhaps even richer. It is idyllically situated on the Downs, not far from the Roman Stane Street, which linked London and Chichester, and it is five miles and a thousand years away from Parham House. George Tupper, a farmer, discovered it on 18 July 1811 when his plough ran over a girl dancer. She was part of the floor mosaic in the dining-room. The Tuppers still own the land, and they have built thatched enclosures over these mid-4th-century mosaics. Thus protected, little Cupids tirelessly pursue their gladiatorial sports, peacocks surround the flowered head of Venus, Medusa's fourteen snakes petrify the observer, and the eagle carries off poor Ganymede. The only one of the four seasons to have survived is Winter, a woman with veiled head and a bare branch over her shoulder. In one corner of this mosaic are the initials TER – Terentius, perhaps the great artist of Bignor.

Catholics and Other Traitors: Arundel Castle

In dramatic tiers, like some Old Master landscape, *Arundel* unfolds its hilly panorama. The Castle and the Cathedral tower mightily over the little town on the Arun. Above the Norman keep flies the flag of the Dukes of Norfolk, the oldest dukedom in the land, and also England's most prominent Catholic family. They rose to the highest offices at court, they made pacts with the wrong side, they fell out of favour, they lost everything, and then they rose again. Three of them died under the executioner's axe, and one died in the Tower. For centuries they took part in the struggle between State and Church, representing both Catholicism and the privileges of the aristocracy. Scenes of this lost world are to be found in Arundel, presented with nostalgic reverence

From the powerful medieval families of Fitzalan and Howard, to whom the castle still belongs, came the sonneteer and enemy of the Tudors, Henry Howard, Earl of Surrey, regarded as the boldest soldier, most melodious poet, and noblest gentleman of his time. The fact that he was a pioneer of blank verse did not, alas, save him. Henry VIII had him executed for high treason – or to be more precise, of 'treasonably quartering the royal arms', a charge even the staid Dictionary of National Biography describes as 'frivolous'. One of his descendants, Thomas

Howard, 14th Earl of Arundel, was England's greatest art collector in the 17th century – a connoisseur of the classics and a patron whom Rubens regarded as 'one of the four evangelists and supporters of our arts'. The Arundel Marbles, which formed part of his collection of antiquities, are now in the Ashmolean Museum, Oxford, but many of his paintings are still with the family at Arundel Castle. Van Dyck's double portrait of 1640 shows him with his wife Alethea, bearing the staff of the Earl Marshal of England. This role of the Grand Master of Ceremonies is hereditary, and is now played by the present Duke of Norfolk, for instance at the yearly State Opening of Parliament. As Earl Marshal, the Duke of Norfolk also has to prepare the coronation of every new monarch, though that has not proven to be too onerous a task in recent years. As Britain's historically most prominent Catholic, the Duke also has an unofficial role as leader of the country's Catholic community.

Thomas Howard, 14th Earl of Arundel, by Rubens

Arundel Castle was almost completely destroyed during the Civil War, and what we see is a 19th-century fortress resurrected around the medieval keep. Inside is a set of spectacular, not to say bombastic, late Victorian interiors, with the occasional late Georgian interlude. Arundel's closest relative is Neuschwanstein in Bavaria, the brainchild of mad King Ludwig. But just as the mountains of Sussex are no competition for the Bavrian Alps, Arundel was the creation of a much more prosaic character, the 15th Duke of Norfolk. With his immense fortune, derived partly from the coalmines of Sheffield, he subsidised Catholic churches throughout the country in the great spate of building after Catholic emancipation in 1829, in support of his long victimised fellow believers. Arundel also owes him its massive neo-Gothic cathedral, designed in 1868 by Joseph Hansom, inventor of that paragon of 19th century modern efficiency, the Hansom Cab. The Castle and the Cathedral together make for a potent if pompous double act of medieval revivalism.

In the northern transept of the Cathedral lies the 13th Earl of Arundel. He died in 1595 in the Tower, after eleven years of imprisonment which failed to break his faith. Four hundred years later, this steadfastness brought him the highest honour his church could bestow: canonization. Previously the bones of St Philip Howard had rested in the nearby Fitzalan Chapel, built in 1380, with a Perpendicular wooden fan vault, whose richly carved bosses still bear traces of their original medieval paintwork. The marble and alabaster sarcophagi date from the 15th to the

19th century, making this chapel one of the greatest galleries of English memorial sculpture. In the proud words of the caretaker, 'Here is history, Sir!' The fact that the Catholic chapel is separated from the (rather ordinary) Anglican parish church by a glass wall, even though they are both under the same roof, is also part of Arundel's history.

One of the tombs has acquired its own history: the early 15th century double effigy of of Richard Fitzalan, 4th Earl of Arundel, and his Countess, inspired Philip Larkin to write what has proved to be one of his most enduring poems, *An Arundel Tomb*. In it Larkin honours the gesture of love: 'One sees, with a sharp tender shock, His hand withdrawn, holding her hand.' But it turned out, long after the poem had already made it to the schoolbooks, that the hands were joined by a Victorian restorer.

Let us, however, leave the distant past. When I went to Arundel I was able to meet the then Duke, Miles Fitzalan-Howard, the 17th in his line. He received me in his study – a small, friendly man with bright eyes and a pacemaker. 'When I succeeded in 1975, we didn't give the castle to the National Trust; we made it into a family trust of our own – Arundel Trustees Ltd. Much better. You keep your independence. We lend our pictures and furniture to the Trust, they insure everything, and there are no death duties.' The retired Major-General chuckled contentedly over his successful manoeuvre. Edward, his eldest son, has rented the East Wing. 'I'm happier to live in my little house near Henley,' said the old gentleman. 'When I stay here at the Castle, I pay the Family Trust ten pounds a night.'

Miles Fitzalan-Howard, 17th Duke of Norfolk

The Duke studied history at Oxford and experienced it for himself during the war and an army career spanning thirty years. Then he sat in the House of Lords, made speeches about abortion and Northern Ireland, and found it frustrating that the Lords had no real power. In Arundel Castle he had his own librarian, but no butler. 'We don't live grandly at all – that's all a myth. I even clean my own shoes.' Does he collect art, like his forebears? 'Can't afford it!' And yet they are supposed to be one of the richest families in the country. 'Rubbish! I've only got one and a half million, say.' Then the impoverished Duke poured me a cup of coffee ('No butler, you see!') and leaves me in the company of his Gainsboroughs. His last words to me, delivered with papal gentility and in German, were: 'Gott segne dich!' (God bless you.)

Not far from this Catholic citadel there is a church with the ceiling of the Sistine Chapel. A local signwriter named Gary Bevans, who specializes in pub signs,

The church at Sompting

copied Michelangelo's frescoes onto plywood in an act that was a mixture of piety and pleasure. The work, which took him five years, was completed in 1993, and is situated in Holy Martyrs at *Goring-by-Sea*. It is not the only curiosity to be found in this region.

On the coast south of Arundel, hidden away at the end of a cul-de-sac, lies *Bailiffscourt*. It's a medieval country house surrounded by old trees, and it was built in 1935 by Amyas Phillips, and the trees were all transplanted here. Nevertheless, Bailiffscourt is genuinely old. It has a 15th-century gatehouse, a 17th-century half-timbered house, 16th-century tapestries, 15th-century oak ceilings. This remarkable jigsaw puzzle was assembled by Lord Moyne (the politician whose assassination in Cairo by Zionists in 1944 was a prime cause of British withdrawal from the Middle East) at a cost of just one million pounds. There are no imitations here – everything is as old as it is new. The only old thing that is not new is a Norman chapel. And you can now stay in this new old house if you want to, because it is a hotel. How often can you stay in an open-air museum?

Another building that looks as if it has travelled for miles is a Norman church tower at *Sompting*, near Worthing on the coast. If this 'Rhenish helm' had been transportable, Lord Moyne would certainly have taken it to Bailiffscourt. Characteristic of churches here, the helm is covered with oak shingles, which have

Sackville chapel at Withyham

to be split, not sawn, because then they last longer – about 100 years. Apart from St Mary's in Sompting, other typical Anglo-Saxon churches are St Andrew's in *Bishopstone* on the Downs near Seaford, and St Nicholas in *Worth*, a village in the Weald (near Crawley). In the main building of Worth Priory, there is a stucco frieze (1897) by Walter Crane, showing the history of transport from the ox-cart through to the motor-car. Crane was a local man – he died at Horsham – and a craftsman who worked within the Arts and Crafts Movement, as well as being an illustrator and an Art Nouveau theorist.

Turner's Hill near Worth offers a picture postcard view over the Weald and *Ashdown Forest*. Hills and heath, covered with gorse, bracken, heather, birch and pine. The Venerable Bede, father of English history, found it 'thick and impenetrable, a refuge for wolves and boar' in 731. From the 15th through to the 18th century, however, the forest was hacked to pieces – oak was needed for ship-building, and charcoal for the iron industry. From the Weald came artistic firebacks, like those at Petworth House, the cannons that fired on the Armada, and memorial slabs as well. The old wrought-iron railings are still to be seen in front of the Sackville Chapel (1680) at St Michael's in *Withyham*, burial-place of one of the great English families. Here, on the edge of Ashdown Forest, lies the Renaissance poet Thomas Sackville, first earl of Dorset (see page 70), whose funeral took place at Westminster Abbey; in 1962 the writer Vita Sackville-West was also laid to rest here. Knole and Sissinghurst, their respective Kentish homes, are not too far away. The village church in Withyham has monuments by some of the finest of English sculptors – Nollekens, Flaxman, and Chantrey. The most striking of all these tombs is that of a boy: 'Here lies the 13th child and 7th son/who in his 13th year his race had run.' With eyes open, lying back on his sarcophagus as if it were a bed, one hand on a skull, is young Thomas Sackville. Kneeling on either side of him are his parents, lifesize figures of grief-stricken marble; the rest of the family are shown in relief on the sarcophagus itself. It is a deeply intimate representation of a scene that indivisibly marries art, life and death. Both the concept and the execution of this tomb are influenced by Italian Baroque sculpture, and it constitutes a new peak in the long tradition of English monuments. It was made by the Danish sculptor Caius Gabriel Cibber for young Sackville's mother in 1677, before he became court sculptor to William III.

A few miles south-west of Withyham, in the middle of Ashdown Forest, lives the most famous bear in the world. Every child between Sussex and Sydney knows Winnie the Pooh and his friends Piglet, Eeyore, Tigger and Kanga, and everybody knows that Baby Roo went missing here. Pooh lives in 160 acres of wood and heath, near *Cotchford Farm* (south of Hartfield). That was the home of A. A. Milne from 1925 until he died in 1956. His plays have long been forgotten, but his children's books became classics: *Winnie-the-Pooh* (1926) and *The House at Pooh Corner* (1928) are best-sellers all over the world. He wrote them for his son Christopher Robin, Pooh's friend, and their adventures at Gill's Lap bring Pooh fans flocking from all corners to see the enchanted places of childhood. From Pooh Bridge they throw sticks into the water, and on the sundial at Cotchford Farm they read with delight that 'This warm and sunny spot belongs to Pooh,/And here he wonders what to do.' There is also a statue of Christopher

Robin, and if you don't know the rest of the dialogue off by heart, you'd better learn it now:

> '...what I like *doing* best is Nothing.'
> 'How do you do nothing?' asked Pooh...
> 'Well, it's when people call out at you just as you're going off to do it, "What are you going to do, Christopher Robin?" and you say 'Oh, nothing,' and then you go and do it.'

Glyndebourne: Picnics and Operas

Every year on November 5th *Lewes* goes crazy. Burning tar barrels roll down the High Street and sink into the Ouse with a loud hiss. The streets of this sober little town on the edge of the Downs are filled with Vikings, Mongols, Red Indians, Tudor ladies, Zulu warriors, waving torches, beating drums, wheeling monstrous effigies of politicians and other pet hates, all of which are finally burnt on a great big bonfire. Fireworks, singing, dancing continue till well into the night. Guy Fawkes' Day is celebrated all over England, but nowhere is it wilder than in Lewes.

Guy Fawkes was one of the leading figures in the Gunpowder Plot of 5 November 1605. Catholic conspirators tried to blow up King James I and both Houses of Parliament, but failed. Guy Fawkes was caught red-handed, and executed, thereby giving the British a great excuse for a party. In Lewes, they had a special reason for celebrating: during the reign of the all-too-Catholic Bloody Mary, 17 Protestant martyrs had been burnt to death there, and so even today 17 burning crosses are carried in the procession, and you can sometimes hear the cry: 'Burn the Pope'.

The little town lies on a hill, and from a distance it still looks much as it did when Daniel Defoe admired it in 1722: 'a fine pleasant town, large, well built, agreably situated in the Middle of an open Champaign country and on the edge of the South Downs, the pleasantest, and most delightful of their kind in the Nation.' Lewes is Chichester's counterpart, being the county town of East Sussex. Despite its by-pass, the traffic is a foretaste of hell, and between the river and the town-centre are two hideous supermarkets. Walking down the High Street, however, is still a pleasure. The buildings are a mixture of periods, styles and materials, with Tudor half-timbering right next to elegant Georgian, fitting together like old married couples. As well as the chessboard patterns of the red and grey bricks, Lewes has more 'mathematical tiles' than anywhere else in Southern England. These are specially shaped tiles pinned to the façade to look like bricks; they are part of a great tax dodge: between 1784 and 1850 there was a special tax on brick houses.

Ditchling: house supposedly belonging to Anne of Cleves

If you go down the steep Keere Street, and manage to avoid breaking your neck on the flint cobblestones, you will come to a traffic sign which tells a story: No Through Road – even though George IV as Prince Regent drove a coach through here for a wager. On the bowling green by the castle, the locals are well nigh unbeatable. It is as undulating as the Downs, and has been so for over 300 years. Once it was the tilt-yard, where the knights from the Norman castle would do their jousting. The castle itself was built by William the Conqueror's son-in-law William de Warenne, who after visiting Cluny, founded the first and biggest Cluniac priory in England, St Pancras Priory, built in 1077 outside the gates of Lewes. Henry VIII's right-hand-man Thomas Cromwell made such a thorough job of sacking it that the cloister and chapterhouse have long since turned into part of the Brighton-Eastbourne railway line. Cromwell, the 'Hammer of the Monks', was beheaded shortly afterwards, having arranged yet another disastrous marriage for the King. Anne of Cleves, the 'Flanders mare', Henry's fourth wife, had a house in Lewes, which is now a local museum. It was part of her divorce settlement, but she never lived there, any more than she did at her picturesque house in *Ditchling*. (Ditchling was the centre of the artistic community that grew around

Glyndebourne in its 1960's heyday, as seen by Osbert Lancaster, who designed for the opera

the purist letterer and sculptor Eric Gill - with goings on that would have scan-dalised locals more than Henry VIII ever did.) In Lewes High Street, the White Hart Hotel proclaims itself to be the Cradle of American Independence, for here the Americans' champion Tom Paine, author of *The Age of Reason* and *The Rights of Man*, founded the Headstrong Club, which engaged in vehement political dis-cussions. Paine lived at Bull House after 1768, married for the second time at St Michael's, and in 1774 emigrated to America, whence he only returned as bones in William Cobbett's suitcase.

In 1956, the writer Malcolm Lowry and his wife Margerie moved into White Cottage in *Ripe*, a few miles east of Lewes. It was his last home. 'We live in an ancient cottage in an ancient village, where there is not even a village idiot, unless you count myself.' But even on the gentle slopes of the South Downs, Lowry still lived under the volcano, in a self-destructive torment of alcohol and depression. In 'The Yew Tree', a pub in the neighbouring village of Calvington, he ordered one more bottle of gin on 26 June 1957. The following morning he was dead, poisoned by alcohol and sleeping tablets. He lies buried in the village graveyard in Ripe.

Nearby, in the green hills of the Downs, lies *Glyndebourne*. John Christie, lover of opera and cricket, married a young soprano and, to keep her in the style to which she had become accustomed, built a little opera house on his country estate, and opened it in May 1934 with Mozart's *Figaro*. Out of this private initiative grew a national institution, the operatic equivalent of Wimbledon. The extremely high musical standards were set right from the beginning by three refugees from Nazism, whom Christie employed to run his Festival: the conductor Fritz Busch from Dresden, the theatre director Carl Ebert from Berlin, and the artists' manager Rudolf Bing from Vienna.

On 28 May 1994 Glyndebourne's new opera house was officially opened – precisely 60 years after the first one, and once again with Mozart's *Nozze di Figaro*. The project was initiated by Sir George Christie, son of the founder, and it was an act of great courage in the midst of a recession. The cost, about £40 million, was raised through private sponsorship and, as with the Festival itself, there was not a penny of government subsidy. The new opera house, designed by Michael Hopkins, is dominated by a bulky, lead-covered fly tower, while the auditorium is in red brick, like the house itself, with open galleries all round and a foyer with a tent roof. There is room for an audience of 1,200, and the acoustics are excellent, thanks to the recycled pinewood panelling. The Festival now runs from the end of May until well into August, and the repertoire has long since gone beyond Mozart, even encompassing works commissioned from Harrison Birtwistle and other leading composers of today.

The most important part of a Glyndebourne opera, however, is the interval. It is 85 minutes long, and worth every second, for if it is not raining, the interval is picnic time and a jolly good time, too. Gentlemen in dinner jackets and ladies in long evening gowns drape themselves opulently over the lawns and gardens of Glyndebourne, staging their own magnificent show with props consisting of woollen blankets, garden tables and chairs, damask cloths, silver-ware, crystal, and even the odd candelabra. From picnic hampers and cool-boxes emerge the smoked salmon and lobster, the truffles and pâté, the champagne, strawberries and cream, and everything else that makes a Glyndebourne opera such a lip-smacking occasion. Meanwhile, the cattle low an attempted musical accompaniment, and all is right with the world.

Virginia Woolf in Rodmell

'I do not know whether pilgrimages to the shrines of famous men ought not to be condemned as sentimental journeys,' wrote Virginia Woolf in 1904, after visiting the Brontë house in Haworth. Now it's her own house that people visit, and although the National Trust have not made *Monk's House* into a literary place of pilgrimage, nevertheless one is bound to have mixed feelings. When you see her bedroom, or her threadbare chair by the fireplace, you feel almost as if you are intruding on something even more personal and private than the lines written in her diaries.

If you leave Lewes and drive along the country road towards Newhaven and the coast, about halfway there you will pass through Rodmell. On the edge of the village, where the riverside meadows begin, is a little church of Sussex flint with a shingle spire, and next to that, right beside the road, is a house with weatherboarding. 'There is little ceremony or precision at Monk's House. It is an unpretending house, long & low, a house of many doors,' wrote Virginia Woolf. There was no running water, no gas, no electricity, but 'an infinity of fruit bearing trees'. And infinite peace and quiet, which is what Virginia Woolf needed when she and Leonard bought the house in 1919.

Today, as then, one enters the cottage from the garden. Leonard only put in the long greenhouse after Virginia's death. The rooms are low and simply furnished. Comfort was never a major consideration for either of them. The table and chairs in the living-room were decorated in the Omega Workshops, commissioned like much of the other furniture from Virginia's sister Vanessa Bell and Duncan Grant, who lived nearby in Charleston Farmhouse (see page 129); most of the pictures, the painted screen, jugs, dishes and glazed tiles came from them as well.

On the mantelpiece is Virgina's onyx pear, and on the tiled table a packet of Petit Voltigeur, Belgian cigarillos of which she was particularly fond. It all seems as authentic as one could possibly expect, bearing in mind the detail in which the household of the Bloomsbury people has been documented. And yet after Virginia died in 1941, Leonard lived on here for another 28 years. It became his house. When he died, it was then rented out to visiting American professors at Sussex University, including Saul Bellow. The interior today is a reconstruction, a sort of authentic compromise. It is as tidy as if Virginia had been the model housewife, but we know that in those days there were books lying everywhere – on the floor, the tables and chairs, both sides of the staircase, right up to the ceiling. After Leonard's death, most of the library was sold off, and the remainder, neatly sorted out, is mainly in the care of the National Trust. After all, their tenants – who live on the top floor – and the awestruck visitors would not wish to be stumbling over books, even if they were Virginia's own.

As the royalties came in, the Woolfs gradually extended Monk's House. They put in a bath and lavatory, hot water, an oil stove, and indeed Virginia was able to write in 1931 that the house was now so luxurious that it even had electric heating in the bedrooms. But with its brick floor and weather-boarded walls, it remained damp and draughty. In the winter of 1940 she wrote: 'Yet the wind cuts like a scythe; the dining room carpet is turning to mould.' Three worn brick steps lead from the kitchen into the garden, to a little extension where she used to sleep. It's a sparsely furnished room, with walls of apple-green, her favourite colour. Vanessa painted the tiles round the fireplace; on one of them a ship is sailing towards a lighthouse – a reference to Virginia's novel *To the Lighthouse* (1927).

'Our garden is a perfect variegated chintz: asters, plumasters, zinnias, geums, nasturtiums and so on: all bright, cut from coloured paper, stiff, upstanding as

Bust of Virginia Woolf at Charleston

flowers should be. I have been planting wallflowers for next June.' In fact, the garden was Leonard's domain, and apart from flowers, there were plenty of vegetables, berries and other fruits. Beneath the chestnut trees in one corner is a white wooden pavilion, with the church just behind a flint wall. The little garden house was where Virginia went to write. The room is tiny, with bare floorboards and a simple table in the middle. On it are her pen, some blue writing paper, a clay inkpot with green ink, and a cigarette packet. You look through the glass window into this room as if you were looking into an empty aquarium.

Life in Rodmell followed a rigid routine: morning, writing in the garden house; afternoon, a walk along the Ouse, sometimes with Pinka her spaniel; then tea with Leonard, endless conversations, long evenings reading by the fireside. In a box under the stairs are the bowls, which were as much a part of Monk's House as Louie the cook. But summers in Rodmell were not quiet, 'I can't say we have had a quiet summer, because Sussex is really only an extension of Oxford Street, and as we are on the wayside, anybody drops in.'

T. S. Eliot was a frequent visitor, and Maynard Keynes, Lytton Strachey, Vita

127

from Sissinghurst, Vanessa with the Charleston clan. The photo albums are full of summer visitors, playing bowls, relaxing, gossiping under the chestnut tree; Virginia is always there with her large, deep-set eyes, and her melancholy mouth. Her niece Angelica Garnett described her, quite unsentimentally: 'Shabby, untidy, wispy, her fingers stained with nicotine, she cared not a straw for her appearance, but by some curious fluke remained both distinguished and elegant.'

Virginia loved to see visitors arrive, and she loved it even more when they left. 'We came back from Rodmell yesterday; & Rodmell was all gold and sunshine. The one dismal element was provided by the human race.' She hated to have to entertain: 'They make the world pinch back.' What she wanted most from Rodmell was the peace and quiet that would enable her to write. Writing was living: 'I thought driving through Richmond last night something very profound about the synthesis of my being: how only writing composes it: how nothing makes a whole unless I am writing.' Whatever she had begun or broken off in London was continued or finished in Rodmell, from *Mrs Dalloway*, her first masterpiece, to *Between the Acts*, her last. Hers was an infinitely subtle quest to express the chaos of emotions, the oscillations of reality, always with microscopic precision and butterfly lightness of touch, as rich and as varied as perception itself. 'And sometimes I suppose that even if I came to the end of my incessant search into what people are & feel I should know nothing still.'

Journeys, invitations, visits – this was a life of never-ending stimulation and over-stimulation, constantly interrupted by illness and by the descent of the 'silver mist', as she described her depressions in her diary. When war broke out in 1939, she and Leonard left London and stayed permanently in the country. But this part of the coast soon became a front line in the Battle of Britain. The army installed searchlights on the Downs. At night the German bombers droned over Rodmell on their way to London. During the day, there were even low-level flights. As a Jew and a Socialist, Leonard knew what would happen to him in the event of an invasion. 'But though L says he has petrol in the garage for suicide should Hitler win, we go on,' wrote Virginia in her diary of May 1940. In September their London house was bombed. Their situation seemed increasingly hopeless, and writing increasingly pointless. 'No audience. No echo. That's part of one's death.' Nevertheless, she finished her last novel, *Between the Acts*.

Exhaustion was now almost total. For a few fleeting moments she could still enjoy the simple pleasures of Rodmell: 'breakfast, writing, walking, tea, bowls, reading, sweets, bed.' But at about 11.30 a.m. on Friday, 28 March 1941, a clear cold day, Virginia went as usual across the garden and the fields, down to the Ouse. This time she did not return. She filled her coat pockets with stones, after leaving a farewell letter behind in the house. It was some three weeks later that children found her body in the river.

Leonard buried her ashes in the garden, under two tall elm trees whose branches

21. Rowland Hilder: Sussex Downs

23. Battle of Hastings, *by Frank W. Wilkin, c. 1820*

22. Battle Abbey

24. *Brighton Pavilion*

25. *Brighton West Pier before the latest fire*

A VOLUPTUARY under the horrors of Digestion.

26. The Prince Regent, caricature by Gillray

28. The Long Man at Wilmington

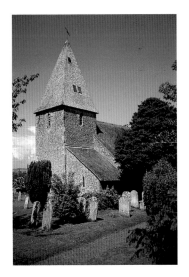

29. Rodmell, 13th century church

27. Hang-glider at Beachy Head

30. Rodmell: bust of Virginia Woolf

31. Charleston Farmhouse: fountain in the garden

32. Charleston Farmhouse: fireplace decorated by Duncan G...

33 & 34. Glyndebourne: garden and interval picnic

35. Mad Jack Fuller's sugarloaf, near Dallington

36 (overleaf). Arundel Castle: a romantic view, c. 1880

37, 38 & 39. West Dean: the house and garden sculpture

Hat Hill Sculpture Park:
40. Wilfred and Jeannette Cass

41. Hat Hill: Give and Take, *by Peter Randall Page*

42. Hat Hill: Space Emptied Out, *by Eilis O'Conne*

43. Petworth: Urn in the park

intertwined. They had always called these trees Leonard and Virginia. One of them was destroyed in a storm, and the other fell victim to Dutch Elm Disease. On the garden wall, beneath a bronze bust of Virginia, the visitor may read her epitaph, taken from the end of her novel *The Waves*: 'Death is the enemy against you. I will fling myself unvanquished and unyielding. O Death the waves broke on the shore.'

Charleston Farmhouse: Bloomsbury in the Country

In a patch of ancient countryside, one part is older perhaps than any. At *Wilmington*, a long-legged giant strides towards you, a long staff in either hand. This is the Long Man of Wilmington, who may only be 18th century, but is probably way, way older – one of the primary spirits of this island in fact. Drawn in the chalk, and renewed beyond memory, he is a link more vivid than most archæological remains with the forebears who were here 'before the Romans came to Rye or out to Severn strode.' Chesterton's rolling road and rollicking verse was all part of a celebration of Englishness in the face of creeping suburbanisation, industrialisation and war; it was particularly focussed in Sussex in the work of his other half, Hilaire Belloc, as well as Edward Thomas and Kipling himself.

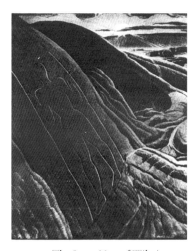

Just in sight of the Long Man, and halfway between Brighton and Eastbourne, a little side-road leads from the A27 into the fields at the foot of Firle Beacon. Where today there are frequent traffic jams, Vanessa Bell in September 1916 was able to cycle the six miles from Lewes Station to *Charleston Farmhouse*. There wasn't even a bus service, so isolated was the farm on the Downs which Virginia Woolf's sister had rented. Initially it

The Long Man of Wilmington, by Leslie Moffatt Ward

was to have been a holiday home and a refuge for her pacifist friends, who instead of military service were allowed to work on the land.

'I suppose it's 17th or 18th century (but my word doesn't go for much)' Virginia wrote to Roger Fry. 'Anyway it's most lovely, very solid and simple in that lovely mixture of frick and flint that they use about here and perfectly flat windows on the walls and wonderful tiled roofs. The pond is most beautiful...' and the reflection of this beige-coloured, rose-covered farmhouse still shines out of the pond, surrounded by irises, meadows and ash-trees. Behind the house are fruit trees and flowers in abundance. Here the young painter lived with her two men, the writer Clive Bell and the painter Duncan Grant, and this triangle was at the centre of all the Bloomsbury Group and their friends, lovers and mistresses. They would meet in Vanessa's farmhouse garden. London came to the country to indulge in an orgy of love and art – the finest flower of English eccentricity to bloom in this century.

The sumptuous development of Vanessa and Duncan's art can best be seen inside the house. Walls, doors and furniture are all covered with figures and decorations, with floral still lifes and nudes, from the firewood box by the hearth to the cupboards, beds and bathtubs. 'Vanessa didn't like tablecloths, and so she painted one here on the round table,' explains our guide. And if she wanted to change the cloth, or it had worn thin, she simply painted a new one directly onto the wooden surface. 'A little housepainting,' she called it when she came across another empty space where she could indulge in her blue, rust brown and reddish yellow.

Grant did not confine himself to his easel either. Over the window of Vanessa's bedroom he painted a cock to wake her, and below the window a dog to watch over her. At the foot of her bed he painted a mask of Morpheus, the god of sleep

Roger Fry, by 'Quiz'

and dreams. Thus the art and imagination of the occupants gradually took over the whole house. They designed screens and lampshades, materials, jugs, plates and tiles. This creative joy could not be confined within the studio; it burst forth into everyday life itself, and is what makes Charleston Farmhouse a very special place.

Bell and Grant did not limit themselves to decorating their own house. They were both associated with the Omega Workshops, founded by Roger Fry in London in 1913. Fry was not much of a painter, but he was the chief æsthetic theorist in the Bloomsbury Group, and as such exercised considerable influence. He was the first to introduce Cézanne, Matisse, and the late French Impressionists to the English public, and he wanted to give new life to the Arts and Crafts Movement with the spirit of international modernism. Young artists like Bell, Grant and Dora Carrington designed furnishings and textiles for the Omega Workshops, mostly with striking colours and abstract patterns. Their best work combined avant-garde sophistication with the naïve freshness of amateur painting. But commercial success did not come their way. After just six years, in 1919, Fry abandoned his artists' cooperative. Omega products are rare nowadays. Of course, you will find them in the Victoria & Albert Museum, and occasionally they come up for auction (and fetch a high price), but nowhere will you find a greater variety of the real thing than at Charleston Farmhouse.

'Now here in the conservatory,' continues our guide after this art-historical digression, 'Angelica Bell first learnt who her real father was.' It was not Vanessa's husband Clive Bell, as she had always thought, but Duncan, the third side of the triangle. In her autobiography *Deceived with Kindness* (1984) Angelica Garnett describes this unusual family life, 'incestuously bound up with each other.' She herself married the writer David Garnett, once the lover of her father Duncan Grant. Duncan himself, shortly before he began his relationship with Vanessa Bell, had slept with her brother. Duncan's cousin Mary Hutchinson, a frequent guest at Charleston, was later Clive Bell's mistress. Vanessa had a big heart and a big household. She was the magnet in this field, but also the central pole around whom the whole merry-go-round of friendships, passions and affairs revolved. Despite all the complications, confusions, deceptions and disappointments, they all remained more or less on friendly terms throughout their lives.

'The atmosphere seems full of catastrophes which upset no one,' observed Virginia Woolf after visiting her sister. 'How much I admire this handling of life.' Husband, lover, children, visitors – and yet Vanessa still had time for her art, which the fragile, childless Virginia could only stand and admire. 'I suppose you are, as Lytton once said, the most complete human being of us all.' She enjoyed her visits to Charleston almost as if they were trips to some kind of intellectual theatre. 'Nessa is (4 miles on the other side of the down) living like an old hen wife among ducks, chickens and children.' But she was never fully at ease in this world of bright colours, duckweed, and free love. Bloomsbury was liberality and libertinage, but in Charleston Virginia smelt something off. Sometimes Vanessa would dive into the slimy duckpond, and 'splash around stark naked without shame and with enormous vigour.' Virginia also describes with mock horror the clothes her sister designed. The colours 'almost wrenched my eyes from their sockets – a skirt barred with reds and yellows of the Vilest kind and a pea green blouse on top, with a gaudy handkerchief on her head, supposed to be in the very boldest taste.' For her, the pigeon-grey sister, this was all too garish. And sometimes she simply felt excluded from this other, painters' world in Charleston. 'There they sat like assiduous children at a task in a bedroom... In front of them was one jar of flowers, and one arrangement of still life.'

Much of what they painted then in Charleston is still to be seen, along with the garden and the interiors which often served as themes or backgrounds for their paintings. Vanessa's finest works are in the Tate Gallery, but she was always in the shadow of her famous novelist sister. The degree to which this depressed her has also been described by Virginia: 'I have seen all the cleverest people, she said, & not one asked me about the South of France. Nobody mentioned painting. I hung two of our latest paintings in Maynard's room & he never noticed them.'

The great John Maynard Keynes, national economist, Cambridge don, noted connoisseur – was he blind to the art of Charleston? Certainly at that time, 1919, he had eyes only for the book he was writing, *The Economic Consequences of the Peace*, and for his dear friend Duncan. Throughout the summer of 1919 Keynes added a new dimension to the *ménage à trois*. He had brought his own servants with him, and they served him breakfast punctually at eight. He wrote till midday, and only then was there time for socialising over lunch, reading *The Times*, doing a little gardening, tea, correspondence – 'all very regular'. It is easy to forget how disciplined these artistic households were when it came to their work. This Liberty Hall was based on a strict Victorian sense of order. The Charleston Bohemians were still middle-class enough to have staff (labour was cheap in those days) and regular mealtimes. But in September 1920 it all broke down.

Maynard Keynes, once more the honoured guest, had insisted that all the clocks be put forward an hour. Vanessa was too good-natured to refuse. Clive, however, insisted on normal time, and in the kitchen there was disagreement and so the kitchen clock stayed as it was. Confusion was total. 'How mad they all are!' It was like a Chekhov play, but instead of it ending tragically, 'everyone laughs and screams and passes on," wrote Lytton Strachey.

Vanessa died at Charleston in 1961, followed shortly afterwards by Clive Bell. Duncan Grant went on living and painting until he was 93. If he had lived much longer, the house might well have become his tomb. 'The house was on the verge

Charleston

of collapse,' recalls Peter Miall, curator of Charleston. 'There was fungus, mildew and woodworm everywhere.' We are sitting in Vanessa Bell's attic studio. A soft northern light is falling on the empty walls, and down below in the garden the irises, columbine and cranesbill are flowering purple and blue, just like Vanessa's pictures. 'This is a unique monument to the lives of two Bloomsbury painters,' enthuses Peter Miall. 'They did work in other houses, but the war and changing fashions destroyed virtually all their interiors. Charleston is the last example of this style to have survived completely intact. That's why we fought so hard to preserve it.'

It was worth every penny of the million pounds the restoration cost. Only since Charleston Farmhouse was opened to the public in 1986 has the other Bloomsbury re-emerged – bright and witty, as sparkling as Leonard and Virginia Woolf's Monk's House was dull. The Charleston interiors have inspired a new generation of English designers. What they saw there struck an answering chord in them. They too wanted to paint the walls and the furniture, and to transform junk into art. The Bloomsbury mixture of genius and the commonplace, and the recycling ethos of the nineties, have come together in a neo-Charleston style of decoration. It's a spontaneous, illustrative style, contemptuous of theory and of minimalist meanness. Charleston Farmhouse is the polar opposite of the Bauhaus. Anglo-Saxon colour versus Teutonic grey.

Nessa, the grey-flecked cat, rubs up against the visitor's legs, as a parting reminder of Charleston sensuality. Then it's time for the final stages of the Bloomsbury trip. Off we go to nearby *Berwick*, where in the early forties the Charleston artists painted the whole church; unusual but, in all honesty, not to our eyes a masterpiece. (At the time, though, Sir John Rothenstein wrote that they 'must be accounted among the best paintings to be made in church or chapel in England during the present century;' and the architect of the church wrote, more simply, 'It's wonderful. It's like stepping out of a foggy England into Italy.') Then to *Firle*, west of Charleston. That is where Vanessa Bell and Duncan Grant are buried. Just as their daughter once noted when she saw them at work in their shared studio, as contented as 'two ducks in a pond', now they lie beside one another in a village graveyard, covered with grass and daisies.

The graves of the two artists are plain and simple, but John Piper's stained glass windows for the Gage family chapel in Firle parish church (1985) positively glow with colour. Charleston Farmhouse is on the Gages' estate, but they themselves live at *Firle Place*. This is basically a Tudor house, but the façade is Georgian, and the interiors would do credit to a museum: English and French furniture, an exquisite collection of Sèvres porcelain, and Old Masters including one of the largest paintings Van Dyck ever made. It may not be spectacular, but for me Firle Place is one of the most beautiful and most homely specimens of the English country house.

Rye: Town on Hill, Painter from Hell

On the south-eastern tip of the Sussex coast, on two hills rising up from the marshes, lie the towns of Winchelsea and Rye. They were both flourishing Cinque Ports, essential to the wool trade, the defence of the coast, and the guardianship of the English Channel. Their prosperity and influence died out when the ports silted up in the 16th century, and today the water is nearly two miles away. 'The two small ghosts of the Cinque Ports family, the pair of blighted hill-towns that were once sea-towns and that now draw out their days in the dim aftersense of a mere indulged and encouraged picturesqueness,' was Henry James' description, and if Rye now has the bustle of a tourist town, there is little changed at Winchelsea as far as picturesque charm is concerned. *Winchelsea* was a garden city 700 years before anyone thought of garden cities. The streets are broad, and the houses and people have plenty of space. You cross a green chessboard on which a game seems to have begun symmetrically but was somehow broken off and left in the Middle Ages. John Wesley, who held his last open-air service here in 1790 under an ash-tree, observed that this was just 'that poor skeleton of Ancient Winchelsea'. We can still see something of the latter if we go down into the vaulted medieval cellars, of which about fifty are still intact. These show clearly that Edward I's concern in establishing the new rectangular Winchelsea in 1283 was not military but commercial: the wine imported from Gascony had to be stored as coolly as possible.

Winchelsea: inside the church

Artists have often been attracted to this place. John Everett Millais was living here when he painted *The Blind Girl* in 1854, with Winchelsea in the background. The actress Ellen Terry had a cottage here, and Joseph Conrad spent a few months here too. There is a marked air of prosperity even today, that intangibility of respectable reserve that Henry James admired despite all his ambivalences about the picturesque.

Between Winchelsea and Rye is *Camber Castle* (1539), one of Henry VIII's coastal fortresses which has remained a ruin in the marshes since the 17th century. Camber Sands are a magnificent sight – when the tide is out they stretch out for what looks like miles; but the tide comes in faster than a cantering horse, so beware. Safely up the hill is *Rye*, a favourite haunt of golfers, sailors and artists, and anyone else with eyes in their heads. The sea has long since ceased to thunder here, but the A259 does its best to make up for that as it winds its way round the hill. The last remaining town gate, Landgate (14th century), tries hard to retain its dignity. Rye is irresistibly romantic. The houses press close together, and rising above the red roofs is St Mary's, a mainly Norman church with two sturdy golden 'Quarter Boys' on the clock (1561) and a stained glass window by Burne-Jones (1891). The cobblestones of Mermaid Street ought long since to have been trodden flat by the endless hordes of admiring photographers. Yachts now lie at anchor in the old fishing port at the foot of the hill, and the tar-black warehouses along the quay are interspersed with apartment houses. Everywhere you will find pubs, bistros, galleries and antique shops. In Lion Street, near the church, is Fletcher's Cafe, the former vicarage whose flat bricks conceal massive 15th-century oak timbers together with an unanswered question: was this or was it not the birthplace of the dramatist John Fletcher? What we know for sure is that he was born in Rye in 1579, and in collaboration with Francis Beaumont wrote plays which at times even rivalled Shakespeare's in popularity. Today Fletcher's pies are better known in Rye than his plays, and the number one literary name here is Henry James. Impressed by the way of life of the English aristocracy, the American novelist settled in Rye in 1898. He rented and then bought the Georgian Lamb House in West Street, and there he lived a bachelor life with dachshund and four servants, until shortly before he died - a bachelor life enlivened by an insatiable social appetite: Conrad, Ford, Kipling, Wells, Beerbohm, Edith Wharton and many others flocked to visit the Master in his nest. The 'open sunny terrace of a dear little old garden – a garden brown-walled, red-walled, rose-covered on its other sides, divided by the width of a quiet street of grass-grown cobbles from the house of its master, is possessed of a little old glass-fronted, panelled pavilion... There is not much room in this pavilion, but there is room for the hard-pressed table and the tilted chair – there is room for a novelist and his friends.' In this little garden house (which was hit by a bomb in 1940) James wrote *The Ambassadors* and *The Golden Bowl*, dictating them to his secretary to type directly on the Remington – a habit that some blame for the convolutions of his later style. After his death, what Wells described as 'one of the most perfect pieces of suitably furnished Georgian architecture imaginable' was taken by E. F. Benson, the member of a distinguished literary family who added to the gaiety of nations with his Mapp and Lucia books. (Another writer who added to the gaiety of nations, in a different sense, was Radclyffe Hall, who penned her pathbreaking lesbian novel, *The Well of Loneliness*, in Rye.)

Henry James is a famous name here. But ask a local if he's heard of Edward Burra. Edward *who*? Rye's most important painter was at such loggerheads with his home town that although the Art Gallery does have his aluminium palette, there is not a single picture of his to be seen. Burra was a realist with the eyes of a surreal satirist. Like Georg Grosz he loved the grotesque and the twilight world of the nightclubs and the characters he saw there. He didn't like Rye, where he lived almost all of his life, and rarely painted it – especially not the picturesque parts. What he did paint, on a grand scale, was the other Rye – the shabby fringes of the town, the industrial waste land, the barren marsh beneath an apocalyptic sky.

He hated the 'mermaid' image of Rye, and deliberately set out to shock the tourists. To stop them gawping through the window, he would sometimes appear behind the glass as the Devil himself, with papier-maché horns on his head and a piece of liver hanging out of his mouth. Burra, who suffered all his life from arthritis and anæmia, lived in Chapel House by the Ypres Tower, now the town museum, but he would frequently quit his provincial nest for the bars of Hastings, Marseille, London or Harlem. In 'Tinkerbell Town' (his pet name for Rye) he always remained an outsider, but in English 20th-century art his place is assured – as one of the country's rare expressionists who managed, like Stanley Spencer, to combine almost egotistical stylistic distortions with an abiding love of the English scene.

There was an Old Person of Rye,
Who went up to the town on a Fly;
But they said: 'If you cough,
You are safe to fall off!
You abstemious Old Person of Rye!'

Hastings: The Conquest

Ever since the hill camps of the Stone and Ice Ages, Sussex has been at the fore-
front of the country's defences. *Pevensey Castle*, between Eastbourne and
Hastings, is a prime example. The Romans called it Anderida. They were then
driven out by the South Saxons, who gave Sussex its name, and they in turn gave
way to the Normans, who built a new castle within the Roman walls, which reach
up to a height of 23 feet. Again and again Pevensey Castle had to be fortified:
against the Spanish Armada, against Napoleon, and then with concrete against
Operation Sealion, the threat of German invasion during the Second World War.
Near the castle is the Mint House (1342), where the Romans used to mint their
coins and where the tourists now spend theirs on antiques.

Pevensey Bay, Norman's Bay: industrial zone, bungalow zone, holiday beach. It
was somewhere around here that William the Conqueror landed on 28 September
1066. To be precise, he stumbled. For heroic tradition has it that he actually fell
quite unheroically on his nose. This might have seemed to his entourage to be a
bad omen, but with remarkable presence of mind William pulled himself up,
showed them his dirty hands, and remarked that he had now taken possession of
England with both hands. What every schoolchild knows as the Battle of Hastings
did not take place at Hastings at all, but six miles further inland at a place called
Battle. (The odds against that must be enormous, as Humphrey Lyttleton once
remarked.) On the uninhabited heath where, on 14
October 1066, after a tactical blunder the Anglo-Saxon
Harold fell, the Norman William erected a high altar
and an abbey. He thus fulfilled his vow and secured
his succession to the throne and his control of the
church. In his own way, Henry VIII did the same
when he dissolved this Benedictine monastery. His
equerry Sir Anthony Browne pulled down the
Norman church and turned the abbey into a manor
house – modernisation 1539-fashion. There is still plenty to see, however – the

dormitory (1120), for instance, and the gatehouse (1338). In the parish church Sir
Anthony lies stretched out on his Renaissance sarcophagus, a man who profited
from his King's dissolution of the monasteries like an estate agent from a redevel-
opment programme. He took Waverley Abbey in Surrey from the Cistercians,
Bayham Abbey near Tunbridge Wells from the Premonstratensians, and
Easebourne Priory near Midhurst from the Augustinians, the last of these enabling
him to consolidate his holdings around his estate at *Cowdray House*. This is where
the British Polo Championships take place every year. In 1793 the last of his line,
the 8th Viscount Montagu, drowned when trying to shoot the Rhine Falls at
Schaffhausen; a few days later the Tudor house at Cowdray went up in flames. No

doubt all this came about as a result of the curse laid by the last monk of Battle Abbey when Henry VIII's Master of the Horse turned him out into the big bad world. Near the school, in a half-timbered house called 'The Pilgrim's Rest' (15th century), you can have lunch and read all about the 'birthplace of a nation'. The Conqueror himself is said to have feasted here off a massive slab of sandstone from the Weald – 'The Conqueror's Stone', which stands in front of the pier at Hastings.

Hastings was the chief of the Cinque Ports in the 12th century, then for a long time was a fishing village, and is now a seaside resort. 'Popular with visitors since 1066,' claims the Tourist Office. 'A kind of résumé of middle class English civilisation,' wrote Henry James, and added that if he were an old lady with a modest income, this was where he would like to spend his retirement. (A less respectable old woman originally from Hastings was Winifred Wagner, *née* Williams. Winifred married the composer's grandson in Bayreuth, and quickly became the most pro-Nazi of the clan. It was she who sent food parcels to Hitler in gaol after the Beer Hall putsch, and gave him the paper on which he wrote *Mein Kampf.*) Despite James Agate's claim that the architectural style of Hastings is 'divided between Early Wedding Cake and Late Water Closet,' there is much of charm. Pelham Crescent (1824), for instance, has an elegant Regency curve, with St Mary's in the middle and the ruins of William's castle on the orange-coloured cliff above, creating an impressive ensemble – spoilt only, it must be admitted, by the souvenir shops.

As land prices on the seafront were obviously pretty high even back in the Middle Ages, the fishermen built their tall, black-tarred wooden huts on very small sites. There are 43 'net shops' for drying nets – neat geometrical structures, a sort of maritime minimalist architecture which is now listed. This part of the Old Town, the Stade, has retained some of the charm that Turner painted and Rossetti reinforced when he married Elizabeth Siddal at St Clement's in 1860. 'Lizzie' often sat for him and the other Pre-Raphaelites. In October 1854 Ford Madox Brown recorded: 'Called on Dante Rossetti, saw Miss Siddall looking thinner and more deathlike and more ragged than ever, a real artist, a woman without parallel for many a long year.' She died in Hastings in 1862, after an overdose of laudanum. Nowadays Hastings has become the last stop for many Londoners with social and mental problems, and the suicide rate is far above the national average.

North of Hastings, however, the English idyll is restored. *Great Dixter*, a medieval hall house just outside Northiam restored by Lutyens (who built a nursery with windows at floor height, so the children could look out at the view) is now the centre of a spectacularly rich garden, the creation of one of the gurus of gardening, Christopher Lloyd. Crazy topiary, a throbbingly colourful sunken garden, and an eye-popping exotic garden add up paradoxically to a vision of real harmony. It is the very embodiment of Kipling's 'Glory of the Garden'. What is more, after all the Royal Oak pub-signs, you can actually have your picnic under a real royal oak, where Elizabeth I preceded you. The oak stands near *Brickwall*, a Jacobean house which is now a school for children with speech impediments. Recorded on the tree is the fact that Elizabeth left her green damask shoes here in memory of a royal picnic on 11 August 1573. Our oaks, say the people of Sussex, live for a thousand years, and they take a thousand years to die. Some, though, will live for ever.

Surrey

We'd rather hang out in Surrey than anywhere else...
Oh yeah, we're behaving ourselves now.
Billie Piper about life with her husband Chris Evans
in a Lutyens house near Godalming

Surrey is variously known as London's Playground and the Stockbroker Belt, neither of which makes it sound particularly attractive. No spot in this county is more than fifty miles away from the City of London, and so vast numbers of people work in London but choose to live in Surrey. It is commuter country – idyll with a rush hour, get-away-from-it-all with eight million fellow Londoners. 'Twas ever thus. At the end of the 17th century, Daniel Defoe described the commuting merchants and stockbrokers, 'who take their horses every morning to London. . . and be at Epsom again every night.' He watched the housing boom in Richmond with mixed feelings. Having a house and garden in the country became all the rage in 18th-century London society. An address on the Thames, say in Twickenham, or in Kew or in Ham, meant that you had arrived. Victorian high society spread further afield, with country houses out on the North Downs. In the 20th century, it was and still is the dream of the middle classes to own a little semi-detached in Surrey, or failing all else, at least to have a Sunday picnic on Box Hill.

Country and capital city – these neighbours are for ever at loggerheads, as Mr Green is forced to give more and more of his land to Mr Grey. No other county in England has changed as much in the last hundred years as Surrey, and yet miraculously it has still preserved an identity of its own. Until 1888, Surrey – the Suthridge (southern district) of the Anglo-Saxon chronicles – had its border on the southern bank of the Thames. Today, however, Greater London reaches out as far as Epsom Racecourse, and soon it will encompass the dormitory town of Woking. One of the smallest counties in England, its density of population is exceeded only by that of London itself and forgotten Middlesex. Ironically, Thomas Robert Malthus, who was the first man to make a global analysis of the population explosion, and who recommended birth control, came from Surrey. So too does the rock guitarist Eric Clapton, born in the village of Ripley ('Let It Rain'). Pop stars like Phil Collins have country homes in Surrey. Their records top the charts, but Surrey holds another record that it is less proud of: 40% of its marriages break down, making it the divorce capital of Europe. Commuting has its perils.

Surrey landscape, from William Robinson's The Wild Garden

Magna Carta and the Devils of Chaldon

Anyone who went up the Thames from London to Hampton Court in the early 18th century saw not only factory chimneys, tall buildings and crowded streets, but also 'the river sides ... full of villages, and those villages so full of beautiful buildings, charming gardens and rich habitations of gentlemen of quality, that nothing in the world can imitate it; no, not the country for twenty miles around Paris, though that indeed is a kind of prodigy'. Daniel Defoe's patriotic delight at the beauty of what was then the northern part of Surrey, but which now belongs to London, was by no means misplaced. He would have gone past Syon House, Kew Palace – country seat of a London merchant – the royal palace at Richmond, Ham House, Hampton Court, and Kingston-upon-Thames, where the Anglo-Saxon kings were crowned in the 10th century. 'The whole country here shines with a lustre not to be described. Take them in a remote view, the fine seats among the trees as jewels shine in a rich coronet; in a near sight they are mere pictures and paintings; at a distance they are all nature, near hand all art; but both in the extremest beauty.' In the vastness of Greater London, these country houses of old Surrey are like oases, remnants of 'the luxuriant age'. Henry VI went up the Thames to *Chertsey* on one last, posthumous sailing trip, when after a turbulent life and a miserable death in the Tower his remains were transported to the Benedictine Abbey in 1471. The Abbey has long since disappeared. Just to the east are the Shepperton Studios, centre of the British film industry – a dream factory that in recent years has produced such hits as *Four Weddings and a Funeral* with Hugh Grant, *Carrington* with Emma Thompson, and *The Madness of King George* with Nigel Hawthorne. Opened in 1932, they are built around the mansion that the first managing director of Harrods built for himself only a few decades earlier.

Not far from Windsor Castle there is a field where the King of England lost a bloodless battle and the Parliament of England laid its foundations. *Runnymede* (near *Egham*) is the name of this historic meadow on the Thames, and the cows are not allowed to graze there as it belongs to the nation. And the nation comes there in droves, makes its tea, plays its cricket, studies its history books, takes its souvenir photos, and tucks into its Magna Carta picnic. On 15 June 1215 King John, surnamed Lackland, spat furiously into the Thames when Stephen Langton, Archbishop of Canterbury, handed him the 63 articles concerning the rights of the barons and the Church. They wanted the return of unjustly confiscated goods, protection against oppression by the Crown, and equal legal rights for everyone. There are four copies of this historic guarantee of citizens' rights against royal abuse: two are in the British Museum, and the others in the cathedral libraries of Salisbury and Lincoln. On the field of Runnymede, between massive oaks, stands a temple built by American benefactors in commemoration of the Magna Carta as

Wall painting at Chaldon

a 'symbol of liberty under law', and as predecessor to their own Declaration of Independence from the colonial motherland. The nearby memorial to John F. Kennedy (1964) was designed by the landscape gardener Geoffrey Jellicoe, as a sort of landscaped allegory in the tradition of John Bunyan's *Pilgrim's Progress*: 'The journey is one of life, death and spirit'. And up the hill is the monument to the members of the RAF killed in the service of that same liberty much later.

At around the same time as the Magna Carta, at the beginning of the 13th century, a little church in Surrey witnessed the creation of a picture which vividly informed the faithful of what awaited them after all their earthly deeds. It depicted the final battle for their souls. If the Magna Carta bears the seeds of the modern era, the wall painting at *Chaldon* summons up the whole spirit of the Middle Ages. The dualism of the time, typified by the struggle between Church and King, King and nobles, nobles and peasants, is reflected by the universal struggle between good and evil, Heaven and Hell. The angels and devils of Chaldon are separated structurally into different fields: in the lower sections of the picture, the devils are making life hell for the damned; at the top is purgatory, where the angels are saving whatever or whoever can be saved; and in the middle, on what is literally a fire escape between the two levels, is a chaotic crowd of souls, some climbing and, God help us, the rest falling. This representation of the Last Judgement and the Ladder of Salvation is not a fresco (that is, painted directly on fresh wet plaster), but was painted onto the dried plaster of the western wall. It may well have been the work of an itinerant monk around 1200. This is the medieval Writing on the Wall, with a simple message illustrated in massive detail – a sort of biblical comic strip for the edification of the faithful, most of whom were illiterate. Hence the naïve directness, the striking silhouettes set against a reddish brown background, the powerful mixture of piety and horror, the raised forefinger and the devilish fantasy, the wailing and the gnashing of teeth contrasted with the hope and the longing for salvation. Chaldon is north of Reigate, on the Pilgrims' Way to Canterbury, and many a pilgrim would have stopped off at the village church of Chaldon and perhaps left with somewhat mixed feelings.

High Schools and Fast Riders: From Claremont to Epsom

Surrey is an urbane county, full of literary figures and associations, not least of course thanks to the proximity of London. There are three great educational institutions in the county that have made a name for themselves for various reasons. They are Royal Holloway College, Charterhouse public school, and the girls' boarding school Claremont. The oldest of these – though still nowhere near as old as Eton or the King's School, Canterbury – is Charterhouse. It was founded in London in 1611 and moved to the country in 1872. The massive Victorian buildings stand like a fortress on a hill overlooking the little town of *Godalming*; 'great pains had clearly been taken,' wrote Osbert Lancaster, an old Carthusian, in his memoirs, 'to select the most wind-swept spur of the Surrey Downs on which to erect an extensive concentration camp in Early English Gothic.' The famous London scholars of Charterhouse are recorded on an ancient gateway: the writers Addison and Steele, the Methodist preacher Wesley, the founder of the Boy Scout Movement Baden-Powell, the composer Vaughan Williams. For Lancaster the saving grace was a tradition of excellence in the graphic arts, examplified by three other old boys, Thackeray, his friend the *Punch* cartoonist John Leech, and the incomparable Max, Oscar Wilde's friend Max Beerbohm. Lancaster imbibed not only their witty line and self-deprecating style, disguising a total mastery of the favourite English medium of black and white, but also the gentle, Establishment-teasing humour. Godalming itself, where Aldous Huxley was born, is the home of Coopers, from whom countless generations of headmasters obtained their dreaded canes in the days when corporal punishment was politically correct. These whippy, pliant sticks were made from willow, ash or ebony. But since 1993

Charterhouse, by Osbert Lancaster

Coopers has concentrated only on what the nation really needs: walking sticks and umbrellas.

In the same decade as the picturesque asymmetry of neo-Gothic Charterhouse, a monumental building in the symmetrical style of the Renaissance arose in the north-west of Surrey. It looked more like a French castle than an English school, but a school it was: *Royal Holloway College*. The wealthy industrialist Thomas Holloway had no intention of lagging behind the wealthy mine-owner Thomas Sutton, the founder of Charterhouse. He made his fortune with pills, and he preserved his name with gigantic buildings: he founded Holloway Sanatorium near Virginia Water, and soon afterwards Holloway College near Egham – both prime examples of Victorian revivalist architecture. Holloway's architect, W. H. Crossland, modelled the Pill King's college on the Loire château of Chambord. He used red brick and Portland stone, and the college has two inner courtyards plus a large number of towers, domes and chimneys. This castle of education was opened by Queen Victoria in 1886, and was one of the first universities for women in England. The founder provided two rooms for each female student. Now the college is open to men as well, and in 1985 Royal Holloway amalgamated with Bedford College in London. In the north wing is the founder's art collection, which he left to his college in order to educate and edify, and which gives a superb picture of contemporary taste. The eighty or so paintings that Thomas Holloway collected between 1881 and his death in 1883 were regarded as masterpieces of his time. Particularly popular were Millais' sentimental historical pictures, the didactic

145

Claremont: Vanbrugh's design

Man proposes, God disposes by Victoria's favourite painter Landseer, and the many hyper-realistic genre pictures of which William Powell Frith's monumental *Paddington Station* (1862) is a fine example. In a move of shocking impropriety, the College decided to ignore the founder's wishes and sold three of the major works in 1993: a Gainsborough, a Constable, and a seascape by Turner. They went to the Getty Museum in California for around £11 million.

The pupils of *Claremont*, a former country house on the border between Greater London and Surrey, do their lessons in royal classrooms. Teacher's desk, slates, and children's desks with inkwells all stand beneath the most elegant plaster ceilings. The scene of today's little classroom tragedies once witnessed the death of a king in exile, and a princess in childbirth. This is a school that has made history. It began privately: Sir John Vanbrugh, the most important architect of the English Baroque, acquired the land in 1708, developed it and sold on to the Earl of Clare. All that remains from that time is the gardener's White Cottage and the crenellated Belvedere (1717) on a hill west of the present house – an early example of 18th-century gothic revival. It was from this vantage point that the house took its name: 'Claremount'. In 1769 Clive of India bought the land, demolished Vanbrugh's house, and commissioned the landscape gardener Capability Brown to build one of the few houses he ever designed (helped, admittedly, by Henry Holland). Built in white brick, neo-Palladian in style it is both simple and noble, and is surrounded by a William Kent park whose tranquillity nothing was allowed to disturb. Hence the only tradesmen's entrance was via an underground passage into which the staff could disappear, like Alice down a rabbit hole. Alas, the owner never had the chance to enjoy this classical home on a hill. Lord Clive was architect of England's dominion over East India, and himself became very wealthy as a result, but he was accused of mismanaging the East India Company's affairs and, although vindicated after one of the great show trials of history, committed suicide soon afterwards in 1774. The next inhabitants of Claremont were a royal

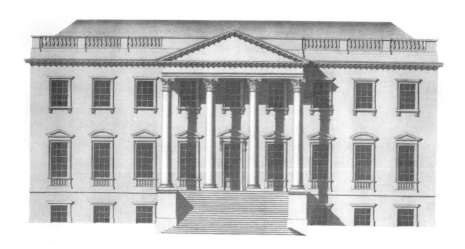

Claremont, as rebuilt by Capability Brown and Henry Holland

couple: Princess Charlotte, only daughter of George IV, and Prince Leopold of Saxe-Coburg, who later became first King of the Belgians. But the happy days of Claremont were short-lived. After just one year, Charlotte died in childbirth (1817). Royal tragedies continued. In the revolutionary year of 1848, Louis-Philippe (as 'Mr Smith') and his wife Marie-Amélie fled into exile, and took refuge in Claremont, where the deposed 'citizen king' died two years later. It seems that only Queen Victoria was happy in Claremont, often spending her holidays there with her beloved Uncle Leopold. 'I passed such a very pleasant time here the pleasantest summer I EVER passed in my life.' In the park you will still find the oak tree from which her swing was swung.

Claremont Park, now separate from the house, is regarded as one of the finest of all early English landscape gardens. Back in Vanbrugh's time, Charles Bridgeman had built a unique turf amphitheatre on a hill. It was planned as a garden decoration, was used for cock-fighting, and is now an open-air theatre for *fêtes champêtres* in the summer. By 1734 William Kent was at work turning the geometrically laid-out garden into a landscape park, with a grotto by the lake and a temple pavilion on the island – the perfect realization of a landscape painting. 'Mahomet imagined an Elysium but Kent created many... he leaped the fence and saw that all nature was a garden,' was Horace Walpole's description of this man who was a mediocre painter, a gifted furniture designer and architect, and a genius of a landscape gardener. The Park became sadly neglected, and if the National

Trust had not taken it over in 1949, by now it would have been 'developed' and Esher would have had another suburb. The National Trust have restored it quite magnificently. Nearby they have also acquired a 1930's house, complete with all its original interiors: *The Homewood* (1937–39), which belonged to the architect Patrick Gwynne. With its flat roofs, white façades and strong horizontals created by the window, this is a classic example of the international style in England.

The time to see *Epsom* – a few miles south-west of Claremont, on the slopes of the Downs – is the first weekend in June, on Derby Day. Apart from upper-class Ascot, this is the highlight of the racing calendar: fashion show, picnics on the grass, caravans, itinerant salesmen, gipsy fortune-tellers, Rolls Royces by the

Epsom in the 1950's

dozen, funfair, here comes the Queen, there go the pick-pockets... and everybody has a bet, and nobody wins except the bookmakers. It's a long day for a short race – just two and a half minutes over the classic distance of one and a half miles. These two and a half minutes, though, are enough to immortalize the name of the horse; Diomed, for example, or Eclipse, after which a pub in Egham has been named. The Epsom Derby has been watched by millions, painted by Géricault, and described by Defoe: 'no sight, except that of a victorious army, under the command of a Protestant King of Great Britain could exceed it.'

In the 17th century, however, Epsom people didn't put their money on horses, but on salt. Epsom Salts and water with wondrous purgative powers made the little town into Charles II's favourite spa and a fashionable resort for London Society. (Pepys came here with fashionable friends: 'I drank the water,' he recorded, 'they did not, but doe go about and walk a little among the women, but I did drink four pints and had some very good stools by it.') When Tunbridge Wells then became more popular, Epsom had nothing left except the Downs and the 12th Earl of Derby. Until he came along, racing in Epsom had been on an irregular basis, but in 1780 he inaugurated the race that bears his name, and since then Epsom has never looked back. The horseshoe-shaped course, a mile and 4 furlongs long with alternating ups and downs, provides an incomparable test for the stars of the stables, and with bets and prize money running into millions, it remains Europe's richest race. The Derby has only been won five times by crowned owners – the last one being in 1909, when Edward VII's Minorou was victorious. Four years later the suffragette Emily Davison threw herself in front of the King's horse Anmer and died from her injuries, a martyr to the cause of women's emancipation. Shergar also made Derby history. He won the race in 1981 for the Aga Khan, was kidnapped the following year – probably by the IRA – and was never seen again. Until recently all the Derby winners were preserved in Epsom's Hall of Fame, audiovisually and in wax, along with their jockeys and trainers, their family trees, and holy relics such as the boots that spurred Lord Derby's Hyperion past the winning-post, or the crop used by Lester Piggott. England's most successful jockey won the Epsom Derby nine times, the first when he was only 19 on Never Say Die.

Box Hill: Picnics and Poetry

'We are going to Box Hill tomorrow,' announces Jane Austen's Emma, and the next day off they all go – the ladies in their carriage, and the gentlemen on horseback – to *Box Hill*, 'where every body had a burst of admiration on first arriving' (*Emma*, Chapter 43). Where Jane Austen's picnickers would have left their horses in 1816 – 'The Fox and Hounds' at the foot of the hill – is now The Burford

Bridge Hotel, and at the weekend you will be mighty lucky to find a parking space. Directly behind it, rising steeply at first but then flattening out into a gentler slope, is Box Hill itself, a ridge as long and as beautiful as a line by Ingres. There are occasional box trees (which gave the hill its name) and junipers, the grass is thick and short, and instead of sheep grazing here, generations of visitors have feasted their eyes upon these rich green pastures. Northwards, in the direction of Leatherhead, the little River Mole has left a hole in the Downs, the Mole Gap, and on clear evenings the distant lights of London shine through this natural peephole. On the summit of the hill, on the other side, there is a classic English panorama: it's not one of those dramatic visions of cliffs and a blue sea lapping against the golden sands; this is a tranquil, broad landscape of green and grey, painted in watercolours, with gentle mists and blurred contours. In the foreground is the little town of Dorking, with the Greensands Hills behind; the Weald is further south, with its endless patterns of fields and forests; then come the South Downs, and the silhouette of Chanctonbury. If the Devil wanted to show an Englishman all the summits of the world, he would find plenty of hills higher than Box Hill, but none with such seductive charms. It's not by chance that the most popular hill in English literature is also the most popular among English people (and among National Trust properties). They flock to it in their thousands to picnic on its broad back. The beech trees rustle, and the birds whistle, and the sausages sizzle, and all is well with the world.

In the autumn of 1817, the son of a London livery-stable keeper registered in what is now the Burford Bridge Hotel, staying, to his delight in the room next to one once occupied by his hero Nelson. The young Cockney's name was John Keats. 'I like this place very much,' he wrote to a friend, 'there is hill and dale and a little river – I went up Box Hill this evening after the moon.' He descended with the last lines of *Endymion* in his head. Fifty years later, the inspiration of the Romantic poet was succeeded by the relaxation of a Victorian fellow-writer, George Meredith, who took up residence at the foot of the hill: 'I'm every morning on the top of Box Hill. I shout ha ha to the gates of the world.' After taking the morning air, Meredith would race down the hill like Apollo from Olympus. No less impressive were the trips he would make in his sulky, drawn by a mule named Picnic. Thus he was already known to the farmers of the region long before his *Diana of the Crossways* made him known to the literary world. The Jacobean Crossways Farm – the setting for this novel, which is concerned with women's rights – lies west of

George Meredith, by Max Beerbohm

Dorking near Abinger, where the novelist E. M. Forster lived and the Hard Edge painter Robyn Denny was born. Flint Cottage, with its bands of red brick, is where Meredith lived from 1867 until his death in 1909, and it remains perfectly preserved, as does the wooden hut which he had built at the end of his garden in order to avoid interruptions from his two children while he wrote – among other things – *The Egoist*. Meredith's grave in Dorking is inscribed with his own favourite lines:

> Life is but a little holding, lent
> To do a mighty labour. It is one
> With heaven and the stars when it is spent
> To do God's aim. Else die we with the sun.

George Meredith spent two years at school with the Moravian Brethren at Neuwied in Germany. In 1864, he was married in the church at *Mickleham*, near Box Hill, and it was in this same Norman church that another famous literary wedding had taken place in 1793. This was the love match of a woman of forty who wrote and lived with passion. Daughter of the famous music lover Charles Burney, Mistress of the Robes to Queen Charlotte, darling of the London salons, Fanny Burney married a French General who had just escaped from the horrors of the Revolution. The house where Fanny met her Chevalier d'Arblay is on the road to Mickleham: *Juniper Hall*, refuge of Talleyrand and other aristocratic émigrés. Madame de Staël was also a guest in this house, whose rooms are still decorated in Robert Adam's arabesque style, as they were in 1793. It is a house from the Age of Sensibility, its façade glowing red behind the mighty cedars of Lebanon. Today it is a residential college run by the Field Studies Council. Fanny had to write constantly to support herself and her husband, and *Camilla* (written 'with no episode but a little baby' as she explained to the King) was such a success that she built a house, Camilla Cottage, just south of Mickleham, on the proceeds.

Near the Burford Bridge Hotel, where the Roman Stane Street and the Pilgrims' Way crossed the Mole, there is a road across Ranmore Common – an ideal spot for walking – which leads to *Polesden Lacey*. One of Fanny Burney's admirers, the Irish dramatist and great parliamentary orator Richard Brinsley Sheridan, bought this country estate in 1797. 'We shall have the nicest place, within a prudent distance of town, in England,' he enthused, and with much eagerness and little experience set about organizing the place. 'It shall be a seat of health and happiness – where she [his beloved second wife] shall chirp like a bird, bound like a fawn and grow fat as a little pig.' In fact, the whole family caught scarlet fever and nearly died. On the site of his house there is now a Regency villa with Ionic colonnades, and it carries no trace of the man who wrote *The School for Scandal* and *The Rivals*, and introduced the word 'malapropism' into the English language.

Sheridan's Walk along the crest of the hill, however, is not only especially beautiful but also retains a literary link, as there are urns on pedestals bearing quotations from Alexander Pope – a Poet's Walk in an English Arcadia. Polesden Lacey itself was enlarged in 1906 and given a completely new interior. The salon especially is a masterly example of taste before the Great War, with resplendent walls and ceilings of white and red and gold, French Rococo furniture, and oriental porcelain – eclectic to a fault, but beautifully so. The lightness and elegance of this Edwardian splendour is in marked contrast to the heaviness of Victorian pomp. Polesden Lacey is where the future King George VI and his bride spent their honeymoon in 1923, and it is also where Mrs Greville's treasures are housed. The Greville Collection is one of the most valuable in Surrey, and contains some especially fine Dutch paintings by Teniers, Terborch, Jan van Goyen, Pieter de Hooch, Salomon and Jacob van Ruysdael, to name but a few. Margaret Greville, a scintillating society hostess of the day, lies buried in the rose garden, next to the dog cemetery.

From Nonsuch to Sutton: Dream Houses, Madhouses

On the northern edges of the Downs, between Guildford and Hatchlands (Admiral Boscawen's house), there is a blot on the landscape: *Clandon Park*. This massive red–brick block has four totally different and equally unattractive façades. With their infallible tastelessness, the Victorians managed to unbalance the front with a pseudo-Baroque *porte cochère*. Could such a graceless building – the country home of the Onslows, no less – really have been designed by a Venetian? Not until one goes inside does one begin to understand the reputation of Clandon Park and its architect Giacomo Leoni, whose Queensberry House in London set the tone for all neo-Palladian town-houses in England. The Marble Hall, a two-storeyed entrance hall, evokes those great receptions of the early 18th century. This is a room that simply lives and breathes Palladio. Two tiers of Corinthian and Composite columns bear the weight of a richly decorated stucco ceiling, around the sides of which are three-dimensional angels and slaves, the work of Italian stuccoists. These harmonise with Rysbrack's antique-style fireplaces and their Bacchus and Diana reliefs (1730). Pedimented doorways lead into the remaining rooms, whose wall coverings and plasterwork are mostly original. The furniture, mirrors, tapestries and porcelain, however, come from another house – Little Trent Park in Herefordshire, home of the art collector Mrs Gubbay, who gave her treasures to the National Trust. The Gubbay Collection is mainly famous for its porcelain: early Chelsea and Derby, Bustelli's Nymphenberg figures, Kaendler's Dresden figures – there is no better place to compare English and German china. But the jewels of the collection are Mrs Gubbay's Chinese porcelain birds of the 17th and 18th centuries. This is an enchanted aviary of exotic and fragile creatures,

The gates to Clandon Park

and is also an early example of Chinese exports to Europe. As for the 4th Earl of Onslow himself, he brought something very special from New Zealand: a Maori meeting-house. This souvenir from the colonies is the only Maori building in England, and the retired Governor used it as a boathouse.

Years ago, I wanted to visit *Sutton Place*, and was kept out by electronic gates and Beware-of-the-Dogs notices. On his country estate between Guildford and Woking, the oil multimillionaire John Paul Getty was not available to the likes of me. Surrounded by six girlfriends, this immeasurably wealthy skinflint spent the last seventeen years of his life here, in a madhouse of jealousy, desire and intrigue. Enraged by his guests' propensity to call far-off places, Getty installed pay-telephones, and he replaced some of the old panelling with plywood. After his death in 1976, another American oil magnate, Stanley J. Seeger, bought the Tudor estate for some £15 million. His idea was to breathe the spirit of modern times into the Renaissance house, and he also commissioned Sir Geoffrey Jellicoe – the doyen of English landscape gardening – to redesign the park and gardens. Jellicoe's designs (1980–86) were intellectually and financially on a feudal scale, unmatched in late 20th-century Europe.

'Landscape art should be a continuum of past, present and future, and should contain within it the seeds of abstract ideas as well as having a figurative meaning.' These were the principles behind Jellicoe's design for the gardens of Sutton Place, based on a system of subtle allegories and analogies. The walled Tudor garden on the west side of the house is complemented by a walled Paradise Garden on the east side. The stepping stones across the lily moat into Paradise are as hazardous as the path taken by the souls in Dante, but once you are there, the reward is a stunning garden of fountains, bowers and scents. Winding brick paths echo the twists and turns of the Tudor chimneys, and through window-like openings in the walls we see the Wild Garden. Jellicoe copied this window motif from Italian Renaissance gardens, which also influenced the long straight paths like the one of pleached limes that leads with classical symmetry to a gazebo. There is a matching path on the other side of the house, with distorted perspectives and absurd proportions, leading to the Surrealist Garden inspired by Magritte, with its five great urns from the dispersed treasures of the Rothschild palace of art, Mentmore.

Lemon trees in buckets, a mighty Atlas cedar, and a constant succession of new and surprising views greet the visitor, as symmetrical walled-in gardens alternate with others that are open and informal. Jellicoe even designed a 'Miró-Mirror' – a swimming pool, originally with a black bottom, surrounded by yellow and blue flowers, with asymmetrical stepping-stones of typical Miró shapes. In another garden, enclosed by dark green yew hedges, there is a pond reflecting the clear, magical patterns of the Ben Nicholson wall, a sculpture in white relief, made from Carrara marble. Nicholson designed it on a 'heroic' scale especially for Jellicoe's garden, but sadly died before it was actually erected. In front of the entrance to the house, where originally there was a gatehouse, there is a double row of American oaks running the full width of the north side, and these lead to an artificial lake, some 12 acres in area, which Jellicoe had dug in the shape of a whale. There were plans for a Henry Moore sculpture on the lake, an avenue of fountains and cascades on the south side, and many other garden wonders, but even Mr Seeger's fortune was not great enough to cover all the dreams of this landscape virtuoso.

In 1986 Sutton Place again changed hands, and the new owner – Frederick Koch, an American industrialist and art collector – made the whole estate over to a Foundation and restored the manor from top to bottom. He followed through most of Jellicoe's ideas, and added some of his own: an elliptical garden, an orchard with rare apple, pear and plum trees, and a sycamore avenue whose foliage glows a rich pink in spring. John Humphris, head gardener at Sutton Place, took a whole afternoon to show me round this gallery of gardens. Ten people are employed to look after them. There aren't many houses left in the world that employ ten gardeners.

The story actually began long, long ago. In 1521 Henry VIII gave the Sutton estate to his junior treasurer and protégé Sir Richard Weston, who built himself a manor in the new Renaissance style, with large windows and richly decorated façades. The best craftsmen of the day, itinerant Italian artists, adorned the walls of Sutton Place with terracotta reliefs, which were a brand new form of decoration at that time.

A few years later, in 1538, Henry VIII decided to build a hunting-lodge outside

Terracotta decoration at Sutton Place

Elizabeth I arrives at Nonsuch, the house 'which of all places she likes best'

the gates of London ('for his solace and retirement'), and of course it had to be finer than Sutton Place, and grander than Cardinal Wolsey's Hampton Court. It had to be a palace without equal, which is why it became *Nonsuch Palace*. It was also meant to rival Francis I's palace at Fontainebleau, which had been begun ten years earlier. Unlike the organic evolution that marked the style of Fontainebleau, Nonsuch was not characterised by any historical courtly style but was a show-place for the international avant-garde. Constructed around two great inner courtyards, the stone and half-timbered walls were covered with stucco sculptures, slates, and 1,300 relief panels all decorated, with some of them even gilded. The designers of this English Sun-King splendour came from France, the foremost amongst them being the Italian Nicolas Bellin, who worked with Primaticcio at Fontainebleau. Henry never saw the completion of his palace (1556), and Mary sold it, but Elizabeth bought it back and spent the happiest moments of her last years there. In 1669 Charles II gave it to his mistress Barbara, Countess of Castlemaine. The royal gift was shamelessly squandered, for Barbara was short of money and so she sold Nonsuch to Lord Berkeley as building materials for £1800. And he proceeded to use this, the most magnificent palace ever built in England, as a salvage yard. By 1702 nothing but a single tower was left; today all that remains of an architectural dream are a few foundations in Nonsuch Park, north of Epsom.

In the hills near the Hog's Back, south-west of Guildford, lies the village of *Compton*. There, in 1891, George Frederick Watts – one of the most popular painters of his time – built a country house called Limnerslease, so that he could escape from the London fog in winter. The house was most remarkable for the fact that the architect forgot to put a staircase between the first and second floors. Watts' wife Mary, a potter, mindful of posterity, had a gallery built to house his paintings, which was opened with perfect timing a few months before he died in 1904. Visitors came in hordes, and the combination of paintings and a perfect Surrey setting remains irresistible, and a fascinating contribution to the history of 19th-century taste, even though today we may feel that the 150 pictures are a monument to misjudgement. In some cases this was Watts' own misjudgement – many of the larger pictures were 'muffins' that had proved unsaleable. But at his peak Watts was hugely successful. His colossal *King Alfred* hangs in the House of Lords, while his allegory *Hope* – a young lady crouched on a globe, sadly twanging the last remaining string on her lyre – was reproduced in countless Victorian living-rooms. All his life Watts regarded his historical and allegorical paintings as the pinnacle of his art. Portraiture was secondary. And yet it is only his portraits that have kept his name as a painter alive. There are over fifty of them in the National Portrait Gallery, and they form a pantheon of Victorian celebrities comparable only to that of his friend the photographer Julia Margaret Cameron. The Watts Gallery in Compton was meant to provide a record of his life's work, but among all the mythical-historical-allegorical clutter, it is only the portraits that truly shine forth as great art. They include one of the actress Ellen Terry, whose

Watts in his garden

marriage to Watts at the age of 16 (he was 30 years older) lasted all of ten months. His self-portrait shows a serious old man with an amazing facial resemblance to his idol Titian – an impression reinforced by his red silk cap.

Unlike Titian, however, Watts was also a sculptor, and his three-dimensional work shows moments of true genius that justify his sobriquet 'England's Michelangelo'. His most famous work is the pulsatingly vigorous *Horse and Rider* made for the Cecil Rhodes monument in South Africa, but familiar to Londoners under the neutral name *Physical Energy* – physicists delight in this name for a sculpture by Watts – in Kensington Gardens.

Poignant and charming as the Gallery is (and it was kept this way for years by Wilfred Blunt, the brother of the spy and art historian Anthony), the really impressive creation here is his wife's life work and masterpiece, the *Mortuary Chapel* (1896–1901) at the top of the hillside cemetery in Compton. This is an extraordinary, original, eclectic mish-mash of a building, externally quite severe, and internally overflowing, loaded with symbols mystic and æsthetic. The building is Byzantine in shape: a narrow, cruciform domed basilica with a Norman entrance; the portal is Norman, with art nouveau angels, and there is a frieze of angels with Klimt faces – art nouveau with Celtic ornamentation. Styles vie with each other in red brick and terracotta. Inside is a twilight world of darkly glowing symbols. The walls are covered with gold and silver, winged messengers, archangels around the Tree of Life, which branches out in an endless art nouveau pattern, *pompes funèbres*, shrine to an artist, monument to an age. Here lies the 19th century. Watts and his wife also lie in the graveyard here. Some of the finest art nouveau gravestones in terracotta were produced by her studio.

Compton's importance to the history of art goes back much further than the Watts chapel. The church of *St Nicholas*, with its shingled broach spire so typical of Surrey churches, has an extremely rare two-storey Norman sanctuary. The sanctuary proper has a low rib vault, above which is a chapel which is open to the chancel but separated from it by a round-arched, wooden balustrade of the same period (*c.* 1180). No one knows what the function of Compton's double sanctuary was, but there are historical parallels in such grand places as St Stephen's Chapel in the Palace of Westminster (the original House of Commons, burnt down in 1831), the Sainte-Chapelle in Paris, and the double chapel at Schwarzrheindorf.

Death in Wonderland: Lewis Carroll in Guildford

Cobbett thought *Guildford* 'the most agreeable and happy looking town,' and I had to agree: in none of Surrey's towns did I feel more at home than here. Perhaps

Watts Memorial Chapel, Compton

it was the mixture of small-town charm and big-city urbanity. Or the beautiful old houses along the High Street. Or the fact that you can so easily slip away into the green of the North Downs and the Greensand Hills. This is 'the ford where golden flowers grew', and even if the Anglo-Saxon name of Guildford has a different etymology, that one will do for me. Here the past is omnipresent – not laid out for the benefit of tourists, but built into the very life and fabric of the town. Guildford is the county town of Surrey, and in recent times has acquired a cathedral (a magnificent building on the hill, by Sir Edward Maufe, *né* Muff, sporting a fine angel recently regilded at the expense of the cellphone company who use it as an aerial) and a university. Roger Fry, England's champion of modern art, knew just what he was doing when he moved to Guildford in 1913.

You cross the bridge over the Wey and climb the long, steep High Street, on which wares and history are displayed in equal measure. The buildings vary in style, but blend together into an architectural unity. The old town-hall clock sticks out on a beam over the street, made in 1683 and still keeping perfect time. Of course, Guildford has not been completely spared the facelessness of much modern architecture, but even its modern buildings can offer the occasional ray of sunshine: the roof terrace of Harvey's Department Store (High Street) has a water-garden designed by Geoffrey Jellicoe, where the clouds admire their own reflections, and islands of grass and flowers lend their colours to a restaurant overlooking the roofs of the town. At the top of the High Street George Abbot, Archbishop of Canterbury, built a red-brick almshouse which looks more like a palace (1619–1622). The four-towered gatehouse, an echo of Hampton Court, leads into a courtyard around which all the houses are grouped – the interiors generally being as Jacobean as the curved gables and the beautifully carved doorway. Today the Hospital of the Blessed Trinity is the home of retired people, and just as they did in George Abbot's time, the men wear flat Tudor hats and coats with the silver emblem of the archiepiscopal founder, who lies buried in what is now the Georgian Holy Trinity Church just opposite. (Abbot was the cause of fine theological controversy at the end of his life, when he accidentally shot a gamekeeper dead while out hunting. Whether this manslaughter was sufficient to disbar him from the see was a point of dispute that continued until his own death; unlike our own laxer times when 'Killer' Runcie occupied St Augustine's chair without demur.) A few buildings further on is Royal King Edward VI Grammar School (1557–86), one of the first places where cricket is known to have been played. The Chained Library, so called because of its ancient chained-up volumes, and the two second-hand bookshops in Upper High Street and Quarry Street, provide an El Dorado for book-lovers.

Guildford has a firm place in Surrey's literary history. P. G. Wodehouse was born here in 1881, creator of the inimitable Jeeves, 'a gentleman's personal gentleman', butler to the equally inimitable Bertie Wooster, the amiable and vacuous

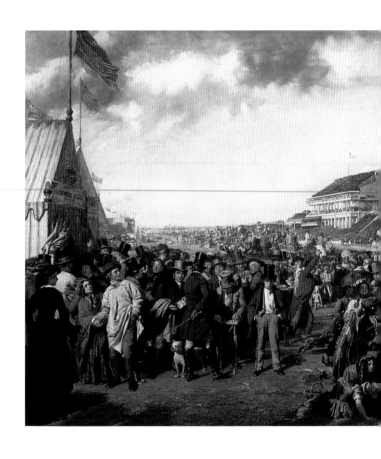

44 (previous page). *Encounter in a Surrey lane*

45. Derby Day *by William Powell Frith*

46 (overleaf) Painshill: lake and folly

47. Munstead House: Gertrude Jekyll's own garden, with house by Lutyens

48. Gertrude Jekyll's Boots, *by Ben Nicholson*

49. Gertrude Jekyll *by Ben Nicholson's father, Sir William Nicholson*

50 & 51. Compton: Watts Memorial Chapel: detail of terracotta exterior (above)
and painted plaster interior (opposite)

52. Wisley: The Wild Garden

53: Wisley: The Laboratory

54. Sutton Place: garden by Sir Geoffrey Jellicoe with White Relief *(1938 et seq.) by Ben Nicholson*

55. Sutton Place: neoclassical urn

56. Sutton Place: dolphin fountain by
Sir Geoffrey Jellicoe

57. Sutton Place: Tudor terracotta tiles

58. Albury, façade by A. W. N. Pugin

59. Loseley: the Library

60. Loseley: Fireplace in the drawing room

61. Loseley: emblem painted for Queen Elizabeth I

*Humpty Dumpty gives
Alice a helping hand*

embodiment of the upper class spirit. Wodehouse's father ('as normal as rice pudding') in fact lived in Hong Kong, and it was only Guildford because Plum's mother was staying with her sister, who was to bring the boy up. Thus Guildford was responsible not just for Wodehouse, but more importantly for one of the great figures of English literature: a Wodehouse Aunt.

A more profound and disturbing world, though full of fairytale charm and sheer nonsense, is that created by an author who came to Guildford in 1868 as a young cleric to find a home for his six unmarried sisters. This was the Reverend Charles Lutwidge Dodgson, but at that time hardly anyone knew that he had another identity. Now we all know him as Lewis Carroll, author of *Alice in Wonderland* (1865). Today no English person can walk past The Chestnuts, a red-brick house in Quarry Street, without recognizing the figures clambering over the letters on the memorial plaque: the White Rabbit with his trumpet, Dinah the cat, Humpty Dumpty sitting on a capital C, and Alice herself with her hand outstretched. At the bottom, in the date of Carroll's death, 1898, the Red King is snoring, watched by Tweedledum and Tweedledee: 'If that there King was to wake ... you'd go out –

bang! – just like a candle!' The colourful enamel figures are based on the illustrations by the Punch cartoonist John Tenniel – the only cartoonist to be knighted. (He was also responsible for the famous Bismarck cartoon of 1890: 'Dropping the Pilot'.) No writer could have wished for a livelier memorial. This Oxford mathematics don and logician would have insisted, however, that he did not live here; on the contrary, he would have said, he died here. It happened during one of his regular Christmas visits, and he is buried in the new cemetery (The Mount). Down the hill, at the foot of the Castle where the Plantagenet princes grew up, is a museum with a large collection (not all on display) of material relating to Lewis Carroll's life and work. Apart from being a mathematician and a writer, he was an amazingly gifted photographer of children. If you need proof that his Wonderland Alice really existed, you will find it in the photos he took of Alice Liddell, whose father was the Dean at Christ Church College, Oxford, where Carroll taught. Alice, so gamine in this picture, lived to a great age and is buried in the astonishing church of St Michael's in Lyndhurst, commissioned by her husband's family, the Hargreaves. Its architect is the idiosyncratic William White, and it contains among other Victorian treasures, some of Morris's finest glass.

Alice Liddell, by C. L. Dodgson

Moor Park or the Love of a Private Tutor

West of Guildford, in the fields on the way to Farnham, lies an abbey where architectural and mistaken literary history was made. *Waverley Abbey* is a ruin and a legend. This was the first Cistercian abbey in England. It was founded by the Bishop of Winchester and some monks from Normandy in 1128, only some thirty years after the order was established in Cîteaux, France. It was an exemplary institution, faithful to all the rules of the order, and set out to cultivate hitherto barren land. The architecture was exemplary too – simple and severe, in the true spirit of this, the biggest and best organized of all the reforming orders. The straight end of the choir, and of the adjacent chapels at the east end of the chancel and transepts, are characteristic of English architecture, but the importance of such Cistercian buildings for the transition from Norman style to English Gothic is not as clearly seen as at Tintern Abbey, or Kirkstall and Rievaulx in Yorkshire, since little of Waverley Abbey survived after 1536. What does remain – parts of the transepts and the vaulted storerooms (13th century) – lies amid ancient oaks in a bend of the River Wey. It's a beautiful spot; though perhaps no longer as perfect as it appeared to one lad at the end of the 18th century. 'When I was a very little boy,' wrote Cobbett, 'I was, in the barley-sowing season, going along by the side of a field, near Waverley Abbey; the primroses and bluebells bespangling the banks on both sides of me; a thousand linnets singing in a spreading oak over my head; while the jingling of the traces and the whistling of the ploughboy saluted my ear from over the hedge... I was not more than eight years old; but this particular scene has presented itself to my mind many times every year from that day to this.' It was the beginning of a love for the country in its every detail, from soil upwards, that is perhaps as great as any other writer of English; but one married to a style of complete matter of factness. The opposite in fact from the romantic adventures of his contemporary, Sir Walter Scott, which are forever linked with the name of Waverley. One would love to connect the romantic ruins of the Abbey to Walter Scott's equally romantic novels, but Scott himself never suggested that there was any such link. Goethe rated these thirty books (started in 1814) as among the finest in all world literature. Their hero, Edward Waverley, caught between the English Hanoverians and the Scottish Stuarts, develops many relationships in the course of his adventures, but never once does he think of, come to, or even refer to Waverley Abbey. The secret seems to be that Scott in his early career spent a great deal of time in Surrey, which became for him the epitome of England – and it was as an English character, the straight man for all the grandeur and romance of the Scottish scene, that he conceived of Edward Waverley.

Not far off is *Albury Park*, one of England's more bizarre houses, in fact 'one of the few to set your teeth on edge,' according to the art historian Christopher Wright. A fine medieval house was palladianized by the Evelyns, classicized by Soane and given fancy Gothic dress by Pugin; the latter was also let loose on the charming medieval parish church, parts of which he redecorated in his most fervent glowing style, 'with glass to knock your socks off.' Historically the most important part is the layout of the garden, where John Evelyn's design for the great patron, Thomas Howard, Earl of Arundel, survives almost intact, complete with the (now disused) canal and tunnel to make an Italianate grotto. Even the no-nonsense Cobbett was enchanted: 'take it altogether, this, certainly, is the prettiest garden that I ever beheld. There was taste and sound judgment at every step in the laying out of this place. Everywhere utility and convenience is combined with beauty. The terrace is the finest thing of the sort that I ever saw, and the whole thing altogether is a great compliment to the taste of the times in which it was formed.'

We are back on literary ground when we visit nearby *Moor Park*. A simple white manor house stands in a long green valley bordered by woodland, and here Jonathan Swift first met his 'Stella'. The author of *Gulliver's Travels* was at the time a young intellectual with no money and no career, but in 1689 he obtained a post here as private secretary to the politician and essayist William Temple. It was thanks to the latter's diplomacy that England was able to enter a Triple Alliance

Jonathan Swift

with Holland and Sweden against the French. Sir William grew tired of court intrigue, and settled down on his country estate at Moor Park. In Swift he found a man who was perfectly qualified to help him write his memoirs and accomplish his occasional political missions right up until his death in 1699. Swift studied in Temple's library, learned during a visit from William III of Orange how to eat asparagus the Dutch way, and wrote his first satires, *Battle of the Books* and *Tale of a Tub*, which brought forth the damning comment from his kinsman John Dryden: 'Cousin Swift, you will never be a poet!' Swift's star, however, rose rapidly after he had met 'Stella'. She was Hester Johnson, who was probably Temple's daughter, and who was eight years old at the time. Swift was her private tutor, and 'instructed her continually in the principles of virtue and honour.' So far as is known, the romance at Moor Park was purely platonic, and the suggestion that eventually they were secretly married in Dublin is pure surmise, for Swift had no interest in marriage or in children. But this complex being, clergyman and cynic, did write the *Journal to Stella*, which shows the importance of the role she played in his life. 'He was always alone – alone and gnashing in the darkness, except when Stella's sweet smile came and shone upon him' (Thackeray).

It was Scott who reported that Swift, in bitter old age, took down a copy of *Tale of a Tub* and sighed 'Good God, what a genius I had when I wrote that book!' William Cobbett would have agreed wholeheartedly. Swift's most famous heir as a radical journalist was born only a few miles from Moor Park 'at the plough-tail and in the hop gardens' of Farnham ('which spot, as it happened, is the neatest in England and I believe, in the whole world'), and he too was a gardener, though at first only a gardener's boy, working at the Bishop of Winchester's residence, Farnham Castle. He might have risen no further, but on hearing another gardener tell of the King's gardens, he determined one June morning to walk to Kew to see them. He reached Richmond in the afternoon with but threepence in his pocket. 'With this for my whole fortune, I was trudging through Richmond in my blue smock-frock and my red garters tied under my knees, when, staring about me, my eye fell upon a little book in a bookseller's window, on the outside of which was written 'TALE OF A TUB; Price, 3d.' The title was so odd that my curiosity was excited. I had the 3d., but then, I could have *no supper*. In I went, and got the little book, which I was so impatient to read that I got over into a field, at the upper corner of Kew Gardens, where there stood a *hay-stack*. The book was so different from anything that I had ever read before: it was something so new to my mind, that though I could not understand some of it, it delighted me beyond description; and it produced what I have always considered a sort of birth of intellect.' He eventually saw the King's garden and even got a job there (the King and his brothers laughed at his strange costume); but Cobbett's greater course was set.

Moor Park later became a mental hospital, then a theological college, and today it belongs to the University of Surrey. There are still a few pictures in the house that hark back to its former occupants, but it was radically rebuilt at the end of the 18th century. More distressing to Swift and Temple perhaps, and certainly to Cobbett, would have been the disappearance of William Temple's geometrical Dutch garden. For Temple was not only a politician and writer of note, but a passionate gardener – his heart was buried in his garden, by the sundial, at his particular request – in his essay *Upon the Gardens of Epicurus* (1692) he made a striking contribution to garden theory:. the concept of Sharawaggi (or Sharawadgi), that is to say, studied disorder. The origins of the term are unknown – it is not Chinese, as he claimed – but it was to have far-reaching consequences in the history of the English garden.

Temple's gardens – and indeed Cobbett's – may have gone, but those of Temple's contemporary, John Evelyn, have fared rather better, as we have already seen at Albury. Evelyn was a co-founder of the Royal Society – the oldest and most prestigious scientific society in England – and was responsible for plans to combat air pollution in London, which was a major problem even in those days. He kept a diary from his eleventh to his eighty-sixth year, recording the history of his life and times, and was truly a man of many parts. Next to his friend Samuel Pepys (who called him 'a most excellent humoured man), he was certainly the most important English diarist of the 17th or perhaps any century, and is buried in St John's, west of Dorking, the town where he was born. The family made their fortune from gunpowder, and their home, Wotton House, is now, satisfyingly, a training school for the Fire Service. It's situated off the main road, in an idyllic valley amongst the Downs. Behind the modernised Tudor house the Evelyns laid out an artificial hill with terraces and a temple pavilion (1650) – one of the earliest Italian gardens in England (Wilton preceded it in 1642). Brother George conceived the garden and left Cousin George to design and supervise it; and John wrote that a true garden was a 'res sacra et divina', a piece of Paradise regained, giving solace to the human mind and soul. He dreamed of a 'noble, princely, and universall Elysium, capable of all the amenities that can naturally be introduced into Gardens of pleasure... the aire and genious of Gardens operate upon humane spirits towards virtue and sanctity.'

Nothing at Wotton survives, the garden at Albury that Evelyn made for the Earl of Arundel is inaccessible, and he never managed to finish his written magnum opus, the *Elysium Britannicum*. But his influence as both a theorist and a practical gardener, plantsman and engineer was profound. A popular descendant from and promoter of such ideas is the Royal Horticultural Society, founded in 1804, the ultimate authority for a garden-crazy nation. Everyone who is anyone in the realm of horticulture will visit their 250-acre headquarters on the A3 near Woking: *Wisley Gardens*. Whatever new plants and flowers are available will be sent out with the coveted seal of approval to all the garden centres in the land, whence they make their way to all the front gardens. On the other side of Woking, in *Brookwood*, is an endless park of graves and mausolea: this is London's necropolis, the biggest cemetery in England. The Victorians were such dedicated worshippers at the shrine of death that a special dedicated train line was built to take mourners direct to Brookwood from London – a creepy subject for a creepy novel, Andrew Bilton's *Necropolis Railway*.

Hermit Wanted: Painshill Park

Only recently has one of the most popular and admired landscape gardens of the 18th century regained its former splendours: *Painshill Park*, near Cobham. It lies within the coils of the M25, the A3 and the A245, a refuge from the carbon dioxide. When Charles Hamilton acquired the land in 1738, it was a barren stretch of heath. He began to lay out a park, at much the same time as Lord Burlington and Henry Hoare were doing the same thing in Chiswick and Stourhead respectively. Gardening was very much in fashion; it was a calling suited to a gentleman. Charles Hamilton, however, was the fourteenth child of an impoverished Irish aristocrat, and was neither rich nor famous. It was his park that made his name. He created it with borrowed money, and before he could build the country house to go with it, he went bankrupt.

The Hermitage at Painshill Park, contemporary drawing

Hamilton lived in Italy for more than three years, and he studied painting there. The result is Painshill Park, the perfect anthology of picturesque land-scapes. In the centre is the 'natural' line of beauty, a serpentine artificial lake, whose bays and islands make the land seem more extensive than it actually is (then over 250 acres, but now only 158). Hamilton spread his surprises out along the shores: the (artificial) ruins of an abbey and a mausoleum, Chinese bridges, a Turkish tent, a Roman temple. Classical and romantic, oriental and western delights merge together in this microcosm – a little green world outside history. The harmony of the place combines all temporal contradictions, and the multi-plicity of styles merges into a whole æsthetic programme. Stourhead is a park of literary asssociations, but Painshill is above all a visual concept, 'a study in time and movement as in a Chinese scroll,' as Geoffrey Jellicoe, Hamilton's 20th-cen-tury successor put it.

Hamilton planted as a painter paints. Contrasts of light, perspectives, sec-ondary motifs – everything was composed according to the rules of art, but at the same time it was all pure nature, from the Alpine wilderness of a gorge filled with spruces to a valley in which the autumn mists were to gather like an open-air stage set. Painshill Park is in the tradition of atmospheric pictures. A Bacchus temple spreads Elysian joy, while a mausoleum evokes the past and the transience of life. Part of the *tableau vivant* in this landscape of the soul was a hermitage – a thatched hut requiring a hermit, for whom Hamilton duly

The grotto at Painshill being restored

advertised: the hermit had to 'continue in the Hermitage seven years, where he would be provided with a Bible, optical glasses, a mat for his feet, a hassock for his pillow, and hour-glass for his timepiece, water for his beverage and food from the house. He must wear a camlet robe, and never under any circumstances, must he cut his hair, beard or nails, or exchange one word with his servants.' The successful applicant, however, found that the role required of the Hermit of Painshill was a bit more than he could stomach: after three weeks, he was spotted in a Cobham pub.

Charles Hamilton was one of the first to plant large numbers of American trees and shrubs, as opposed to individual showpieces. He used tulip trees, magnolias, azaleas, and different types of cedar. He planted a vine, bred Jacob's sheep, and behind the ruined Gothic abbey he ran a brickworks. But none of this was profitable enough to enable him to pay his debts, and in 1773 he had to sell the park which had been his life's work. In the same year, a view of Painshill even appeared on the magnificent dinner service the Wedgwood made for Catherine the Great. Horace Walpole, Elizabeth Montagu, and other prominent trend-setters in

London Society loved the park (though Walpole disapproved of the temple on the bizarre grounds that the Goths would not have built a summer house) and two future American Presidents, John Adams and Thomas Jefferson, visited it in 1786 during their tour of English gardens.

Today it is not the historical importance of this garden that arouses our immediate admiration, but its magnificent restoration. After the Second World War, it was practically forgotten and completely neglected; the exquisite pavilions and bridges had fallen into total disrepair. At last, local people took things into their own hands. In 1981 they set up a Trust, and began to restore the park. The fact that this was carried out so accurately was due partly to archaeological findings, and partly to William Gilpin's sketchbook of 1772, as well as a number of other documentary sources. Plants were dated, paths and buildings reconstructed, the Gothic temple with its filigree ogee arches was reinforced with a steel frame, and on a slope beside the lake the Turkish tent is once again shining out in white and blue and gold. The most difficult thing to restore was the island grotto. With stalactites of plaster embedded with chips of calcite, fluorite and gypsum, this fairytale grotto was Hamilton's most spectacular creation. Hundreds of volunteers, students, and long-term unemployed people worked alongside the experts in restoring Painshill – a wonderful example of British team spirit, not to mention the British passion for gardens.

Edwin Lutyens: Country Houses for the Leisured Classes

Since Cobbett rode through Southern England and published his influential *Rural Rides* (1821-1830, first published in Cobbett's newspaper *The Political Register*), no county has changed more than Surrey. The symbiosis between thrusting suburb and yielding countryside created a new type of landscape at the end of the 19th century: the 'High-Class Suburb' (Pevsner). In places like Virginia Water and St George's Hill in Weybridge, you can't see the houses for the trees. They are hidden behind tall hedges, tucked away in their own piece of forest. At the beginning of this new development, it was a woman with the same gardening zeal of a John Evelyn who gave the new country houses their new gardens. Her name was Gertrude Jekyll. It was also Gertrude Jekyll who gave a decisive push to the career of a young architect. Her protégé began by building country houses in Surrey, and ended with monumental constructions in India. He was Sir Edwin Lutyens.

When he unscrewed the top of his walking stick, out came a ruler. Sir Edwin was a perfectionist, and wherever he went, he was always planning and drawing. For his own home he designed a dining-table with a slate, and every guest was given a piece of chalk. He hated holidays, especially by the sea, and his only hobbies were playing patience, fishing, and doing *The Times* crossword puzzle. He

was happiest in London, where he was born in 1869, the tenth of thirteen children. His father was an officer, and a painter who specialized in horses. Lutyens became England's most successful architect since Christopher Wren. He built houses and castles, palaces and banks, churches and war memorials. His finest houses lie hidden in the English countryside, his most massive work is the Viceroy's House in New Delhi, and his most poetic the doll's house he made for Queen Mary in Windsor Castle. He grew up with the unlimited repertoire of Victorian styles, had an Edwardian clientèle with almost unlimited means, and was still planning imperial-style buildings at a time when the Empire was on the verge of breaking up. His most gigantic project remained incomplete: Liverpool's Roman Catholic Cathedral, which was to be twice the size of St Paul's, with a dome even bigger than that designed by Michelangelo for St Peter's in Rome.

When Lutyens died in 1944, British architectural journals were published with black borders, as if the King had died. The funeral was in Westminster Abbey and he was buried in the crypt of St Paul's, the bier passing what he considered his greatest work, the sublimely simple and subtle Cenotaph in Whitehall, the focus to this day of Britain's remembrance ceremonies. Yet by comparison with all this grandeur Lutyens' influence was curiously muted. His fame had never spread to the Continent, for he was a lone wolf, not at the beginning but at the end of a stylistic era. He was never a pioneer of modern architecture like Frank Lloyd Wright or Mies van der Rohe, and he was no innovator like Mackintosh or eccentric like Gaudí. In short, he had no place in the history of modern architectural development and the international style. Only recently has he been rediscovered as the grandfather of postmodern architecture.

Lutyens was in tune with the Arts and Crafts Movement and with a very English tradition of country house architecture. Therein lay his roots, his greatness, and his limitations. He admired Norman Shaw and Philip Webb and their attempt 'to bring England back to craftsmanship and tradition'. He was twenty when he built his first country house, Crooksbury House near Farnham. In the same year, 1889, he first met the 45-year-old Gertrude Jekyll in a Surrey garden. It was the beginning of the most successful partnership in the history of English gardens. Lutyens learned a great deal more from Jekyll than she from him. He called her his Horacle, and showed her every single one of his designs right up until the day she died. 'Aunt Bumps' not only introduced the beginner to potential clients, but also taught him above all about the organic relationship between house and garden. 'So naturally has the house been planned that it seems to have grown out of the landscape rather than to have been fitted into it,' wrote Edward Hudson,

Lutyens, by Quiz, shown at the peak of his official career, designing Delhi. The Viceroy's Palace is seen in the background

171

Tigborne Court, Surrey

founder of *Country Life*, describing Deanery Garden, the house Lutyens built for him at Sonning in Berkshire.

A few years earlier, in 1895–97, he had designed Munstead Wood for Gertrude Jekyll – a house in the wooded hills of *Munstead* above Godalming. He also built her some smaller cottages for her staff, including the Swiss gardener and the butler. In her book *Home and Garden*, Gertrude Jekyll enthused over the virtues of Munstead Wood: 'an honest building, whose only pretention is to be of sound work done with the right intention, of material used according to the capability of its nature and the purpose designed, with due regard to beauty of proportion and simplicity of effect.' Even William Morris could scarcely have paid a greater compliment to the young Lutyens than did the normally strict and highly critical Miss Jekyll. Of the whole house, she said, 'in some mysterious way it is imbued with an expression of cheerful, kindly welcome, of restfulness to mind and body, of abounding satisfaction to eye and brain.' In her new house, Gertrude Jekyll felt so much at home that it was as if she had never lived anywhere else.

The typical Lutyens house gives the impression that it has been standing in its setting for hundreds of years. This was achieved by using local materials and old techniques of craftsmanship. Lutyens reinforced this ageing effect with a collage of different, contrasting motifs from architectural history. Nevertheless, his individuality always outweighed his eclecticism. That is very evident at Tigborne Court, which he built in 1899 for the chairman of an insurance company. It is situated on the A283, near *Witley*. Its façade has three Elizabethan pointed gables and an Ionic loggia, flanked by two low wings with very tall chimneys, whose sharp edges are in marked contrast to the concave side walls. The geometry of it all is dramatic, sophisticated, elegant and eloquent, right through to the surface materials: rough-hewn masonry, broken up by bands of flat brick, rather like the *opus spicatum* of Roman walls.

Lutyens loved to endow ordinary architectural features with extraordinary proportions: he built chimneys taller, gables longer, and arches wider. This makes his houses slightly mannered but completely his own. It was this architectural dramatization that Frank Lloyd Wright – who was born in the same year as Lutyens – especially admired. It was the ability 'so characteristically and quietly to dramatize the old English feeling for dignity and comfort in an interior'. Lutyens himself regarded Queen Anne houses as the embodiment of Englishness and classical discipline. This can be seen most vividly in The Salutation, a red-brick house which he built in Sandwich, Kent, in 1911. Its giant chimneys and hipped roof only serve to enhance the atmosphere of harmony and peace. In addition to such individualistic neoclassical houses – Lutyens, an irrepressible punster, called this his Wrenaissance – he built Lindisfarne Castle in Ireland, and Castle Drogo on Dartmoor, one of the last castles to be built in our modern age, a paradoxical combination of conservatism and the avant-garde.

Lutyens was a child of his time, the short but glamorous age of Edward VII, and with the accompanying *folie de grandeur* it was only natural that he should be the man asked to design the government buildings in New Delhi, which in 1912 replaced Calcutta as the new seat of government in India. In the Viceroy's House, his masterpiece, he combined in the grand manner themes from the European Renaissance and elements of Hindu architecture. 'That will be the finest ruin of them all,' commented Clemenceau when he visited New Delhi. Gandhi called the palace a white elephant and Nehru mocked at its pomposity, but Le Corbusier, before he designed his own Indian town Chandigarh, went to see New Delhi and admired Lutyens' 'extreme care and great talent'.

For a man of such big ideas, the architectural modesty and social involvement of the garden-city movement in England had little to offer. In Hampstead Garden Suburb (1908–10), there were constant complaints about the dimensions of his houses. This architect for the leisured classes built just one working class housing estate, Page Street in Westminster. But he did design children's rooms with windows at floor level, so that crawling babies could have a view, and he even designed a circular children's room, according to his daughter Mary, so that no child could ever be made to stand in a corner.

Sir Edwin, always known as Ned, was basically a shy man with a youthful charm and wit. He married the daughter of a Viceroy, but Lady Emily had little interest in his work or in sex. What attracted her was theosophy. She took advantage of their time in Delhi to pursue Mrs. Besant and the strange Bishop

Leadbeater, who in turn led her to the handsome youth Krishnamurti. It was she who was responsible for Krishnamurti's education in England. Despite all these distractions, the Lutyens managed to produce five children, and bore their marriage with a heroism that might even have bordered on love.

Edwin Lutyens died in London in 1944. His rediscovery began in 1977 in Washington. At a dinner celebrating the 50th anniversary of his British Embassy building, Philip Johnson – doyen of American architects – confessed himself to be a convert and new admirer of Lutyens. 'Today, Lutyens represents everything we find delightful,' said Johnson, whose AT&T building in New York, a skyscraper with a Chippendale gable, made him into a leading light of postmodern architecture. A year later, on the occasion of an exhibition at the Museum of Modern Art, the *New York Times* declared the Englishman to be 'a giant of 20th-century architecture'. The great Lutyens retrospective of 1981 in London provided grist to the mill of the traditionalists, led by Prince Charles, champion of a new Domestic Revival. This well-earned revaluation of Lutyens, however, might well degenerate into nostalgia, which would be very much at the expense of contemporary architecture.

Nowadays you can buy a curved Lutyens garden-bench called 'Sissinghurst' – the pride and joy of many a back garden – or a bulky but comfortable Lutyens Napoleon chair, and various other items of Lutyens furniture manufactured under the watchful eye of Candia Lutyens, the master's granddaughter, who is a London stockbroker. Ocasionally you can even buy Lutyens houses – modern antiques for sale on the housing market. They are all listed, and indeed no other 20th-century British architect has so many of his buildings on this roll of honour. Looking at them is sheer pleasure, and nowhere are they so densely grouped together as in Southern England. You can even get rooms in a Lutyens hotel: Little Thakeham in Sussex (north of Worthing) was built in 1902 as a country house, but has been run as a luxury hotel since 1979. It also has a wonderful garden in the style of Gertrude Jekyll.

Surrey is not, however, exclusively Lutyens territory. Here you can also find what have now become classic examples of country house architecture by his colleagues Norman Shaw, Philip Webb, and Charles Voysey – pioneering work which at the turn of the century was regarded as European avant-garde. The architects of the Domestic Revival preferred local building materials and rural traditions of construction, which constituted a new naturalness in architecture. Their style was simple, large-scale without being monumental, comfortable but not luxurious, designed as homes and not as showpieces. Norman Shaw's houses are homely and spacious, brick with tile-hanging, for instance, Banstead Wood (1884–6) south of Epsom. Charles Voysey's houses are similar – extensive, with large low roofs, completely incorporated into the landscape, and generally with interiors designed entirely by himself. 'In the category of qualities of general need we should put repose, cheerfulness, simplicity, breadth, warmth, quietness in storm, economy of upkeep, evidence of protection, harmony with surroundings, absence of dark passages or places, evenness of temperature, making the home the frame to its inmates, for rich and poor alike will appreciate these qualities.' This was what Voysey regarded as good building, and with such magnificently situated houses as Greyfriars (1896) near *Puttenham* at the foot of the Hog's Back, this son of a heterodox vicar from Yorkshire became the most influential British architect on the Continent. Hermann Muthesius, the co-founder in 1907 of the *Deutscher Werkbund* ('work league' a William Morris-inspired group that aimed to raise the standard of German design) and of the garden town of Hellerau, was sent by the Prussian Ministry of Trade to London to study architecture and design, and through his own work and publications (*Das englische Haus*, 1904), he made this style of country house popular in Germany as well.

In the forest and on the heath around *Haslemere,* where Surrey and Sussex and Hampshire join together, there is a beauty spot and a poet's corner. This is where George Eliot used to come, to escape from London, and her descriptions of English provincial life owe their vivid subtleties not least to her observations of this part of Surrey. She and the married man with whom she – shockingly – lived, and who was the catalyst of her creativity, George Lewes, rented a house (now divided, but with one half called 'Middlemarch') in Shottermill where she wrote *Middlemarch* under a yew tree that can still be seen in the garden. It was a charmed existence for them. 'We have a ravishing country round us, and pure air and water – in short, all the conditions of health, if the east wind were away. We have old prints for dumb companions – charming children of Sir Joshua's, and large hatted ladies of his and Romney's. I read aloud – almost all the evening – books of German science, and other gravities. So you see we are like two secluded owls, wise with unfashionable wisdom, and knowing nothing of pictures and French plays.' This was the calm

George Eliot

background needed by what Virginia Woolf called 'the troubled spirit, that exacting and questioning and baffled presence who was George Eliot herself' to create one of the greateast and most instantly acclaimed novels in English. Despite Eliot's scandalous private arrangements, it was recognized as one of the great works of the moral life. Preachers quoted it in their pulpits; an Archbishop was caught keeping it in his hat to read during long sermons. Virginia Woolf herself called it

Aldworth, where Tennyson entertained Henry James, Turgenev and Gladstone amongst others;
designed very much with his involvement, and here drawn by him in 1889

'the magnificent book which with all its imperfections is one of the few English novels written for grown-up people.'

Eliot and Lewes did not manage to achieve total seclusion however. 'Tennyson, who is one of the "hill-folk" about here, has found us out,' she had to announce, not altogether happily. (He needed no invitation to launch into a reading of *Maud*, wherever he might be.) He lived only a few miles over the border, in the house that he had built on the Blackdown Hills, Aldworth. Tennyson had grown to resent the crowds who gathered to catch a glimpse of him at Farringford, and the site he chose was so isolated on its high plateau that there was no road to get to it, only cart tracks. Here he was able to consecrate his now-assured social position with a gothic house with crenellations and heraldry; and also with the unprecedented luxury of a bathroom, an innovation so exciting that the poet took to having three or four baths a day. Tennyson wrote his last poems here, including *June Bracken and Heather*, dedicated to his wife Emily:

> There on the top of the down,
> The wild heather round me and over me June's high blue,
> When I looked at the bracken so bright and the heather so brown,
> I thought to myself I would offer this book to you,
> This, and my love together,
> To you that are seventy-seven,
> With a faith as clear as the heights of the June-blue heaven
> And a fancy as summer-new
> As the green of the bracken and the gloom of the heather.

It was at Aldworth that Tennyson died, and there is a memorial window at St Bartholomew's in Haslemere (1899), commissioned from Burne-Jones by the poet's friends, despite Tennyson's known dislike of Pre-Raphaelite versions of his work. Burne-Jones chose the subject of Sir Galahad, since Tennyson had written many of his Arthurian poems at Aldworth. It is a poet's corner; another window commemorates Gerald Manley Hopkins, whose parents lived nearby. And, in this same church, protected by glass, is a delicately coloured silken altar cloth by William Morris, with a choir and orchestra of angels. Since the angels are making a guest appearance in Haslemere, they are of course playing those ancient instruments which Arnold Dolmetsch had been making and collecting since the turn of the century, and whose sounds had reverberated from this village in Surrey to appreciative ears all over the world.

The Dolmetsch Festival has been taking place in Haslemere since 1925. For lovers of old chamber music, this week in July is the equivalent of Glyndebourne for opera-lovers. Thanks to Arnold Dolmetsch, we can now hear Bach, Handel, Telemann, Purcell or Locatelli in Haslemere and on countless records just as their contemporaries heard them, on the instruments for which the music was composed. This rediscovery – like the reappearance of the recorder in the rooms of all well-brought-up children since 1910 – is the pioneering achievement of a man who came from a family of organ and piano makers, and who found the spiritual and technical inspiration for his work in the Arts and Crafts Movement. It was at William Morris's suggestion that he built his first faithful reproduction of a harpsichord, and when Morris fell ill in 1896 and was on his deathbed, he sent for Dolmetsch to come and play the flute and the viola da gamba. These ancient instruments, examples of Dolmetsch's outstanding musical skill and technical craftsmanship, are exhibited along with other prototypes from musical archæology in his former workshop at Jesses House, Grayswood Road. This is now the home of his son, Carl Dolmetsch, who is a flautist and has directed the festival since his father's death. He told me that the music used to have a strange effect on the local people, but now the Haslemere Festival brings in the tourists, and the instruments from the Dolmetsch workshops (in the King's Road) are famous throughout the world of music.

Stoke d'Abernon, near Cobham in North Surrey, is another village that is famous for music-lovers. In 1963 Yehudi Menuhin opened a music school there. 'England was the ideal place to start such a venture because of the quality of the English approach to life, the teamwork, the tolerance, the lack of rigid authority and the encouragement and dignity given to the human being.' Violin, cello, viola and piano are taught here, and one of the most famous old boys is Nigel Kennedy. 'At this school,' Menuhin told interviewer Robin Daniels, 'we are trying to build a community on a foundation of wholeness, uniting the musical life, spiritual search, intellectual attainment, a sense of giving and sharing and mutual understanding,

and a broad view of life, social, artistic, scientific, philosophical.'

Pilgrims of a different kind also make their way to Stoke d'Abernon: the legions of brass-rubbers who are drawn here by the earliest English brass, Sir John d'Abernon (far left). Almost fifty years later than the oldest surviving brass of all (Bishop Ysowilpe, 1231, in Verden, Germany) Sir John still lies in his original stone setting, with his lance and his once blue shield, the very model of a medieval knight captured by a matchless work of art. Next to him is his son (left), who died 50 years later; part of his armour is plate, for the chain mail of his father was already out of fashion then. He also has a most unmilitary swing in his hips, an artistic rather than a personal affectation however, as it is a distant echo of the sweet International Gothic style that was then sweeping Europe.

Queen of the Flowerbeds: Gertrude Jekyll

In her heavy apron, leather lace-up boots, and battered straw hat she walked into garden folklore. She was stocky, robust, short-sighted, a lifelong spinster, a battle-axe, and a workaholic. But she had the finest of ears, and the most sensitive of noses. It is said that she could tell a tree from the sound of its leaves rustling, and she could distinguish between kinds of roses by their scent. She was Gertrude Jekyll, Queen of the Flowerbeds. More than anyone else, it was she who determined the form and character of the 20th-century English garden. David Austin created a pink rose called 'Gertrude Jekyll' as recently as 1986, which may perhaps give some slight idea of her everlasting popularity.

She was born in London in 1843, the daughter of a well-to-do family, and was educated at the Art Academy in South Kensington. By the time she left, she was master of the whole range of Arts and Crafts: painting, sewing, metalwork, photography, woodwork, and stone-cutting. Only in her mid-40s, because of her failing eyesight, did she turn from painting and flower embroidery to the art of gardening. Ruskin's combination of art with nature was her guiding principle: 'Planting ground is painting a landscape with living things,' she wrote, 'and, as I hold that good gardening takes rank within the bounds of the fine arts, so I hold that to plant well needs an artist of no mean capacity, and his difficulties are not slight ones, for his living picture must be right from all points and in all lights.' As opposed to the Victorian gardens with their straight lines and their bright colours, Jekyll used the subtle shades that she admired in Turner's paintings, systematically applying scientific theories of colour. Instead of rectangular, formal beds, she planted mixed borders, bringing together flowers and shrubs, winter and summer,

Father and son: the two Sir John d'Abernons at Stoke d'Abernon

How exotics were planted before Robinson: and opposite, how he recommended growing the green hellebore in the wild garden

in a varied, relaxed harmony. She took inspiration from the gardens planted by Surrey farmers all around her home at Munstead Wood, and also from the writing of William Robinson.

Robinson, the great creator of the 'natural' English garden (in fact made up of the spoils of half the world) lived in Gravetye Manor (where his garden is currently being restored). His most influential book, first published in 1870, was '*The Wild Garden*, or, our *Groves and Gardens* more beautiful by the *Naturalisation* of *Hardy Exotic Plants*; being one way onwards from the *Dark Ages of Flower Gardening*, with suggestions for the *Regeneration* of the *Bare Borders* of the *London Parks*.' The subtitle says it all – including the revelling in the imperialist reach that rings a strange, unnatural note today. But the impact on the British æsthetic can scarcely be overestimated – nor the impact on the British landscape. The Wild Garden 'is best explained,' he wrote, 'by the winter aconite flowering under a grove of naked trees in February; by the Snowflake, tall and numerous in meadows by the Thames side; by the blue Lupine dyeing an islet with its purple in a Scotch river; and by the blue Apennine Anemone staining an English wood blue before the coming of our blue bells.' Not a 'wilderness', nor even a 'picturesque garden', let alone 'a garden run wild', but a desire for a consciously created 'fair garden and new and beautiful pictures – painting with the living colours brought from all over the world'.

Robinson himself had an acute response to plants in the wild, and this æsthetic of a 'natural look', combined with a refined appreciation of the purely artistic value of colours and massing, was a profound influence on Gertrude Jekyll. She worked with him on his magazine, *The Garden*. But where he started off life as a practical gardener, she was an artist, trained at the Slade and who knew both Morris and Ruskin. She refined Robinson's art with an instinct for the right plants, combinations, colours and textures that amounted to genius. From 1883 onwards, she used her own 15 acres of wood and heathland in Surrey to plant a garden that became the bedrock of all her books and all her designs. Like the house of Bargate stone that Edwin Lutyens had built for her, *Munstead Wood* became a household name. 'A Lutyens house with a Jekyll garden' – this was the combination that made them into the dream pair of 20th-century English landscape gardening. Their partnership sprang from shared roots, the Arts and Crafts Movement, and a common aim – the unity of house and garden, nature and art. The harmony was unfolded through a whole network of correspondences and contrasts, and the more uniform the materials, colours and shapes, the more exciting was the relationship between vegetation and architecture, between the fixed frame and the ever growing, ever changing natural picture. Ponds, steps, sunken lawns, pergolas, yew hedges – all of these became trademarks of the partnership. Some purists might complain that Lutyens made too much use of stone, with his terraces, stairways, and paved paths, but these areas are a delight to the eye, with their striped patterns of brick and slate, like dark grey tweed, and they serve to set off the sheer beauty of the flowering borders. Perhaps the prime example of Jekyll's virtuosity is the garden at Hestercombe, in Somerset, where her flowerbeds are simply the perfect complement to Lutyen's geometrical framework.

Gertrude Jekyll designed over 100 gardens with Lutyens, and another 260 all over the world. She never saw most of them, either before or afterwards. Generally drawings, information, and samples of soil sent by her clients would suffice for her to make detailed plans. Her fellow gardener Russell Page noted with admiration her grasp of the nature of soil, water and growth. Unlike the designs of the feudal landscape gardeners, Gertrude Jekyll's ideas could be applied even to the homes of the more modest middle classes. There are thousands upon thousands of small gardens in England that have followed her example without needing the fourteen gardeners who worked for the owner of Munstead Wood. Between 1899 and 1925 she wrote fifteen books, constantly reprinted, especially *Colour Schemes for the Flower Garden*. Her enduring influence is certainly due more to these books than to her gardens, for none of the latter have remained completely unaltered. How could they? That is in the nature of Nature (quite apart from the nature of new owners). Even if the overall structure has survived, the plants themselves have been drastically changed. Perhaps about two dozen gardens are something like the originals. Strict historians may maintain that even Hester-combe is a posthumous creation, but it is the only garden that has been restored with utter fidelity to her instructions. And what of Munstead Wood, where she lived until her death in 1932, together with her three maids

Munstead Wood; opposite, her
favourite pussy cat arrangement

and her seven cats?

'Miss Jekyll rather fat, and rather grumbly,' observed Vita Sackville-West, when she visited the living legend there in the summer of 1917. Then comes the somewhat barbed comment: 'Garden not at its best, but can see it must be lovely.' After Gertrude Jekyll's death, successive owners altered the garden until it became unrecognizable. But in 1992 the present owner, the banker Sir Robert Clark, gave the go-ahead to his (one and only) gardener to restore the garden to its original state. Since then, Stephen King has followed Gertrude Jekyll's plans 'as far as possible'. Those plans, incidentally, form part of the Reef Point Gardens Collection at the University of California. In the Spring Garden there are narcissi, tulips and irises, wallflowers and primulas, creating a range of colour from red and pink, through blue and yellow, to a cool white. In the adjacent Summer Garden, roses, peonies and delphiniums, lilies, lupins and bellflowers, forget-me-nots and spurge, all carefully graduated, create their own characteristic sequence of colours. Stephen has also planted birch trees between the rhododendrons, and – his pride and joy – he has recreated the Primrose Garden with a dozen different species.

Just a few paces away from her garden, Gertrude Jekyll lies buried in the shade of the church at *Busbridge*. The stained glass windows are by Edward Burne-Jones and William Morris & Co (1899), the rood and chancel screen by Lutyens (1897). Over thirty years later, the great architect also designed Gertrude Jekyll's gravestone, as well as that of her brother. 'Artist, Gardener, Craftswoman' is the inscription, along with the proud words of Horace: 'Non omnis moriar' (I shall not altogether die, Ode III, 30). Roses and begonias grow on her grave, and her garden boots stand patiently in Guildford Museum.

Hampshire

*A happy country in the four elements, if culinary fire may pass for
one, with plenty of the best wood for fuel thereof. Most pure and
piercing the air of this shire; and none in England hath more
plenty of clear and fresh rivulets of troutful water...
As for the earth, it is both fair and fruitful*
Thomas Fuller, *History of the Worthies of England, 1662*

You walk through the countryside, then you go to the river, and you finish up on the village green. That's the Hampshire way: nature, fishing, and cricket. And if you want three places in Hampshire to epitomise these three great British obsessions, then go to a museum, a grave, and a pub. We must get our priorities right: the pub first. On the Downs north of Portsmouth, near *Hambledon*, you'll find 'The Bat and Ball'. The sign at least helps us ignorant continentals to understand the basics: the bowler propels the leather ball in the direction of the batsman, who has a club which looks half cudgel and half paddle, and with which he tries to hit the ball. What happens next is a ritual of rules and runs, played out on lovingly tended grass by twenty-two men in white. It is a sport for philosophical contemplation, often stretching into days of wild excitement which the uninitiated misconstrue as unadulterated tedium. Its code of honour is so deeply ingrained that the phrase 'That's not cricket' is taken to cover all aspects of unfairness and dishonesty. Many famous writers, artists, and public figures have a love of cricket that amounts to a passion, and it's a game that's played by people of all ages and all social strata. Next to death, the English regard it as the greatest leveller, even though a favourite differentiation is still 'Gentlemen' and 'Players'. It all began in the middle of the 18th century, when the game as we know it today was first

The Bat and Ball

played on a field opposite 'The Bat and Ball'. Although the origins of the sport go back at least to the 13th century, it was the Hambledon Club that put it on its modern footing. The star player of those times was one John Nyren, and so it is to him that we raise our glasses in his own inn, 'The Bat and Ball'.

'Sir Henry Wotton was also a most dear lover and a frequent practiser of the art of angling; of which he would say 'twas an employment for his idle time, which was then not idly spent ... a rest to his mind, a cheerer of his spirits, a diverter of sadness, a calmer of unquiet thoughts, a moderator of passions, a procurer of con-

Idsworth: grand wall paintings in a lonely downland church

tentedness; and that it begat habits of peace and patience in those that professed and practised it.' This was written in the middle of the Civil War by the 'Prince of Fishermen', Izaak Walton. He lies buried in the transept of Winchester Cathedral, where in 1914 the fishermen of England and America dedicated a window to him, for was he not their patron saint? The enduring popularity of this London iron-monger is due not to the biographies he wrote of some of his contemporaries, important though these are, but to his book *The Compleat Angler* (1653).

One anonymous early reader wrote in the margin, 'Of this blest man, let his just praise be given, Heaven was in him, before he was in heaven,' and in fact next to Bunyan's *Pilgrim's Progress*, it is the most widely read book in English literature. Just as there is far more to angling than pulling a fish out of the water, there is far more to Walton's book than a discussion of how to do it. This is a work full of rural delights, reflections, songs, dialogues, which Charles Lamb praised as being 'the very spirit of innocence, purity and simplicity of heart'. 'Let us be going, good Master, for I am hungry again with fishing.' With this Angler's Bible in our bag, then, let's find ourselves a little spot beside a trout-rich Hampshire river – the Itchen, Avon, or Test. Then afterwards we'll go to the Houghton Fishing Club, the most exclusive in England, at the Grosvenor Hotel in *Stockbridge*, and we'll tell them all about the one that got away.

Another book to achieve all-time best-selling status was the Reverend Gilbert White's *The Natural History of Selborne* (1789), which made the name of his village famous all over England. It has never been out of print since, and was even translated into German only three years after its first publication. If it had only been what its title proclaims it to be, a mere description of local flora and fauna, present-day readers would certainly not come flocking to the Gilbert White Museum at The Wakes, the house where he lived for over forty years until his death in 1793. 'This sweet delightful book', as Coleridge described it, was also a favourite of Constable's. White's letters to nature-loving friends are full of observations on the state of the weather and of the soul, the topography of his rural surroundings, and the love of life that we always associate with the countryside.

Title page cartouche from the first editions of The Compleat Angler

But White was more than a charming writer; he was also a serious scientist and his pioneering approach to field observation, detailed and above all local, was a real contribution to scientific knowledge and method. 'The more confined your sphere of observation, the more perfect will be your remarks,'

General view of Selborne from one of the many 19th-century editions of the Natural History

he once wrote. The immediate application was to improve agriculture, but the combination of rigour with delight in 'the wonders of Creation, too frequently overlooked as common occurences' is an inspiration to naturalists everywhere. These 18th-century perspectives are timeless – and they have particular appeal to our 21st-century preoccupations, for with his precise, gentle observations of Nature's cycles, White can be seen also as one of the pioneers of the ecological movement's motto, 'Tread lightly'.

No image of White survives, so we have no idea of what he looks like; but the Wakes is little changed and full of his spirit. Growing once more in his garden, which has only recently been restored, are rugosa roses, columbine and cowslips, cranesbill and hellebore, vetch and lady's mantle. And behind Gilbert White's garden, a path leads up the hill to a landscape closely akin to paradise.

Jane Austen's Tea Table and Wellington's False Teeth: From Chawton to Stratfield Saye

In the foothills of the Downs, right next to Selborne, is the village of *Chawton*, where there lived a writer whose popularity today matches even that of Dickens: Jane Austen. Chawton's charms are typical of many Hampshire villages. Its red brick, half-timbered houses have thatched roofs that reach right down over the windows like ear-muffs. In the age of the stagecoach, Jane Austen's house was an inn on the main road from London to Southampton. It was to this 17th-century brick house that the country parson's daughter from Steventon moved with her mother and sister Cassandra in July 1809, after four years of constant removes. They were delighted:

> Our Chawton home, how much we find
>   Already in it to our mind:
> And now convinced, that when complete,
>   It will all other houses beat
> That ever have been made or mended,
>   With rooms concise or rooms distended,

she wrote to one of her brothers. At Chawton Jane spent the last eight years of her short life (before she was moved to Winchester to die), unnoticed by her neighbours, writing at a tiny, three-legged tea table in the family living-room. From here came *Mansfield Park*, *Emma* and *Persuasion*. Her early warning system for unannounced visitors was a creaking door (and it still creaks). This functioned so well that during her lifetime, her novels were all published anonymously. It was not that she wrote anything scandalous. The problem was simply that it was regarded as not quite respectable for a woman of her social class to be writing at all.

Jane Austen doll, Chawton

Jane Austen lived in the country, but apart from its beauty the countryside plays as little a part in her novels as migration from the land, the Industrial Revolution, or the Napoleonic Wars. It was not that she was not aware of the wider world: her brothers led active lives, and one was an admiral. As she wrote to Edward, the closest to her, who owned the neighbouring manor house: 'What should I do with your strong, manly, spirited sketches, full of variety and glow? – How could I possibly join them on to the little bit (two inches wide) of ivory on which I work with so fine a brush, as produces little effect after much labour?' On that piece of ivory she painted love and marriage (though she herself never married) with all the attendant confusions and complexities of middle-class life. 'It makes me most uncomfortable to see,' wrote W. H. Auden, 'an English spinster of the middle class,/ Describe the amorous effects of "brass",/ Reveal so frankly and with such sobriety/ The economic basis of society.' Realistic, ironic, sometimes biting, and never sentimental, Jane Austen's world is a restricted, domestic one, but it is not a cosy one, either emotionally or socially; her heroines are always trying to create their own lives and find their own values, and the effort can at times be rough on them. The models for her characters were to be found in the villages west of Steventon – places like Ibthorpe and Hurstbourne Tarrant – and in Bath, where she reluctantly lived for a time, and in the worlds of her five brothers. 'That young lady has a talent for describing the involvements and feelings and characters of ordinary life which is to me the most wonderful I ever met with,' wrote her contemporary Sir Walter Scott, when Jane Austen died in Winchester in 1817, at the age of forty-two. On her grave in the northern aisle of the Cathedral stands the simple inscription 'England's Jane'. That was what Kipling called her, and that is what she has continued to be, as English as cream teas and the National Trust. The Austen industry is flourishing. Millions of people were hooked by the BBC serialisation of *Pride and Prejudice*, and they flocked to the film of *Sense and Sensibility* with Hugh Grant and Emma Thompson (who said 'I hope she knows how big she is in Uruguay,' when she accepted her Oscar for the film). She's even big in Silicon Valley: the owner of an American computer firm has bought the lease of Chawton House, Edward Austen's house, and has restored it. Now she is turning it into a centre for the study of women's literature in the 18th and 19th centuries.

Wellington

While Jane Austen was at home, at work on her little piece of ivory, England was shuddering at the thought of a Napoleonic invasion. But after the Battle of Waterloo in 1815, a grateful nation offered their successful commander any country house he chose. Among others, Wellington had a good look at Bramshill House, on the Berkshire border, one of the biggest Jacobean country houses in England, but then in 1817 he decided to take the nearby *Stratfield Saye*, with its fertile farmland. His friends were somewhat dismayed, since they felt that this simple, mid-17th-century house was not grand enough. The Duke, however, was by no means as modest as the exterior of the house might make him seem. The drawings displayed in one of the corridors show that he was planning a Waterloo Palace as majestic as Vanbrugh's Blenheim Palace, which the nation had given to John Churchill after his victory in the War of the Spanish Succession against Louis XIV. But times had changed, and even heroes had to tighten their belts: Parliament only granted him £600,000, which was not enough for his grand palace. Thus he had to rest content with grandeur on a smaller scale, much to the fiscal relief of the present owner, the 9th Duke of Wellington, who has opened his national heritage to the public.

The Iron Duke installed one of the first English central heating systems at Stratfield Saye, as well as flowery blue porcelain lavatories with flush – an unheard-of luxury in those days. His great-great-grandson has not hung back either. His modern luxury is a swimming-pool next to the music room. The taste of the Iron Duke is evident straight away in the entrance hall, where one is greeted by the captured *tricolore*. There is glory everywhere, in the Louis XVI furniture, the Rococo stucco ceilings, the French wallpaper, the bronze and marble busts everywhere (even one of Blücher, who some might think gave him victory at Waterloo). After the pomp and circumstance of glorious war, Wellington died in 1852 in the relatively spartan surroundings of Walmer Castle in Kent. Twelve black horses drew his funeral car, a triumphal carriage more than 20 feet in length, made out of 18 tons of bronze taken from cannons captured at Waterloo. This mighty specimen of Victorian funeral art was originally in the crypt of St Paul's, but is now at Stratfield Saye. The collection of paintings that Napoleon plundered from Ferdinand VII of Spain and Wellington plundered from Napoleon is now mainly at Apsley House, his London residence.

One remarkable feature at Stratfield Saye is the print room, and in particular the Gallery. From floor to ceiling there are prints of landscapes, sport, and history, actually stuck directly on the wall – a Regency fashion which Wellington took over from the previous owner, who at the end of the 18th century had wallpapered the Gallery with gold-framed prints mostly of scenes from Shakespeare. In the passage leading to the billiard room are relics of the hero of Waterloo: two sets of false teeth, earpieces, snuff boxes, and a lock of his hair in a brooch worn by Queen Victoria. Under an oak tree in front of the house lies his valiant horse Copenhagen, buried with full military honours in 1836. The inscription on his grave expresses the hope that Copenhagen and the Duke will ride victoriously into Heaven together. The name of Wellington has been planted far beyond the confines of his country estate, in the form of the Wellingtonia, the massive Sequoia tree first introduced into England from the Sierra Nevada a year after his death. If this is not enough to remind you of the great man, then put on your wellington boots.

From Stratfield Saye, take the A33 past 'The Jekyll and Hyde Inn', and head for *The Vyne*. Unobtrusively situated in a hollow, The Vyne, with its warm red bricks forming diamond-shaped patterns, is a typical Tudor country house (*c.* 1520). It was built by William, Lord Sandys, Henry VIII's Lord Chamberlain and one of the few courtiers not to lose his head. 'I am an honest country Lord,' he says in Shakespeare's *Henry VIII*. Not only was he honest, but he also had taste and flair. For his house Sandys designed one of the very first Long Galleries, and he had it panelled entirely in oak with some 400 decorated panels containing the carved coats-of-arms and initials of his family and friends, including Henry's Tudor rose and Queen Catherine's pomegranate. Sandys decorated the chapel with stained glass windows, one of which shows Henry VIII kneeling beside his patron saint, Henry II of Bavaria. The glowing colours were created by Netherlandish artists in Basingstoke. Next door, in the Gothick chapel, is the magnificent 'Tomb

The summerhouse at the Vyne

Chamber' designed by John Chute to commemorate his ancestor Chaloner Chute, Speaker of the House of Commons: a wonderfully graceful monument on which the body, though dressed in full ceremonial fig, seems almost to be relaxing in a field rather than on a sarcophagus (*c.*1780).

Chaloner Chute, who acquired The Vyne in 1653, was no less innovative than his predecessor. The Corinthian portico facing the lake gives the north façade a classical character, and it was the first of its kind at any English country house (*c.* 1655). It was designed by John Webb, related by marriage to Inigo Jones, whom he called 'Unckle' and whose pupil he also was. The design is reminiscent of

Palladio's Villa Barbaro in Maser, a full half century before Lord Burlington's Palladianism became fashionable. The Vyne reached its last architecural peak in the second half of the 18th century, with the staircase hall. In a very narrow space, it reveals a fascinating variety of perspectives and rhythms, full of Georgian elegance, with a gallery of Corinthian columns and a coved ceiling. It seems more like the entrance to a temple or a theatre than to a country house – indeed one contemporary called it 'the Grecian theatric staircase.' The architect of this cool magnificence was none other than the owner of the house himself, John Chute. But his best and most avant-garde ideas were put into operation elsewhere: at Strawberry Hill, the house of his friend Horace Walpole.

Walpole's room at The Vyne was called Strawberry Parlour, and he would gladly have converted the whole house to Gothick, and not just the ante-chapel. '[Chute] was my council in my affairs,' Walpole acknowledged after the death of his friend, 'was my oracle in taste, the standard to whom I submitted my trifles and the genius that presided over poor strawberry!'

Crusade against War: Stanley Spencer in Burghclere

There is a late and refined echo of Strawberry Hill at *Mottisfont Abbey*, west of Winchester. This former Augustinian monastery in the Test Valley, surrounded by oaks and plane trees, has a great deal more in common with The Vyne than just its Gothick elements. Lord Sandys acquired it in 1536 – in exchange for the villages of Chelsea and Paddington! – tore down large sections of the monastery (founded in 1201), and built himself a residence in what had been the nave. Even when the Abbey had turned into a Tudor country house, it continued to undergo drastic alterations, the most interesting being in 1938-39: Rex Whistler was commissioned to design a new drawing-room in the south-west wing. This became a positive feast of visual delights and deceptions, a showpiece of trompe l'œil where all the decorations are painted, mostly in grisaille: the slender columns, the reliefs in the stucco ceiling, the trophies, the curtains, and, most masterly of all, a niche with a smoking urn, books, lute and glove – all real enough to grasp. This is a game played with space and surfaces, with Gothick decorations and Baroque illusions. The anachronisms of the art perfectly mirror the anachronism of a 20th-century feudal lifestyle. The illusions are as social as they are optical, and the decorations are like an ironic comment on conditions that are no longer what they seem. Mottisfont was Whistler's last major work for an English country house. He was killed in Normandy in 1944. Down in the rose garden is one of the great collections of historical roses, including the red rose of Lancaster and the white rose of York.

Decoration by Rex Whistler at Mottisfont Abbey

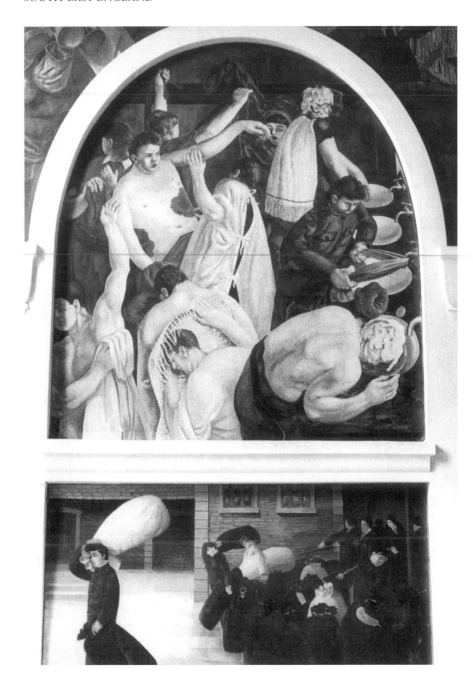

Stanley Spencer: the Sandham Memorial Chapel in Burghclere, looking towards the Resurrection *(above); the* Arrival in the Field Hospital *(left)*

Only a few years before Whistler painted his elegiac drawing-room, a chapel in Hampshire was consecrated that contained murals considered to be the finest Expressionist works in England. This is the Sandham Memorial Chapel in *Burghclere*, a village south of Newbury on the Berkshire border. The plain brick exterior and the ordinary rectangular interior might lead you to expect the conventional memorial decor of biblical stories. The shock is therefore all the greater when you find yourself confronted with the brutal historical reality of the First World War: camp, field hospital, trenches, and all the appalling truths of armed conflict apart from actual battle scenes. The chapel at Burghclere is a memorial with a difference – a remembrance of suffering, disturbing and in no way consolatory, except for the gentleness of the painting itself. The crosses swarm out of the east wall above the altar, and the fallen rise from their graves, but even this vision of the Resurrection is more connected with infernos than with paradise. There is no triumph. Nothing but the end of a tragedy. Where is Christ? The Son of Man is a tiny white figure in the background. In Giotto's Arena Chapel in Padua, and Michelangelo's Sistine Chapel, God appears in all His majesty, Lord and Judge of the world. But not here in Burghclere. There are no saints or sinners, no heroes or villains – nothing but helpless victims. Lieutenant H. W. Sandham died in 1919 from injuries received during the war when he was fighting in Macedonia. Stanley Spencer, son of a Berkshire organist, knew all about the war in Greece: he had served there and had immediately afterwards started making sketches for a chapel. He showed these to Mrs. Behrend, who was so impressed that she and her husband, a rich businessman, offered to pay for the chapel to be built. Spencer's first reaction to their offer was 'What ho, Giotto!'; his second, even more characteristic was: 'Thank you very much, but that's not good enough.' Given the chapel and a house to live in while working, Spencer worked unremittingly in Burghclere between 1926 and 1932. There are 19 pictures in three rows, one above the other, divided by arches. Spencer painted the whole cycle in oil on canvas, which he stretched out over the wall, rather than painting frescos which seldom last in the English climate. The colours are dull, and fragmented like the scenes themselves – grey, brown, beige, with just a very occasional red or blue. These are everyday scenes, viewed as if from a parachute, which gives them an extraordinary immediacy. The vanishing point of the foreshortened perspectives is Mannerist, the faces are Brueghel-like, the abstract representations suggest the new functionalism, but the expressiveness and the precision of the whole cycle are unmistakably Stanley Spencer. This is a record of the Macedonian campaign, and it is a crusade against war. The original designs for Burghclere are in the Stanley Spencer Gallery in Cookham in Berkshire, where he was born.

Andrew Lloyd Webber: A Museum for the King of the Musical

The musical hit of 1971 was *Jesus Christ Superstar*. It was the first worldwide success for a 23-year-old composer named Andrew Lloyd Webber. One year later, he bought himself the regulation status symbol: a country house. *Sydmonton Court*, a few miles south of Burghclere, is not, however, the showcase for Andrew Lloyd Superstar. He has plenty of prestige addresses elsewhere, including a villa on the Côte d'Azur, and an apartment in Trump Tower, New York.

Sydmonton is a Tudor house with later additions, architecturally unpretentious, surrounded by fairly nondescript hills and fields. 'Quite ordinary countryside' – which is what makes it typically English in the eyes of Lord Lloyd-Webber. Of course, 'Englishness' is as fictitious and romantic a concept as a Lloyd Webber musical – the phantom of a long-gone rural, patriarchal, aristocratic society. This knowledge, however, does not hinder the peer from fulfilling his own dream of Little England in Sydmonton. A vital feature of the fulfilment is preserving the countryside, or at least the 6,000 acres of it that belong to him. They include the rabbit country of Watership Down, the area around Nuthanger Farm where Richard Adams's classic animal story takes place (1972). Lloyd Webber has planted over 30,000 trees here. And there is another passion this Conservative patriot shares with all the old lords of the manor. No, not hunting – he is too pacific – nor drinking – though he once had one of the great collections of wine. Very quietly at first, but subsequently hitting more and more headlines, he has built up a private art collection that in its field is second to none.

In 1992 he spent £1.65 million on *Contradiction: Oberon and Titania*, a major work by the Victorian painter Richard Dadd. A year later he acquired Dante Gabriel Rossetti's portrait *A Vision of Fiammetta*, and in 1994 James Tissot's *Le Banc du Jardin*. In the same year at a Christie's auction he bought four monumental tapestries depicting the Legend of the Holy Grail, designed in 1890 by Burne-Jones and made by Morris & Co. During just three weeks in winter 1994, Lloyd-Webber spent over £10 million on Victorian art. Since then his collection has grown to about 300 pictures – paintings and drawings by Holman Hunt, Alma-Tadema, Edward John Poynter, Edward Burne-Jones, John Everett Millais, as well as Lord Leighton's *Dante in Exile*, Arthur Hughes' *Ophelia*, and other works by major and minor artists of the period. Then of course there is a Picasso portrait from the Blue Period, bought in 1995 for a mere £18.5 million, and Canaletto's *Old Horse Guards Parade* for over £10 million ('to save it for the nation') – which he has lent to the Tate Gallery.

The financial scale is perhaps not the most surprising thing about Lloyd Webber's passion. After all, as a composer and impresario, 'Andrew Lloyds Bank' is believed to be worth around £400 million (increasing every day through royalties of about £100,000), which makes him one of the 25 richest men in Britain. The astonishing thing really is his obsession with Victorian art. Some would say that it corresponds to his music: emotional, story-telling, the same smooth mixture of love and death, the cult of beauty, romantic escapism. This may be true of his musicals, but it is certainly not true of his art. Lloyd Webber's fascination with the Pre-Raphaelites, even if it does spring from an affinity with their rather gloomy, sentimental and theatrical view of the world, began at Westminster School when he saw the Victorian stained glass in the medieval Abbey. His interest was further inflamed by John Betjeman's plea for a reassessment of Victorian architecture. From Morris's church windows it was just a small step to the pictures of the Pre-Raphaelites. At the age of 15 he bought his very first Rossetti drawing for just £12. 'But the picture I really wanted (he confessed to *Radio Times)* was one of the greatest Rossettis ever. It cost £15 and my grandmother wouldn't lend me the money. There was another picture for £50, *Flaming June* by Lord Leighton, probably worth £4 million today.' Things have changed a great deal since then, as is evident from the auction prices amongst other things.

With the passing years, Lloyd Webber's æsthetic fascination has turned into a patriotic mission. He has set out to track down the few important Pre-Raphaelite works still in private ownership in America and Australia, and to bring them home to England. Some may call it another example of English eccentricity, but the fact is that he now has the world's finest private collection of Victorian paintings. It is a single-minded or, in the best sense of the word, insular mission and collection, confined to a single stylistic age which coincided with the peak period of the lost British Empire, but this is Englishness at its shining best. The pictures tell their own story now to the Lord of Sydmonton Court and his visitors.

In 1994 Lloyd-Webber announced a plan to build a museum on his estate. It is to be a 280-foot tower of glass and iron, in neo-Gothic style, designed by himself with the help of Rod Hackney, one of the Prince of Wales's favourite architects. The idea has run into the sands, which is a pity: it would have been a museum tower in the tradition of Victorian follies, with about twenty floors, where some of his pictures would have been on show to the public. An enthusiastic amateur's collection would have been on its way to becoming a national institution. Recently he has announced his intention of leaving the collection to the nation, keeping it at Sydmonton. Whether the tower will be resurrected remains to be seen, but it will certainly be a bucolic day out.

Due west from Sydmonton is another impressive example of Victoriana. This is *Highclere Castle*, home of the Earls of Carnarvon. The neo-Elizabethan palace with its massive central tower, corner towers and turrets was designed by Sir Charles Barry in 1842-9, at the same time as he was building the Houses of Parliament. It is all a con – the vast structure is just a stone face applied to a Georgian brick house that is still there underneath. The interiors are a curious miscellany too, ringing the changes on all the predilections of the Victorian historical imagination, from Gothic through to Rococo; the glorious main hall (1862) is by Barry's draughtsman Thomas Allom.

The owner's racehorses graze quietly in the park designed by Capability Brown (1774–1777). The last Lord Carnarvon was a successful breeder and manages the royal stables. In 1988 his butler was looking through a cupboard, and found 300 burial gifts from the Valley of the Kings in Thebes. These were the long-lost souvenirs of Lord Carnarvon's grandfather, the 5th Earl, the amateur archaeologist who made the most important find in the history of Egyptology. For years he steadfastly financed Howard Carter's search for the tomb of Tutankhamen, until at last in November 1922 the two of them stood in front of a burial chamber that had been sealed for 3,000 years. 'Do you see anything?' asked the Earl. 'Yes,' replied Carter, laconically, 'wonderful things.'

The City Beneath the Cornfields: The Romans in Silchester

After the invasion of 43 BC, the Romans left quite a few tracks in Hampshire: the coastal defences at Portchester, the villa at Rockbourne, and the town of *Silchester*

Silchester
1. North Gate
2. South Gate
3. East Gate
4. West Gate
5. Gate
6. Postern

A. Forum
B. Church
C. Temple
D. Baths
E. Inn
F. Court
G. Amphitheatre

are three typical forms of Roman settlement. *Calleva Atrebatum,* the forest town of the Atrebates, stands east of the present village of Silchester (between Basingstoke and Reading) on a plateau that is easy to defend and is well supplied with water – ideal for a Roman settlement. But where is it? We can walk round it, and we can go through it, but we can't see it – not even its foundations. Where there were once four thousand people living in an area of 100 acres, there is now a cornfield. Beneath the waves of corn, long since hidden from view, lies the most thoroughly researched Roman town in England. When it was excavated at the end of the 19th century, Wellington's son managed to take away two of the mosaic floors for the entrance hall at Stratfield Saye.

The plan of the town made by the archæologists is so detailed that the former inhabitants could easily find their own homes down below the fields. They would

199

be amazed to see how their rubbish dumps have been scrutinized to provide items for the little Calleva Museum and the larger museum in Reading – items illustrating various facets of their rural life and their handicrafts. In the centre of the town was the forum, with colonnaded shops on three sides and the town hall on the fourth, where both the market and the courts were situated. In the south-east district, *insula XXXIII*, were the baths, one of the oldest buildings. Its façade fell victim to Roman town-planning after the 1st century, when a new road system was introduced whose chessboard pattern can clearly be seen from the air. The north-eastern corner of the town was the entertainment area, with wrestling and animal-baiting in an amphitheatre right by the walls; the earthwork tiers, which were covered with rows of wooden seats, can still be seen. There were five temples, two of which lie under the graveyard of St Mary's (13th century), and even a little Christian church. Nearly all the houses had gardens, and the more prosperous ones had an atrium, mosaic floors, glass windows, a bathroom and hypocaust heating. This was where the Atrebates lived, one of the Belgic tribes from Northern Gaul, together with Romanised Britons whose princes held the reins of power, although they were answerable to Roman administrators. All that one can see now are some exterior earthworks and the walls, which encompassed the town in a polygon instead of the usual rectangle. Large section of these walls, which extend for 1½ miles, are covered with earth or overgrown with bushes and trees, like some massive, ancient hedge. The natural appearance mirrors the natural end of this provincial Roman town, where the roads to and from London, Chichester, Winchester, Dorchester and Old Sarum converged. *Calleva Atrebatum* simply lost its political and economic importance after the 5th century: the inhabitants abandoned it, and that was the end of Silchester.

As neither Anglo-Saxons nor Normans ever settled in the town, unlike Winchester for instance, its Roman ground-plan is more perfectly preserved than anywhere else. There are in fact about eighty known Roman towns in England and about 500 Roman villas. The Romans were great farmers, who cultivated the first vines in England and introduced cherries, peaches and figs, and they were also fine exponents of the country-house culture. Aristocrats and officers, and also rich farmers and merchants were the owners. They furnished their villas with urban tastes and comforts, decorating them with mosaics and frescos, and equipping them with baths, atrium and underfloor heating. They had fountains and statues in their gardens, and cultivated *ars topiaria*, the art of shaping evergreen plants into figures that is still so familiar. One of these Roman villas was excavated in *Rockbourne*, south of Salisbury. The finds from more than seventy rooms fill a complete museum, and give us a very good idea of what country life was like in Roman Britain.

In the broad harbour of Portsmouth, on the tip of a flat tongue of land, lies *Portus Adurni*, the Roman fortification of *Portchester*, which is almost too picturesque to be a military installation, and is certainly too beautiful ever to be destroyed. It was, however, captured several times in spite of its strategic position, which in fact turned out to be something of a trap. The walls and their battlements look seemingly impregnable, as if the Romans were still there and had not already pulled out by 370 AD. Portchester Castle is the only Roman camp in Northern Europe whose walls have been completely preserved. They are 20 feet high, made of flint with horizontal bands of stone and brick, and were built in the late 3rd century. The ground-plan is almost square (approximately 200 yards each way) and there are twenty bastions. It's a model fortress in the chain of coastal forts that also included Richborough and Reculver. When the Normans came, eight hundred years later, they took over the walls intact, but put in new gates and, as at Pevensey Castle, built a fortress within the fortress – the massive square tower in the north-west corner. This was in the reign of Henry I, who extended Portchester Castle to make it a royal fort surpassed only by the castles at Dover and Corfe. Diagonally opposite the keep he founded an Augustinian abbey in 1133; the abbey buildings were torn down, but the monastery church of St Mary's remains beauti-fully preserved, with its Norman colonnaded doorway and its font. At the end of the 14th century, Portchester Castle was no longer militarily up to date, and so Richard II built a fortified palace (1396–99) next to the keep. Henry V was living here in 1415 when he assembled his army of 10,000 men on the wide lawns, in preparation for his French campaign;

> Then forth, dear countrymen; let us deliver
> Our puissance into the hand of God,
> Putting it straight into expedition.
> Cheerly to sea; the signs of war advance
> No king of England, if not king of France.

And indeed after his victory at Agincourt, he returned triumphantly as king of two countries. Later the French were to have unpleasant memories of Portchester Castle, because in Napoleon's time the fortress and keep were filled with prison-ers-of-war, who scratched their names on the walls, and whiled away the time making model boats that are the toast of collectors everywhere.

Portsmouth and Southampton: The Great Ports

After Fareham, the M27 becomes almost like a drive-in cinema, as you find your-self gazing out over a panorama of Portsmouth. On the peninsula in the foreground you can see the walls of Portchester Castle, in the bay beyond are the white sailing boats, and further still are the grey ships of the Royal Navy with a phalanx of oil storage tanks, docks, and towering cranes and pylons punctuating

HMS Victory

the skyline. There are few harbour panoramas in the world to match the size of this one. Portsmouth is an island, like England itself, and was once called the 'glory and the bulwark of these kingdoms'. Plymouth was the port of admirals, Elizabethan explorers, and merchants, but Portsmouth was the country's chief naval base after the Armada. With the Dutchman Bernard de Gomme, one of the best military engineers of his time, Charles II began a massive programme of fortification in Portsmouth, and at the same time (1662) he married Catherine of Braganza in Garrison Church, Penny Street.

Fortifications were continually strengthened, until under Queen Victoria's Prime Minister Lord Palmerston, Portsmouth and Gosport opposite became a single stronghold. Whoever controlled the Solent between the Isle of Wight and Portsmouth would control the Channel, and whoever controlled the Channel would control England. Historians of military architecture can really go on the warpath in Portsmouth, from the Round Tower (*c.* 1415) and the Square Tower (1494) at the harbour entrance to the Old Town, past the long curtain walls and the royal bastion – the only remaining original de Gomme fortifications – and down to Henry VIII's Southsea Castle (1538–40). From there you can make your way to Fort Cumberland (1746/86) in *Eastney*, and then up the limestone hills of

Portsdown, where you can visit Lord Palmerston's Fort Widley (*c.* 1868) and Fort Nelson, with a view over Portsmouth and the Solent. From the waves of the latter rise four more of 'Firebrand' Palmerston's bastions, like giant buoys on the water. Not one of Palmerston's 'follies' ever fired a shot in anger. The steel-plated Fort No Man's Land in the Solent (*c.* 1860) is now an exclusive island residence, complete with indoor swimming-pool and helipad.

It was not by chance that Operation Overlord was planned in 'Pompey'. It was here that the main contingent of the Allied invasion force had assembled in order to storm Hitler's 'Fortress Europe'. The story of 6 June 1944 is recorded in minute detail at the D-Day Museum on Clarence Esplanade. And just like the Norman Conquest, the momentous events of that day have been woven into a 'tapestry'. The 'Overlord Embroidery' (started in 1968) stretches about 100 yards long – surpassing the Bayeux Tapestry in length if nothing else.

Since the end of the Cold War, the importance of this naval port has been confined to its history. There is a correspondingly high unemployment rate. Once the docks were the beating heart of the town and its very *raison d'être*. Indirectly, the same applied to its most famous writers. Samuel Pepys was Secretary to the Admiralty for several years, George Meredith was born here, the son of a naval tailor, and John Dickens was a clerk in the navy pay office when his son Charles was born in 1812 in the almost rural suburb of Portsea. Today the little Georgian brick house, No. 393 Old Commercial Road, is a Dickens Museum surrounded by new housing estates. In one of the rooms is the green chaise longue on which Dickens died 58 years later in Gad's Hill (see page 38). Sir Arthur Conan Doyle was an unsuccessful doctor in the seaside resort of Southsea when he wrote his first Sherlock Holmes novel, *A Study in Scarlet* (1887).

Portsmouth – where Isambard Kingdom Brunel was born, builder of railways, ships and bridges – is a town of industrial rather than ecclesiastical architecture. Typical of its charms are the docks, with their Georgian brick warehouses. This is basic, functional architecture of solid proportions and stark beauty. In the Royal Dock, not far from where Henry V put into operation the first dry dock in the world, lies Lord Nelson's flagship *HMS Victory*, a triumph of ship-building and a monument to the age when Nelson was a hero and Britannia ruled the waves. After 47 glorious years on the high seas, *Victory* lost her last battle – defeated by woodworm. The 3,000 oaks from which she was made in Chatham have been replaced by tropical hardwoods. Her double now relives the Battle of Trafalgar from the peaceful haven of the dry dock. Her Majesty's cadets take visitors through the three cannon decks to the spot where, on 21 October 1805, Nelson died. A Trafalgar sail, shot to pieces, is revered like a holy relic. These historic

Overleaf, detail from the panorama of Portsmouth by the Bucks, c. 1740,
complete with Jolly Jack Tars and a man being 'pressed' into service

docks also contain another naval *pièce de résistance*: the *Mary Rose*, Henry VIII's flagship. On 19 July 1545 she sailed from Portsmouth to fight the French, and before the King's own eyes, sank with 700 men aboard. More than four hundred years later, in October 1982, the *Mary Rose* was raised in one of the most expensive salvage operations in the history of maritime archæology. One can see not only the restored wreck of the great four-master, but also the various finds made in sand and silt that enable us to reconstruct in detail the life of a sailor on board a Tudor warship.

Portsmouth has about 184,000 inhabitants, and neighbouring *Southampton* has some 205,000. Gradually they are coming closer and closer to forming a single coastal megatown. Southampton, if one might quote Samuel Johnson's subtle distinction, is worth seeing but not worth going to see. Pass through it, perhaps, and enjoy your departure along the strait to the Isle of Wight. Southampton is the port for the great ocean-going liners, and over the years has witnessed more emotional scenes of welcome and farewell than most other ports. It was from here that the *Titanic* set sail in 1912 on her fateful maiden voyage to New York. The quays and docks extend for over six miles. Today, there are great empty spaces. Tomorrow perhaps it will all be a theme park, or a computer centre – who knows? The Blitz shattered Southampton even more than it did Portsmouth. St Michael's is the only surviving medieval church in the city centre; other relics of Old Southampton are the Tudor House in Bugle Street, Bargate (the northern city gate), God's House Tower in the harbour, and the arcades of the city wall with the ruins of King John's, a Norman merchant's house. They are all impressive, but out of context in an efficiently but facelessly reconstructed city. There is very little convincing modern architecture. The Nuffield Theatre (1961) by Basil Spence, situated on the University campus, is one of the exceptions, as is Norman Foster's School for Occupational Therapy (1995, Burgess Road). Southampton is an industrial city, but it was also the birthplace of the Pre-Raphaelite John Everett Millais and the pop-artist Allen Jones, and for anyone interested in the arts the Guildhall Art Gallery in the Civic Centre is a major attraction. Among its treasures are the *Perseus* cycle by Burne-Jones, a fine collection of contemporary pottery, and above all an outstanding collection of modern English art, from paintings by the post-Impressionist Camden Town Group, founded in 1911 and led by Walter Sickert, to Nash, Spencer, Lowry, Nicholson and Sutherland.

Netley Abbey: What To Do With Ruins

Between Hampshire's two biggest and busiest towns, as if to balance things out, lie the peaceful ruins of two monasteries: Titchfield and Netley Abbey. Both were founded in the first third of the 13th century by the Bishop of Winchester, and both were rebuilt as mansions after 1536. *Titchfield Abbey*, the last of 33 Premonstratensian monasteries founded in England (1232), is dominated by a stately gatehouse with four crenellated corner towers, built by Henry VIII's Lord Chancellor Thomas Wriothesley right in the middle of the church nave. The refectory became the hall, and the cloister turned into the inner courtyard (1542). In this Tudor palace, Shakespeare visited his patron, the 3rd Earl of Southampton, and probably also performed some of his plays there. Shakespeare dedicated his sonnets as well as other poems to this controversial courtier, and was paid for doing so. The Bard would not have trod the boards here, however, but the tiles: there are very few places with so many perfectly preserved medieval floor tiles in their original setting (see p. 6).

Flymo at Netley Abbey

Flowers, birds, chessboard patterns, heraldic motifs like the lion, tower and double eagle – they are all as beautiful and as clear as William Morris's early designs.

Unlike Titchfield Abbey, the Cistercian *Netley Abbey* (1239) has almost completely shaken off the mansion that had been imposed on it. The monastery ruins stand in all their radiance, as if the profane interlude had never taken place. 18th-century engravings and visitors' accounts provide records of what the abbey originally looked like. 'All variety of windows wrapped round and round with ivy – many trees are sprouted up amongst the walls and only want to be increased with cypresses!... in short, they are not the ruins of Netley, but of Paradise.' Horace Walpole's enthusiasm was shared by his friend Thomas Gray, who wrote the *Ode on the Death of a Favourite Cat, by Drowning* for Walpole, but is immortal for the *Elegy Written in a Country Churchyard*. Gray visited these ruins in 1755, the same year as Walpole, author of the Gothick novel *The Castle of Otranto* and leading figure in the Gothic Revival through his little 'castle' of Strawberry Hill. Melancholy was the new cult, the Picturesque was the new man-made paradise, and Netley Abbey the cathedral of the new taste. Ruins were good for the soul. And the ruins of Netley Abbey so delighted the landowner Thomas Lee Dummer that in 1770 he pulled down sections of the transepts and built them up again as an artificial ruin on his estate at Cranbury Park, north of Southampton. This was picturesque and practical at the same time, because he had his gardener live there. The Romantics saw ruins as a symbol, and as an idealised setting. The bat and owl replaced the horrors of infinity and eternity, and everyone rushed to visit Gothic ruins and read Gothic novels. The latter in turn made places like Netley Abbey into showplaces for the imagination. Wasn't that Melmoth the Wanderer scurrying through the door? Was this the arm of the monk Ambrosio reaching through the shattered tracery? Two years before the publication of Matthew Gregory Lewis's *The Monk* (1796), the most popular of all the Gothic novels, London audiences had revelled in an opera entitled *Netley Abbey* at Covent Garden. The ruins were the subject of odes and elegies, and Peacock's satire *Nightmare Abbey* (1818) could have been called 'Netley Abbey'. By 1840 there were even ruin festivals with tea and dancing at Netley Abbey, which must have scared any remaining ghosts right off.

What of today? Today the ruins are as sprightly as a pensioner after live-cell therapy. Netley Abbey is a model ruin, administered by English Heritage, cared for like a vintage limousine, and as safe and secure as a brand new bank. Such is the changing fate of collapsed buildings. The walls and columns have been freed from ivy, and once more one can see the architecture, with its Early English lancet windows. We look coolly and objectively at the structure itself instead of whipping up our own emotions; we are interested in layers of style not of soul. This is a return to rationality, to the clear dimensions against which the æsthetics of the romantic ruin had rebelled. Now a whole army of mowers impose 'lawn and order' on Netley Abbey. It all has an air of permanence, and is as scrubbed and sterile as a hospital ward. There are regular examinations, diagnoses, and injections of cement to prevent decay. This is conservation as geriatrics. The ruins are objects from the past, suitable for study but not to be interpreted as symbols of transience. Sight has taken the place of vision. All that comes out of the experience now is a few photos. The sentimental traveller in the 18th century had time to bury himself or herself in the rich atmosphere; today's tourist wants a few quick facts, and a readymade mood, because after all, this is just an open-air attraction with a touch of nostalgia. You can even get made-to-measure ruins now, quite immune to future catastrophe, as built by New York architects in the mid-1970s for a chain of American mail order firms – guaranteed collapse-free ruins as advertised, although to be fair they were also a protest against the dull sterility of modern city architecture.

At the beginning of the 1960's, a London banker applied a different form of treatment to ruins when he acquired the country estate of Stratton Park (remodelled by George Dance jun., 1803–6), near *East Stratton*, north of Winchester. Instead of rebuilding this neoclassical manor house, he pulled as much of it down as he was

62. Sir Stanley Spencer, Self-portrait

*64. Izaak Walton, memorial window
in Winchester Cathedral*

*63. Previous page. Fishing on the
Test*

*65. Gilbert White in waxwork at
Selborne*

*66. Selborne: Gilbert White's
garden and sundial*

67. Grange Park, by William Wilkins, now home to opera

68. The Vyne: principal staircase

69. Winchester Cathedral

70. Initial from the Winchester Bible

71. Winchester Cathedral: Crypt with Sounds II *(1992) by Anthony Gormley*

73 & 74. The New Forest: general view (above) and sketchers at work (below)

72. Opposite: Netley Abbey ruins

75. *Beaulieu*

76. Hurst Castle

77. Hurst Castle: lighthouse

78. Osborne House: dining room

79. Osborne House: walled garden

80. Carisbrooke Castle, from an old postcard

81. Overleaf: The Needles

Stratton Park

legally able to, leaving the listed portico standing as a ruin, but building behind it a modern house of steel, glass and brick (Gardiner and Knight, 1965), linked to – or separated from – the old structure by a pond, which runs as a stream through the house. A modern arrangement, where the constructive and destructive urges are in balance. The unfluted Doric columns of the portico form a classical framework for the view from house to park, completely in the tradition of the picturesque. The same banking family also owned The Grange (remodelled by William Wilkins from 1809) near *Northington*, south-east of Stratton Park. This Greek temple of a coun-try house is a wonderful example of the 'Greek Revival', though Wilkins generally lacked the sense of grandeur of his contemporaries Schinkel and Ledoux (look at his dreary National Gallery façade in London). The Grange, set among fields and woods, has been restored and is now home to an opera festival.

England's Old Capital: Winchester

For centuries the capital of England lay on the River Itchen and not on the Thames. Kings, wool merchants, pilgrims all flocked to Winchester. When the Romans left *Venta Belgarum*, it became the capital of the Anglo-Saxon kingdom of Wessex (the land of the West Saxons). By the time the Normans arrived, it had already been the capital of all England for 200 years, so favoured because of its proximity to the Continent and to English Normandy. Today, it is a small city

Alfred burns the cakes: an illustration from a 19th-century German guidebook to Britain, picking up on the Victorian rediscovery of Alfred and his subsequent heroization

stretching out from the west bank of the Itchen to the surrounding hills, but it is also one of the most prosperous in the country, since many of London's top civil servants, judges and bankers live there.

In the reign of King Alfred, Winchester blossomed culturally, rather like Aix-la-Chapelle under Charlemagne a century earlier. It is hardly a coincidence that Alfred is the only English King that the country cares to call 'the Great'. Without Alfred, it is arguable that England would not exist: not because of his sword and his ships, though his achievements as a soldier are true enough, but because he more than anyone made the English language possible and with it absorbed all those dangerous and successful invaders, the Danes and later the Normans. Winchester was the site of Alfred's capital, and his most signal victory, the baptism of Guthrum.

That, at least, is the traditional view of Alfred, based on the contemporary biography by the Welsh monk Asser. Some historians have called it a myth, have questioned Asser's veracity, called the invention of England the imposition by the victors of a new brand name on the history of the British archipelago. The most enthusiastic of the mythmakers were the Victorians, and the statue in Winchester is a fine memorial to them. As the Lord Mayor pronounced when dedicating it for Alfred's millenium, 'Since it is acknowledged that the English-speaking people still derive great and incalculable benefits from Alfred's indefatigable works... it was felt that the memorial to "the hero of our race" should be worthy not only of the city and neighbouring counties but also of the Anglo-Saxon race.'

From Alfred's statue , the High Street with its colonnaded shops (The Pentice) leads through the 13th century *Westgate* (No. 2 on the map in the inside back cover) up to the administrative centre of the county town. This was once the site of the fortress where William the Conqueror kept the Domesday book of 1086, which formed the basis of his taxation policy and is the most important source of information about English life in the 11th century. Today it is kept in the Public Record Office in London. William had himself crowned in both capitals – London and Winchester. It was only after the reign of Henry III, who was born in Winchester, that London became the sole capital. Nevertheless, Charles II commissioned Christopher Wren to build him a royal palace in Winchester, for his 'autumnal field diversions' – and for keeping an eye on his navy, for he hoped to be able to see Spithead from the high cupola that was planned. This rival to Versailles was begun in 1683, and in 1685 the King was able to exclaim 'I shall be so happy this week as to have my house covered with lead!' The prophecy was fulfilled, for he was taken by a seizure shortly after and was in his lead coffin within a week. The unfinished palace ('the worst thing I ever saw of Sir Chrisopher Wren's,' grumbled Horace Walpole, 'a mixture of a town hall and a hospital') stood until the end of the 19th century near Henry III's *Great Hall* (3), the only surviving section of the medieval royal residence. This broad hall, with its three aisles, its slender columns of Purbeck marble, and its open roof trusses, was the scene of festivities and trials: the wedding feast of Mary Tudor and Philip II of Spain, the trial of Sir Walter Raleigh, and many sessions of the English Parliament. On the west wall hangs something that looks like a giant dartboard but actually represents King Arthur's legendary Round Table. The 25 sections, reserved for King Arthur's knights, are painted in the Tudor colours of green and white. The central Tudor Rose, where King Arthur sits enthroned, is not an anachronism but is simply the emblem of Henry VIII, who had the oak tabletop restored in 1522 for the State Banquet held in honour of the Holy Roman Emperor Charles V in the Great Hall. This Round Table is mentioned in Caxton's edition of Malory's *Morte Darthur* (1485) as proof of the existence of King Arthur, but we modern sceptics will enjoy it more as a medieval wheel of fortune. Radio carbon tests and massive research suggest that the table was made almost eight hundred years ago for Edward I, as part of elaborate events celebrating the foundation of his dynasty. Sixty years later, in 1340, Edward III had wanted to found his own Order of the Knights of the Round Table (abandoned in favour of the Garter) and he had the legs lopped off, the top painted and the result hung up. Henry's restoration was intended to impress his Imperial guest with the ancientness of British kingship and historical overlordship.

The quest of Sir Lancelot and Sir Galahad and the Knights for the Holy Grail used at the Last Supper was a courtly romance with a religious basis – a literary counterpart to the popular pilgrimages of the Middle Ages. Since the 9th century pilgrims from all over England had come to Winchester to visit the shrine of St Swithin. Only after the martyrdom of Becket did they take the opposite route along the Pilgrims' Way and head for Canterbury. This, together with the rise of London as the political capital, was the second great turning-point in the history of Winchester.

Behind the High Street is the start of the Cathedral Close – a green with avenues of lime trees, and local people and tourists relaxing among the gravestones; it's a resting-place for the living. Nothing disturbs the peace here, and even the Cathedral seems gentle and restrained. *Winchester Cathedral* (4) has no imposing west façade like Wells, and no towering spire like Salisbury. Defoe thought it looked as though the spire had fallen off and the stump of the tower had merely been roofed over in order to keep out the rain. But what the Cathedral lacks in height it makes up for in length – dimensions made necessary by its double life as a

Winchester: cathedral precincts
1. *Close wall*
2. *Castle wall*
3. *St Swithun's Gate*
4. *Pilgrims' Hall*
5. *Remains of Prior's House*
6. *Deanery*
7. *Site of the Cloister*
8. *Mound.*
9. *Millstream*
10. *Wolvesey Palace*
11. *Wolvesey Castle*
12. *Site of the Saxon Old and New Minsters*
13. *High Street*

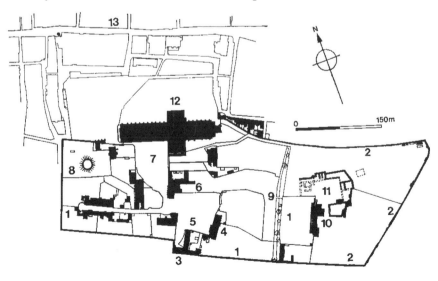

Winchester Cathedral: view from a German 19th century guidebook

cathedral and a Benedictine monastery church (a peculiarly English combination). Lay people prayed in the nave, while the monks stayed on the east side. Stretching for 555 feet, this is the longest medieval church in Europe. What we now see is the third cathedral, begun in 1079. The two Anglo-Saxon minsters stood next to one another directly to the north of the present nave. The bones of the Anglo-Saxon kings Edred, Egbert and Æthelwulf, as well as Rufus and Cnut, lie in colourful chests in the choir, no doubt in some disarray after Cromwellian vandalism. 'These monsters of men, to whom nothing is holy, nothing is sacred, did not stick to profane and violate these cabinets of the dead and to scatter their bones all over the pavement of the church,' one shocked contemporary wrote. Apart from the crypt and the arcades of the chapter house next to the Cathedral, the purest sections of the building begun by Walkelin, the first Norman Bishop of Winchester, are the transepts. These are the most perfect example of early Norman architecture in England. The galleries are almost as high as the arcades – round arched with cubiform capitals. Conquerors can plan on a massive scale, but it takes a master builder to conquer materials and space in such a manner. After 1394, William of Wynford, who built Wells Cathedral, reconstructed the nave of Winchester Cathedral in the Perpendicular-Gothic style, with pointed arches and fan-vaulting. (There is, incidentally, another monumental piece of Norman architecture a few miles south-west of Winchester, with an absolute jewel of an interior: Romsey Abbey.)

To see such a cathedral properly, one needs weeks rather than days, unless one can share the load like the mythical American couple: 'You do the outside, and I'll do the inside.' The interior is simply a mass of treasures: Pilgrims' Gate, with the wrought iron filigree work of the grille between transept and choir (11th century); the wall paintings (c. 1230) and Morris & Co.'s stained glass windows (1909) in the north transept; the choir stalls and their richly figured misericords (14th century); and most striking of all, the Norman font of black Tournai marble, depicting scenes from the life of St Nicholas, a masterpiece made by Flemish sculptors. Stoically, in contemplative mood, a lifesize lead figure by Anthony Gormley stands in the waters of the crypt (1992). Winchester's bishops have princely renaissance monuments, but there is also an ordinary worker commemorated here: William Walker was a diver, who for six years dived down into the ground water under the Cathedral in order to give it new foundations. Concrete and 900,000 bricks replaced the original raft of beech trees. It was one of the most spectacular architectural rescue operations of modern times (1906–12). The Cathedral Library records the glory of the medieval school of illumination. One of the most valuable manuscripts, the Benedictional of St Æthelwold (975-80), with its lavish acanthus borders, is now in the British Museum in London. For two hundred years the miniaturists of the Winchester School were among the finest artists in England and indeed in Europe. They reached their zenith in the middle of the 12th century, when Bishop Henry of Blois – brother of King Stephen, and next to Becket the most controversial of contemporary church leaders – had the Vulgate copied out in a magnificent edition of the Bible that took six monks many years and indeed was unfinished. The initial letters in the Winchester Bible show the extraordinary range and scale of these miniatures. The figurative style is partly stiff and hieratic, partly rhythmic and fluid, betraying Byzantine influence that probably filtered here via the Norman-Sicilian Benedictine monastery of Monreale. One is simply bowled over by the religious and artistic imagination that can compress the whole history of Creation, right through to the Last Judgment, in a single initial letter – the 'I' with which Genesis begins and which is here spread over the entire page. The vegetable-dye colours are as fresh as when they were first applied, as if the illumination wanted to compete with the enlightenment brought about by the text.

Winchester Cathedral: part of the Perpendicular vaulting

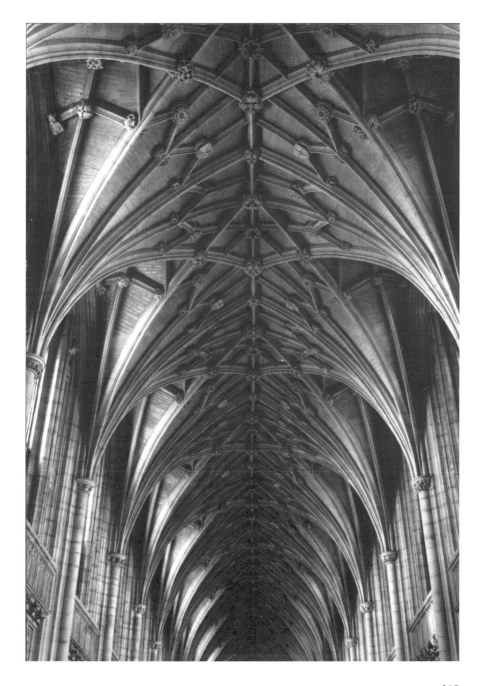

Winchester Cathedral: monument to Joseph Warton, headmaster of the College, by Flaxman, 1801: 'as neat as Piero della Francesco,' said Pevsner. One of Flaxman's most successful funerary monuments, intimate yet imposing

There is a similar radiant clarity in the voices of the Winchester choirboys, who have been singing evensong here every evening for centuries. The stones of Winchester come alive with the sound, which transcends all the boundaries of architecture and history.

Winchester College (5), surrounded by walls of flint, is a world on its own within the Cathedral precincts. Tradition here is alive but not oppressive. The pupils carve their names on the cloister columns just as they have done for centuries. The founder of this, very arguably the oldest public school in England, was William of Wykeham, who as Bishop and Lord Chancellor for two different Kings had seen that both Crown and Church needed people properly trained for governance. He founded New College, Oxford, and then a little later in 1382, as a preparatory stage, Winchester College. Systematic education from public school through to university was a new concept, and this acted as a model that was followed some sixty years later by Henry VI, when he founded both Eton and King's College, Cambridge. Public schools were primarily for the deserving, but the sons of the nobility, and later of anyone who could afford to pay, were soon admitted, if only around the edges. By the 19th century their task, formulated above all by

Thomas Arnold, was to inculcate 'muscular Christianity' and the morals of the gentleman; Arnold, though headmaster of Rugby, sent his son Matthew, poet and educationalist, to Winchester. By around 1400, Winchester College had been laid out on a more lavish scale than any other school in Europe, round two huge inner courtyards. Like New College in Oxford, it was designed by the royal stonemason William of Wynford, who had a place of honour at the Bishop's table. William of Wykeham's motto, 'Manners makyth man', is perhaps somewhat cryptically reflected by the school uniform. The seventy Scholars, who live in the College wear black gowns, while the more numerous Commoners, who live in the city wear sports jackets, grey flannels and boaters. One famous Wykehamist was Edward Young, a clergyman's son from the nearby village of Upham, whose poem *Night Thoughts* (1742-45) had a Europe-wide vogue in its day. It brought some consolation to a century wrestling with scepticism: 'By night an atheist half-believes a God,' Young observed. It was admired by Klopstock and Robespierre, and illustrated by Blake; today all that we remember is the phrase 'Procrastination is the thief of time.' Another influential figure at Winchester is seen in a painting called *The Trusty Servant,* which has spawned many pub signs if not butlers: he is a symbolic figure with tools, weapons, a pig's head and stag's feet.

In August 1819 John Keats came to Winchester in the hope of improving his health. Every day he would wander along the bank of the Itchen to the surrounding hills, whose air was worth 'sixpence a pint' (a great deal for an impoverished poet). It was a period of constant inspiration: 'my mind is heap'd to the full, stuff'd like a cricket ball – if I should strive to fill it more, it would burst.'

The Trusty Servant

One walk on September 19 felt particularly rich. 'How beautiful the season is now How fresh the air. A temperate sharpness about it. Really without joking, chaste weather – Dian skies– I never like'd stubble fields so much as now – Aye better than the chilly green of the spring. Somehow a stubble plain looks warm – in the same way that some pictures look warm – this struck me so much in my Sunday's walk that I composed upon it.' That composition was the ode *To Autumn*. Keat's biographer, W. J. Bate, says 'each generation has found it one of the most perfect poems in English.'

> Where are the songs of Spring? Ay, where are they?
>   Think not of them, thou hast thy music too, –
> While barred clouds bloom the soft-dying day
>   And touch the stubble-plains with rosy hue...

The Wayfarer's Dole being dispensed in c. 1900

Keats was 24, and had less than two years to live.

Keats was less enraptured by the works of man; the Cathedral, though beautiful, 'to me is always a source of amusement'. and the stately grey Hospital of St Cross and Almshouse of Noble Poverty, 'a very interesting old place, both for its gothic tower and alms square, and for the appropriation of its rich rents to a relation of the Bishop of Winchester'. Trollope made this scandal of 1808 into the basis for *The Warden*. Now the buildings breathe only peace and charity. It is England's oldest almshouse, founded by Bishop Henry of Blois in 1136, and the Brothers of St Cross, pensioners in ruffed caps and sweeping robes, still distribute the

Wayfarers' Dole of 'a horn of beer and a crust of bread' to visitors (it's included in the entrance price).

Opposite St Cross on *St Catherine's Hill*, surrounded by the walls of an Ice Age hill camp, is a labyrinth mysteriously carved in the grass, covering an area of some 100 foot square. Was it a game, like the maze at Hampton Court, or a sort of ritual dancefloor, or a religious symbol like the tiled labyrinths of medieval churches? Like Theseus, we could do with an Ariadne to give us a clew.

New Forest: Where the Wild Ponies Are

There are wild ponies grazing among the ferns and gorse, and violet rhododendrons flowering among the pines and oaks. 'This New Forest is simply lovely. I should like to have a house in it and dispeople the rest like the Conqueror,' wrote the romantic poet Robert Southey. Indeed, after his marriage in the village church at *Boldre* in 1839, he settled down on the fringes of the New Forest at Burton, near Bournemouth. The *Nova foresta* is by no means new. It dates back long before William the Conqueror, who passed Draconian laws to make it into exclusively royal hunting grounds, though the fattest deer ever shot here was his own son William Rufus. Today the only hunting that goes on among the trees and over the heath is by the ponies, on the look-out for picnic leftovers. The ponies belong to the 'commoners', some 300 local people whose centuries-old privileges include the right of pasturage. The New Forest itself, however, which covers an area of 145 square miles between Southampton and the River Avon (the Dorset border), remains almost exclusively the property of the Crown. For years environmental groups have been trying to have this hikers' paradise turned into a National Park, which it now effectively is.

The capitals of the slender Purbeck columns in St Michael's, *Lyndhurst*, reproduce the leaves and fruits of the New Forest. Above the altar of this Victorian church, the masterpiece of the underrated architect William White, shines the New Jerusalem in all its Pre-Raphaelite glory of dark red, blue and green, interspersed with radiant white. Edward Burne-Jones designed these windows in 1862 for his partner William Morris. This was quite literally piecework: he was paid £1 for each musical angel in the trefoils, and £3-5 for the larger angels and saints. The man who arranged for this masterpiece to be created at Lyndhurst was the immensely popular painter Frederick, Lord Leighton, who trained in Frankfurt, and himself painted a somewhat conventional, neoclassical fresco on the wall below the east window: the lifesize figures of the Wise and Foolish Virgins. At the time, 1864, this monumental painting created a furore in the art world, since it was the first fresco to be painted in any English church since the Reformation. In the churchyard at Lyndhurst is the Hargreaves' family vault, where Alice Hargreaves, née

Liddell, lies buried, dreaming perhaps of the Wonderland she inspired.

The roots of Britannia's rule over the waves lay in the land, and many of her ships grew up in the New Forest. In *Bucklers Hard*, on the bay at Beaulieu, the 2nd Duke of Montagu established a model settlement, Montagu Town, where sugar from the West Indies was to be imported and refined. When the business went bust, the sugar refinery was turned into a dockyard. England needed merchant ships for her colonies and warships to fight the French, and the Royal Dockyards in Portsmouth were completely overloaded. They needed assistance – to be precise, they needed another sheltered harbour with enough wood in the hinterland. They needed Bucklers Hard. In 1749, shortly before the Seven Years War, the idyllic River Beaulieu became a busy shipyard where the great vessels were built with which Nelson fought and won his most famous battles, such as *Agamemnon*. At times there were more than 4,000 workers employed at Bucklers Hard. The market-like street between the brick houses was not broad enough for the quantities of wood that had to be stored and dried here. It needed some 1,000 oaks to build a single ship – a fact which caused Nelson's Admiral Collingwood to fill his pockets with acorns which he indefatigably planted whenever he was back on dry land. Seventy years earlier it did not seem so critical: Daniel Defoe cheerfully opined that England could easily accept commissions from the rest of the world: 'If we were employ'd in England, by the rest of the world, to build a thousand sail of three deck ships, from 80 to 100 guns, it might be done to our infinite advantage and without putting us in any danger of exhausting the nation of timber.' But the iron industry in the Weald needed vast quantities of charcoal, and the needs of housing swallowed up whole forests. The New Forest itself might have been totally razed had it not been for the fact that the middle of the 19th century saw the launch of the great iron steamships. Bucklers Hard closed its docks, until the Second World War, when minesweepers were built here and part of the Mulberry Harbour used in the invasion of Normandy. Now the only boats built here are the yachts that sail from Beaulieu to the Solent and the Isle of Wight, or round the world like Francis Chichester's *Gipsy Moth* which was anchored here. Henry Adams's house has become 'The Master Builder's House Hotel'; the 'New Inn' at the other end of the village is a maritime museum, with Nelson's baby clothes and Chichester's charts; and the workers' homes are a holiday resort. All that is left of the past at Bucklers Hard are the tides and the colours – the green forests, the white sails, and the red brick houses.

The Beautiful Bodies of Beaulieu

There is no more uplifting walk in the New Forest than the path from Bucklers Hard to *Beaulieu*. You stroll along the river, through the sparse oak forest, and between the village and the mill-pond you come to the house where once the abbey stood. 'Beaulieu' means beautiful place, and so it is. In 1024 the Cistercians came here, cleared the forest, and founded a monastery. After the Reformation the refectory became a parish church, and the gatehouse was turned into Palace House. Once it was all an oasis of peace and quiet, but today Beaulieu has half a million visitors a year, and is right up in the Top Ten of all English country estates. Why? It's certainly not because of the art collection, which would fit into an attic at Blenheim Palace; and it's not because of the house itself, which would barely constitute a gatehouse at Warwick Castle. Lord Montagu realized that when he inherited the place in 1951. But there was something else he realized too: old cars are more attractive to most people than Old Masters, and the biggest miniature railway in the world would bring in more visitors than a collection of miniature paintings. Lord Montagu had also spent enough years advertising English chocolate to know how to advertise an English country estate. If you can't offer still lifes, hold a steam fair instead. If Capability Brown never gave you a landscape garden, then put a monorail on what you've got, and get it to stop at your picturesque abbey ruins. What is the point of having an invisible ghost of 1538? Much better to have a solid Rolls Royce Silver Ghost of 1909. An old Banqueting Hall is a good idea, but a medieval banquet is an even better one, complete with Beaulieu wine, which His Lordship actually manages to sell to the French. Although the abbey is in ruins, you can still see monks. Two of them, straight from Madame Tussauds, are standing guard to the accompaniment of Gregorian chants on tape. This is the happy sound of Beaulieu, Lord Montagu's pleasure grounds. There are about 250 vintage cars and famous racing cars in his *National Motor Museum*, including such record-breakers as Donald Campbell's *Bluebird*, and classics like the white Auburn 851 of 1935, which Marlene Dietrich sat in when she was filming *Désirée*. Intoxicated by all these beautiful bodies, I splashed out on Graham Hill's *Lotus* at the exit – and hung it on my key-ring.

Reginald
Cleaver.

Isle of Wight

The inhabitants of this Isle were wont merrily to make
their boast, that their case was happier than all others,
because they had neither hooded monks nor
cavilling Lawyers, nor yet crafty foxes
Old proverb quoted by William Camden,
Britannia, *1610, tr. Philemon Holland*

It's summer, and the Solent is shining in all its splendour. This narrow strait between Hampshire and the Isle of Wight is now in full sail. In the haze of Southsea, Palmerston's island fortresses are dozing, occasionally disturbed by the roar of a hovercraft grinding its way to Ryde. At a more leisurely pace the ferry makes its way between Lymington and Yarmouth at the other end of the Solent, where Henry VIII's Hurst Castle stands on a long tongue of land, opposite Fort Victoria. We are now on the Isle of Wight – colourful as Alum Bay, an island for strategists and geologists, for luxury-loving sailors and TB patients, prison for a King, home for a Queen, haven for happy Victorians.

Dickens worked here on *David Copperfield*, Macaulay on his *History of England*, and Karl Marx lay here sunbathing. Marx came to the island three times for health reasons. There is sea air all around, 500 miles of footpaths, and every path leads to the sea. Myrtle, fuchsias, geraniums all grow in the wild, so mild is the climate. This is the ideal place for open-air concerts. Two weeks after Woodstock, in 1969, Bob Dylan and Joe Cocker set the whole island swinging, and the next year it practically sank under the weight of the infamous 1970 Isle of Wight Pop Festival. Jimi Hendrix, Joan Baez, Jethro Tull, Leonard Cohen, The Doors, The Who – they were all there (though Hendrix announced that he had only just woken up before stumbling through one of the most lacklustre sets of his career). Foolishly the festival was held under Afton Down, giving free radicals and other hippies the perfect opportunity to see the acts without paying. About 250,000 fans came – more than double the population of the island, and the chaos was such that no-one dared revive the idea until 2002.

Cowes Week: The Kaiser Makes Himself Unpopular

Up until the middle of the Stone Age, the Isle of Wight – the Roman *Vectis* – was part of the mainland, and the Solent was still a river, not a strait. The island owes

Tennyson with his nurse on Freshwater Down, a few months before his death

its main attraction to this geological fracture. The regatta at *Cowes* is held every year, and every two years there is the race for the Admiral's Cup, which first took place in 1851. At the beginning of August, anyone and everyone with a sailing boat or even just a sou'wester descends on Cowes. It's no longer confined to the 'enjoying classes', as G. M. Trevelyan once dubbed the pleasure-loving members of High Society. But when Cowes Week, the climax of the yachting season, is over, Cowes sinks back into its small-town lethargy for the rest of the year. This sailors' Mecca has its Kaaba at the top of Victoria Parade: Cowes Castle, Henry VIII's coastal fortress and now the headquarters of the most exclusive sailing club in the Commonwealth, The Royal Yacht Squadron (1815). Prince Charles is a member. When J. M. W. Turner was the guest of the architect John Nash at East Cowes Castle in 1827, his host commissioned him to paint the 'Royal Yacht Squadron Regatta'. Where Nash's country house once stood, there is now an estate of bungalows. One year after Heligoland was exchanged for Zanzibar

Queen Victoria in old age

(1891), the noble sailors of the Royal Yacht Squadron elected a new member: Kaiser Wilhelm II. Two years later the Kaiser won the Queen's Cup in the English yacht *Thistle*, which he had bought and renamed *Meteor*. From then on, every summer the Kaiser's white yacht *Hohenzollern* was to be seen in Cowes Bay next to the smaller, black *Osborne* which belonged to his uncle, the Prince of Wales. Their Royal Highnesses did not, apparently, merely exchange pleasantries from beneath their sailor's caps, and gossip in Cowes sailed freely on the wind. The Kaiser called his uncle, the future Edward VII, 'an old peacock', and the latter named his considerably vainer rival 'the boss of Cowes'. As he complained, the dashing nephew from Germany evidently intended to take full control of Cowes Week himself. Even Queen Victoria, Kaiser Wilhelm's grandmother, turned up her nose at these demanding family visits. Once her grandson ruined a banquet held in his honour at Osborne House, simply because he insisted on finishing the regatta, no matter how late it was and even though everything was totally becalmed. For all his love of England and the English, this Prussian was singularly lacking in good old English refinement. What was worse, Admiral Tirpitz was busy devising naval policies in Berlin which increasingly took the wind out of the Kaiser's sails. Nevertheless, Germans are in Wilhelm II's debt for 'Kieler Woche', the regatta in Kiel, which is based – of course – on Cowes Week.

The Kaiser could scarcely have found himself nicer lodgings during his visits than *Norris Castle*, opposite Cowes on the other side of the Medina. This is a castle built in the medieval style (*c.* 1800) by James Wyatt, with Georgian comforts, towers, battlements, and a dash of Anglo-Rhenish romanticism; it is separated from the water by nothing but a green slope, but is at a very respectful distance from Osborne House, the summer residence of Wilhelm's greatly esteemed grandmother. And it has a view over the Solent that is even more imposing that the one he would have had from the bridge of his yacht. The Kaiser would dearly have loved to buy Norris Castle, which he would no doubt have renamed 'Burg Hohenzollern'. The Kaiser's shower, incidentally, was one of the first in England, installed by the Duke of Bedford, at imperial command.

Osborne House: How Victorian was Victoria?

In 1840, three years after her accession, the 21-year-old Queen Victoria married Prince Albert of Saxe-Coburg. Windsor Castle, Buckingham Palace, and the Brighton Royal Pavilion were at their disposal, but they wanted a private house, 'quiet and retired'. In 1845, when Friedrich Engels published *The Condition of the Working Classes in England*, the royal couple's desperate search for a place of their

Osborne House

Indian craftsman at work in the Durbar Hall

own came to an end. *Osborne House* was to be their new nest. It still has a surprising family informality and warmth.

The Prince Consort, who had been reminded of the Bay of Naples by the view over the Solent, got together with the London architect and land speculator Thomas Cubitt, and together they designed a country house with two campaniles, a loggia, and terrace gardens, all in an Italianate style that is now a familiar model for town-halls, railway stations, spa hotels and suburban villas all over the world. The new Osborne House was finished in the same year as Paxton's Crystal Palace, the monumental construction of glass and iron erected for the Great Exhibition of 1851 in London. Victoria's Osborne House was a kind of private equivalent to this public demonstration of style, and both in their own way represented Victorian taste.

England had reached the peak of her economic expansion and her industrial prowess. English furniture puffed out its chest with pride, and gave itself luxurious curves and flourishes and decorations. Every item set out to be bigger, finer, richer than its neighbour. Design became ever more ornamental, styles competed with

The Queen's bedroom

one another and were ever more extravagant. The rich could do everything, had everything, and flaunted everything. Queen Victoria's private chambers are as crowded as the cabinets of the Victorian middle classes: vases, pictures, souvenirs from the Empire. This was the culture of bric-à-brac. Every inch is covered. Empty spaces are as unacceptable as straight lines and smooth surfaces. All the expensive knick-knacks on the mantelpieces and the sideboards, and indeed throughout the interior are a battle against the dreaded void, as if the Victorians were terrified of even the smallest gap. The age of cast-iron gave itself a base of false marble and a cover of gold leaf; it impressed and imitated, it costumed itself and coloured itself, carved and curved its way to happiness, until along came the true Puritans and waved the flag for functionalism. Before the opening of the Great Exhibition of 1851, Queen Victoria wrote in her diary: 'so much care has been taken and the manufactures of our people show such good taste.' Victorian naturalism coupled with a love of keepsakes resulted in some strange mementoes. Under a glass cover, not unlike a cheese cover, lie marble copies of Prince Albert's hand and Princess Victoria's foot. When the Prince Consort lay back in his bronze

Whippingham: the royal church

bathtub with mahogany edges, he could look up at the wall and see his children, photographed in theatrical costumes. Goethe was also in Albert's bathroom – a scene from *Götz von Berlichingen*, painted by Prince Albert himself. The Prince Consort, in effect the Queen's private secretary, was President of the Society of Arts, and himself collected Italian primitives – Fra Angelico – and German sophisticates like Franz Xavier Winterhalter. He ran his estate like a little German principality, with a school, hospital, and social welfare for his employees. His admiration for the work of the Nazarenes (a group of German painters not unlike the Pre-Raphaelites) was shared by William Dyce, who had joined them in Rome, studied Late Romantic history-painting in Germany, and revived fresco-painting in England. In the stairwell at Osborne House is his fresco *Neptune Resigning to Britannia the Empire of the Sea* (1847): contemporary history dressed up as patriotic myth.

The Victorians plundered styles as liberally as they plundered their colonies. In 1877 Victoria had become Empress of India, and so Indian butlers waited on her at Osborne House, and Indian Maharajahs came to visit her there. The portraits of these servants and princes adorn the Durbar Wing, whose Indian stucco decorations were partly designed by John Lockwood Kipling, Rudyard's father. In the park is a Swiss chalet, imported – from America – as a playroom for the royal children. In front of it are seven little gardens with flowers and vegetable patches, from which they were to learn the rudiments of housekeeping. English Heritage has recently restored these educational gardens as accurately as it has restored the whole Victorian park. After the early death of her Prince (1861), Queen Victoria left all his rooms unaltered, and when she herself died in 1901 at the age of 81, her own rooms remained equally sacrosanct, witnesses to an age that bore her name. It had been the favourite home of a queen whose 63-year reign was the longest in English history.

In *Whippingham*, one mile south of Osborne, on a hill overlooking the Medina, stands the royal church, built (1854-62) under the watchful eye of the Prince Consort himself. Inside is a fine screen by Britain's neglected Art Nouveau master, Alfred Gilbert, as well as tombs of royalty and hangers-on. Don't overlook a little painting with a large history: Lavery's once famous *Angel of Mons*, an icon of the First World War.

After all this Victorianism, *Quarr Abbey*, on the main road to Ryde, comes as a breath of fresh twentieth-century air. It is a masterpiece of Expressionist brick architecture, designed in 1911/12 by one of the monks, Dom Paul Bellot, for a community of French Benedictines who left France at the turn of the century and settled here on the site of the old Cistercian abbey. Today Quarr Abbey is a popular centre for meditation, with daily Gregorian chants; we trippers can find the gardens open and teas available.

Freshwater: Mrs Cameron's Camera

The route from Bembridge to Alum Bay at the other end of the island is as scenic as can be, with cliffs and beautiful beaches. This is a holiday coast with Victorian memories. Not everywhere has as many as *Shanklin* in Sandown Bay. There is a fountain with lines contributed by Longfellow, and a 'Pickwick's Pub', an 'Oliver's Kitchen', and even 'Keats Ladies Hair Stylist' next to the boarding-house where Keats stayed in 1819 (where he wrote to Fanny Brawne 'I will imagine you Venus tonight and pray, pray to your star like a Heathen'). Old Shanklin's thatched houses with carved gables, those typical Victorian *cottages ornées*, are to be seen all over the island. Landslides have created a particular form of coastline here, with so-called 'undercliffs' – broad terraces beneath the cliffs themselves. *Ventnor* is regarded as the English equivalent to Madeira, but I found its suburb of *Bonchurch* more cosy and romantic. Swinburne spent his

Weather vane, Bonchurch

childhood here in East Dene House, where the 'golden-haired lad' played with Dickens' children, and he lies buried in the churchyard of St Boniface.

The most popular Victorian poet on the Isle of Wight was Alfred, Lord Tennyson. Indeed he was so popular that in 1867 he had to leave the island to escape the autograph and souvenir hunters (He moved to the winter house he had built himself in Aldworth (p. 176); on one of the crossings of the Solent between houses he composed *Crossing the Bar.*) 'King Alfred' lived from 1853 onwards in Farringford House, high above *Freshwater Bay*. 'A miracle of beauty' was his description of the view. He rented the house until the proceeds from his comedic-philosophical poem *Maud* gave him the means to buy it. 'That was the poem I was cursed for writing! when it came out no word was bad enough for me! I was a blackguard, a ruffian and an atheist!' The house has now become a hotel, very high class and rather dull. In front of all the crenellations and neo-Gothic pointed windows stands the Wellingtonia planted by Garibaldi, who visited Tennyson in 1864. Jenny Lind, the Swedish Nightingale, sang in the drawing-room, and Sir Arthur Sullivan played some of his compositions there. Lewis Carroll listened to Tennyson describing his dreams and based the *Mouse's Tail* on one of them. Even Prince Albert came to Farringford from Osborne House to enjoy a literary cup of tea. In Tennyson's library, now a television room, is a cabinet with his pipes, nightcap, and poet's black cape. With his cape billowing and his broad-rimmed hat on his head, Tennyson would climb the hill – now called Tennyson Down – in all weathers, right to the top where his admirers have erected a Celtic cross of Cornish granite in his memory.

The route along the cliffs leads west to the *Needles*, three huge (and famously dangerous) chalk rocks jutting out from the sea, and to Alum Bay with its cliffs of many colours, the different strata of which provide a visual record of geological history. In the other direction lies Freshwater Bay, and if you had gone walking there in the 1860's, you might well have run into a very determined lady. 'I'm Mrs Cameron. May I take a photograph of you?' she would have asked. Julia Margaret Cameron was a lady of good family who in 1863, at the age of 48, was given a camera by her daughter 'to amuse herself'. The amusement turned out to be hard work. Glass plates had to be covered with collodion, and made sensitive to light with silver nitrate. Mrs Cameron turned her coalshed into a darkroom, and her glazed henhouse into a studio. From then on, no tourist and no guest of her neighbour Tennyson was safe from her camera – not Charles Darwin on his summer holidays in Freshwater, not Crown Prince Friedrich of Prussia, not Carlyle, not Newman, not Tennyson himself. In her only play, *Fresh Water* (1923/35) Virginia Woolf drew a satirical

Portrait by Julia Margaret Cameron

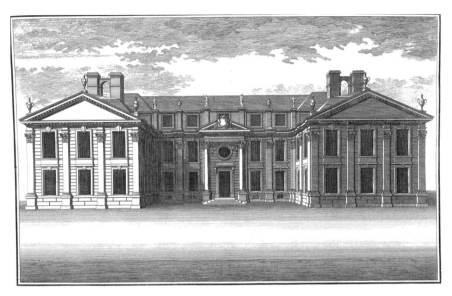

Appledurcombe House

portrait of her camera-mad great aunt and of the artists' clique of Freshwater Bay. Mrs Cameron's maid Mary posed countless times for her as the 'Island Madonna', and the porter on Yarmouth Pier was immortalised in the role of King Arthur when in 1874 she illustrated Tennyson's *Idylls of the King*. Her soft, artistic and very poetic portraits make up a Who's Who of Victorian society, and the majority were taken at Dimbola Lodge, Freshwater Bay, where she lived from 1860 to 1875. This bright hilltop house, named after the Camerons' tea and coffee plantations in what was then Ceylon, is now a museum and exhibition centre run by the Julia Margaret Cameron Trust.

There are some small country houses on the Isle of Wight, such as *Nunwell* and *Arreton*, and the magnificent ruins of *Appledurcombe* (c. 1710–13) with its Baroque architecture, and there is also *Carisbrooke Castle*. This castle has a Norman keep and Elizabethan bastions, and was the official residence of the governor. There was one person who did not enjoy the wonderful view of the island: King Charles I. Charles had escaped from Hampton Court, but wanted to stay on British soil, so he gave himself up to the governor of the Isle of Wight, much to official embarassment. Initially he was allowed to move freely round the island, but after he had some botched attempts to spring him from the island, he was confined to Carisbrooke. There the only distraction granted to him was a bowling green within the castle walls. He attempted once more to escape, and failed dismally. In trying to climb out of a window, he got stuck between the bars. At the end of 1648, Charles I was brought to London. Cromwell considered the scaffold of Whitehall to be safer than 'Carisbrooke's narrow case'.

Tennyson's manuscript of Crossing the Bar

Crossing the Bar.

Sunset & evening star,
   And one clear call for me.
And may there be no moaning of the bar,
   When I put out to sea,

But such a tide as moving seems asleep,
   Too full for sound & foam,
When that which drew from out the boundless deep
   Turns again home.

Twilight & evening bell,
   And after that the dark!
And may there be no sadness of farewell,
   When I embark!

For tho' from out our bourne of Time & <u>Place</u>
   The flood may bear me far,
I hope to see my Pilot face to face,
   When I have crost the bar.

Kings and Queens of England

Glossary of Architectural Terms

Apse Semi-circular or polygonal end of a church or section of church

Atrium Originally an open, colonnaded inner court in a Roman house; in Christian architecture, a colonnaded court in front of the west door of the church

Balustrade A series of small, vertical piers used to support a rail on stairs, balconies or roofs

Barrel Vault Simplest form of ceiling, consisting of a series of semicircular sections

Basilica Church with three or more aisles, of which the central one is higher than the others and contains windows to let in light. In early Christian architecture this was the favourite form, and set standards for all western church architecture even in its later developments

Buttress A pillar built at an angle to the wall to strengthen it and to resist its outward thrust

Caldarium The Roman warm bath, usually to the south to let in as much light and sun as possible

Capital The very top of a column, pillar or pilaster with decorative patterns, figures or plants

Cathedral Close The area all round a cathedral, generally including a wide stretch of lawn and surrounding buildings. In the middle ages the precinct was under ecclesiastical jurisdiction. The lay-out and architecture are typical of English cathedral cities

Chancel Area containing High Altar, reserved for the choir and clergy, and some steps higher than the nave. Often separated from the nave by a screen or rails

Chantry or Chantry Chapel A memorial chapel in which, until the time of Henry VIII, a mass to be said (or sung – *chanter*) for the soul of the person who endowed it. In English cathedrals such chapels are nearly always built between pillars in the nave or chancel, whereas on the Continent they tend to be extensions.

Chapter house A separate room in a cathedral or monastery set aside for meetings of the clergy, so called because a chapter of the Bible would be read. The Cathdral Chapter is the body of resident clergy.

Chinoiserie European imitations of Oriental art

Cloister Covered walk round inner court of monastery or cathedral

Coffered ceiling Flat or vaulted ceiling, decorated with sunken round or rectangular panels; the decorations are often gilded reliefs

Crossing Intersection of transepts, chancel and nave of a church

Crypt Underground chamber at eastern end of church for relics, tombs of saints and martyrs

Decorated Style (*c.* 1300-1400) Typically English form of Gothic (2nd period) with flowing convex, concave lines (ogees) and elaborate ornamentation

Early English Style (*c.* 1190-1300) First period of English Gothic, with severe, narrow forms and emphasis on the vertical (e.g. lancet
windows)

Fan vaulting Ceiling construction where the ribs radiate out in a fan shape from a central point, characteristic of English late gothic

Hall church Church in which all the aisles are of more or less equal height

Hypocaust Heating system for Roman baths. From an underground heating room, hot air is circulated through spaces beneath the floor and through pipes in the walls

Keep Central tower of a Norman castle with tiny apertures and no visible entrance. Used as refuge during sieges and also as residence

Keystone Topmost stone in an arch or vault, often decorated

Lady Chapel Chapel dedicated to the Virgin Mary; often after *c.*1200 an eastern extension of the chancel

Long Gallery On the top floor of Elizabethan country houses, it runs the full length of the house and was used for games and entertainment in bad weather

Nave The main body of the church between the west entrance and the chancel

Perpendicular Style (*c.*1350-end of 15th C.) Peak and final period of English Gothic, with filigree vaulting, clear and simple forms and proportions developed from complete mastery and reduction of all preceding forms

Pilaster Vertical, rectangular column attached to wall or other area, with base and capital

Portico Porch in front of main entrance, borne by columns and usually surmounted by a pediment

Retable Wall behind altar containing panel or shrine

Retro-choir Section east of the choir, often used to contain the shrine of the saint

Rib Projecting member which supports other sections of a vault

Rose window In Gothic architecture, a round window with tracery radiating from the centre

Tracery Geometrical Gothic ornamentation, initially only in large windows, but later also on walls, gables etc.

Transept Between nave and chancel, one of the two extensions north and south that form the crossing in a cruciform church

Trompe-l'oeil (French: deception of the eye) Objects or views painted in such a way as to appear three-dimensional

Tudor Style (*c.*1520-early 17th C.) Mixture of Late Gothic elements with Italian and German Renaissance

Tympanum Arched area above a doorway, generally with sculpture in relief

Further Reading

Arnold, Eve, *Eve Arnold in Britain*, London 1991

Betjeman, Sir John, *Sir John Betjeman's Guide to English Paris Churches*, rev. and updated by Nigel Kerr, London 1993

Bisgrove, Richard, *The Gardens of Gertrude Jekyll*, London 1992

Boogaart, Pieter, *A272: An Ode to a Road*, London 2000

Brown, Jane, *Gardens of a Golden Afternoon: The story of a partnership: Edwin Lutyens and Gertrude Jekyll*, London 1982

Cannadine, David, *The Decline and Fall of the British Aristocracy*, London 1990 (rev. ed. 1992)

Cheatle, J. R. W., *A Guide to the British Landscape,* London 1976

Clifton-Taylor, Alec, *The Cathedrals of England*, London 1967

Clifton-Taylor, Alec, *The Pattern of English Building*, London 1987

Cobbett, William, *Rural Rides* (1830 and later)

Collins, Wilkie, *Rambles Beyond Railways*, London 1851

Compton, Susan (ed.), *British Art in the Twentieth Century: The Modern Movement*, London 1987

Cook, Olive, *The English Country House: An Art and a Way of Life*, London 1974

Davies, Norman *The Isles: A history,* London 1999

Defoe, Daniel, *A Tour through England and Wales (1724-26)*, London and New York 1959

Dixon, Roger and Muthesius, Stefan, *Victorian Architecture*, 2nd ed. London 1985

Drabble, Margaret and Lewinski, Jorge, *A Writer's Britain,* London 1971

Eagle, Dorothy and Carnell, Hilary, *The Oxford Literary Guide to the British Isles,* Oxford, 1977

Fisher, Adrian and Georg Gerster, *The Art of the Maze*, London 1990

Fleming, Laurence and Alan Gore, *The English Garden*, London 1979

Freeman, *Literature and Locality,* London 1963

Girouard, Mark, *Life in the English Country House: a social and architectural history*, Harmondsworth 1980

Girouard, Mark, *The English Town*, New Haven and London 1990

Godwin, Fay, *Our Forbidden Land*, London 1990

Grigson, Geoffrey, *The Faber Book of Poems and Places*, London 1980

Hadfield, John (ed.), *The Shell Book of English Villages*, London 1985

Headley, Gwyn and Meulenkamp, Wim, *Follies, Grottoes and Garden Buildings*, London 1999

Hewison, Robert, *The Heritage Industry*, London 1987

Hunt, John Dixon and Peter Willis, *The Genius of the Place: The English Landscape Garden 1620-1820*, London 1975

Hutton, Graham and Edwin Smith, *English Parish Churches*, London 1976

Hyams, Edward Solomon, *The Changing Face of England*, Harmondsworth 1974

Jackson-Stops, Gervase and James Pipkin, *The English Country House: A grand tour*, London 1984

Jackson-Stops, Gervase and James Pipkin, *The Country House Garden: A grand tour*, London 1987

Jacobs, Michael and Malcolm Warner, *The Phaidon Companion to Art and Artists in the British Isles*, Oxford 1980

James, Henry, *English Hours (1905)*, London 1960

Jekyll, Gertrude, *Classic English Gardens*, New York and London 1995

Jenkins, Simon, *England's Thousand Best Churches*, London 1999

Jenkins, Simon, *England's Thousand Best Houses*, London 2003

Lutyens, Mary, *Edwin Lutyens*, London 1980 (rev. ed. 1991)

Marsh, Kate (ed.), *Writers and their Houses*, London 1993

Morley, Frank, *Literary Britain*, London 1980

Newby, Howard, *Country Life: A Social History of Rural England*, London 1987

Nicolson, Nigel, *Great Houses of Britain*, London 1973

Palmer, Alan and Veronica, *Royal England*, London 1983

Pevsner, Nikolaus, *The Englishness of English Art*, London 1955

Pevsner, Nikolaus, *The Buildings of England*, 1951 onwards

Priestley, J. B., *The English*, Harmondsworth 1975

Rackham, Oliver, *The History of the Countryside*, London 1986

Rackham, Oliver, *Illustrated History of the Countryside*, London 1994

Randall, Gerald, *Church Furnishings and Decoration in England and Wales,* London, 1980

Richmond, I. A., *Roman Britain*, Harmondsworth 1963

Schinkel, Karl Friedrich, *English Journey*, (ed. David Bindman and Gottfried Riemann), Yale 1993

Soper, Tony and Le Mesurier, Brian, *A Natural History Guide to the Coast*, London 1993

Spens, Michael, *The Complete Landscape Designs and Gardens of Geoffrey Jellicoe*, London 1994

Taylor, John, *A Dream of England: Landscape, Photography and the Tourist's Imagination*, Manchester 1994

Theroux, Paul, *The Kingdom by the Sea: A Journey Around the Coast of Great Britain*, London 1983

Thomas, Nicholas, *A Guide to Prehistoric England*, London 1976

Trevelyan, George Macaulay, *English Social History*, Harmondsworth 1984

Trueman, A. E., (rev. J. B. Whittow and J. R. Hardy) *Geology and Scenery in England and Wales,* London, 1971

Whybrow, Marion, *St Ives 1883-1993: Portrait of an Art Colony*, Woodbridge 1994

Wilson, Simon, *Holbein to Hockney: A History of British Art*, London 1979

Practical Information

Some Practical Hints A-Z

Accommodation There is something for all tastes and budgets, from camping sites to castles. The cosiest type, particularly practical and economic for the go-as-you-please tourist, is Bed and Breakfast (B & B), which may also offer a unique insight into other people's private lives. See the annually updated *Good Bed and Breakfast Guide* (Which? Ltd.); many people swear by the various guides published by Alastair Sawday (*Special Places to Stay, British Bed and Breakfast, Bed and Breakfast for Garden Lovers*, etc.: www.sawdays.co.uk).

English hotels are relatively expensive, in some cases unashamedly so bearing in mind their quality. Ask to see the room and don't necessarily take the first one offered (it's often second best). See *The Good Hotel Guide* (Vermilion) and *The Which? Hotel Guide* (Which? Ltd). For luxury hotels at luxury prices, contact the Pride of Britain Hotels, Courage Farm, Foxley, Wilts. SN16 0JH, tel. 01666 824666, fax. 01666 825779, www.prideofbritainhotels.com.

A better value alternative, often in historic family houses, is the 200-plus private guest houses listed by Wolsey Lodges, 9 Market Place, Hadleigh, Ipswich Suffolk IP7 5DL, tel. 01473 822058, fax. 01473 827444, www.wolsey-lodges.co.uk.

Unusual accommodation in restored historic houses can be rented from the Landmark Trust (Shottesbrooke), Maidenhead, Berks. SL6 3SW, tel. 01628 825925, fax. 01628 825417, www.landmarktrust.co.uk.

Almost 300 beautifully situated holiday homes, from farmhouses to castles and water towers, are available from the National Trust (Holiday Cottages, PO Box 536, Melksham. Wiltshire SN12 8SX).

If you want real peace and quiet, e.g. in monasteries, hermitages, meditation centres, you'll find a selection in George Target's original guidebook *Out of this World* (1985, still in print). For groups and conferences, a very good deal is offered at university halls of residence during the vacations, i.e. mid-March to mid-April, and mid-June to early October. Information from: Venuemasters, The Workstations, 15 Paternoster Row, Sheffield S1 2BX, tel. 0114 249 3090, www.venuemasters.co.uk.

Angling There are plenty of facilities on coasts and rivers. See the annual handbook *Where to Fish* (Harmsworth Publishing). Licences may be obtained from local tourist offices.

Hampshire boasts two of the most famous trout rivers in the world, the Test and the Itchen. These are of the type called chalk streams, clear spring-fed rivers that have been carefully managed for their trout fishing for 150 years or more. Casting for and landing a wily chalk stream trout remains one of fly fishing's ultimate challenges. The imitative dry fly and the nymph, two of the principal methods used today, were developed here in Victorian times, and there is a strong sense of history as you walk the banks that so many famous anglers of the past have walked before.

Although most chalk streams can be reached in little over an hour from Central London, don't think you can simply turn up and fish – these waters are all privately owned and access is not only expensive but in peak season needs to be booked well in advance. Your own private chalk stream 'beat' for a day will cost anything between £80 and £200 per person. Famous Fishing (01722 716210, www.famousfishing.com) is an outfitter that can arrange either single days or extended trips on a range of chalk streams, with knowledgeable guides/instructors and full equipment where required.

Season: Trout 15th April-15th October
Grayling: 16th June-15th March

Cycling England's gentle countryside is ideal for cyclists, and more and more cycle tracks are being laid, particularly along canal towpaths. For detailed information, contact Cyclists Touring Club (CTC), Cotterell House, 69 Meadrow, Godalming,

'The bicycle menace'

Surrey GU7 3HS, tel. 0870 873 0060, fax. 01483 426994, www.ctc.org.uk; and for the current state of the national network of cycle trails, see Sustrans, 35 King St, Bristol BS1 4DZ, 0845 113 0065, info@ sustrans.org.uk, www.sustrans.org.uk

Drink For a long time it used to be said that English people didn't drink when they were thirsty, but they were thirsty when it was time to drink. The pubs operated under Puritanical licensing laws, but since 1988 these have been relaxed to the extent that the English may now drink from 11 a.m. till 11 p.m. from Monday to Saturday. Country pubs, however, still tend to have a natural break between 2pm and 6pm.

Draught beer is neither as cold nor as foamy as on the Continent, and there are distinctions between ales and bitters, stout (stronger) and lager (lighter). Free houses do not offer free beer, but since they are not tied to one brewery, they do offer a wider choice. It's always worth asking for local beers: Faversham (Kent) for instance has two local breweries – Fremlins (founded 1764) and Shepherd Neame (founded 1698). In Sussex it's King and Barnes (Horsham), and Gale's in Hampshire. The Campaign for Real Ale continues to encourage the enthusiastic appreciation of good beers (and now ciders and perries too) and produces an annual guide book, *The Good Beer Guide*; www. camra.org.uk.

The Romans tried, and so of course did the Normans: wine-making in England can be regarded either as a sport or as an eccentricity.

Nevertheless, it's on the increase, perhaps because of the mild climate in the south, or perhaps because the English have strange tastes. Try 'Surrey Dry' from Denbies, the 250-acre vineyard north of Dorking (A24). For further information,

'"Qu'est ce que c'est, ce toad in the hole?"'

contact The English Vineyards Association, Church Road, Bruisyard, Saxmundham, Suffolk IP17 2EF, tel. 01728 638080, fax. 01728 638442. But don't drink and drive.

Eating Out Somerset Maugham thought that anyone who wanted to eat well in England would have to eat three breakfasts a day. With the regrettable advance of the so-called Continental Breakfast, that is no longer true, but complaints about English food (and weather) are equally anachronistic. 'The miracle of English cuisine: flavoursome, juicy and sensuous' (*Die Zeit*) can be enjoyed even in the villages and small towns of Southern England. Fresh ingredients from the garden or the market, and international sophistication make these gourmet restaurants well worth a detour. See the annually updated *Good Food Guide* (Consumers' Association, 2 Marylebone Rd, London NW1 4DF), which has been a gourmets' bible since its first publication in 1951. The same association publishes a *Vegetarian Good Food Guide*. Michelin, Gault-Millau and others also produce guides to food in Britain.

English Heritage (EH) This organization was founded and is partly financed by the government, though it works independently. It owns and administers over 400 historic sites and buildings, including Stonehenge and Dover Castle. It protects and maintains houses and gardens, prehistoric monuments, and even telephone kiosks from the 1920's, as well as castles, ruined abbeys, industrial and municipal sites. It also gives grants to the National Trust, historic churches and important private estates. London headquarters: Fortress House, 23 Savile Row, London W1X 2HE, tel. 020 7973 3000, www. english-heritage.org.uk.

For an annual subscription members get free admission for themselves plus unlimited numbers of children to all EH properties, plus reduced price admission to many other sites, as well as a magazine etc.

Visitors from outside the UK can buy an Overseas Visitors Pass for a week at £15 – excellent value.

In recent years, the concept of English Heritage has become an important issue. The increasingly popular, practical but not always unproblematical relationship between conservation and tourism was trenchantly analysed by Robert Hewison in *The Heritage Industry* (London 1987), in which he argued against the complete commercialisation of the past: heritage seen as the enemy of history. Subsequent developments have not invalidated his thesis.

Folly Fellowship Founded in 1988 to help promote the awareness and enjoyment of follies, and where necessary, 'to protect lonely and unloved buildings of little purpose from being rationalised and destroyed'. As well as setting up a database to record these 'grace notes in the symphony of our landscape', the Fellowship organises visits and lectures and celebrates once a year at an annual summer garden party. For more information contact the Membership Secretary, the Folly Fellowship, 7 St Catherines Way, Fareham, Hants PO1 8RL, or visit www ffellowship.fsnet.co.uk

Gardens and Parks Southern England is a paradise for gardening enthusiasts, as indeed is the rest of England. In addition to the public gardens owned by the National Trust and other institutions, about 2300 private gardens are open to the public at least once a year.

Garden-spotting is a national sport, with particular kudos for those who visit one on its only open day (better still, on its very first open day). A useful aid is the annually updated *Gardens of England and Wales*, published by the National Gardens Scheme, Hatchlands Park, East Clandon, Surrey GU4 7RT, tel. 01483 211535, www.ngs.org, which lists private gardens open for charity. Short descriptions of over 900 British gardens, with addresses and recommended visiting season, are published in the *Good Gardens Guide* (Frances Lincoln), also updated yearly. A history of both traditional and unusual English gardens is Penelope Hobhouse's *The Private Gardens of England* (London 1986); a more general history is Jane Fearnley-Whittingstall's *The Garden – An English Love Affair* (London 2002).

A redundant London church houses the only Museum of Garden History (St Mary-at-Lambeth, Lambeth Palace Rd, London SE1 7LB, tel. 020 7401 8865, fax. 020 7401 8869, www.museumgardenhistory.org, open daily 10.30-5.

National Trust (NT) Three English philanthropists – a social reformer, a clergyman, and a lawyer – founded the

'National Trust for Places of Historic Interest or Natural Beauty' in 1895. This highly influential private institution is financed by members' subscriptions, donations, entrance money, foundations, and a whole chain of flourishing souvenir shops and tea rooms. After the Crown and the State, the National Trust is the third biggest land-owner in Britain (612,000 acres and 600 miles of coast). It owns, administers and restores castles, country houses, estates, farm-houses, gardens, forests, battlefields, bird sanctuaries, pubs, dovecotes, industrial monuments, barns, mills, cider presses, and whole villages and islands. It has over three million members, some 50 million visitors a year, and an annual turnover of £200 million, which makes it the most powerful conservation body in England.

Its acquisitions have a not inconsiderable influence on the tastes and values of the nation. This most admirable and most enviable institution does, however, have its critics.They dub it The National Dust, and accuse it of one-sidedly preserving the

New Forest ponies

traditions of the aristocracy and the pastoral past – a 'fossilisation of taste' (*Observer*). Until the seventies, the Trust's main focus was on saving historic houses that were under threat, but since the mid eighties it has concentrated more on protecting nature and the countryside. This 'green policy' has rescued some of the most beautiful British landscapes, which include about a sixth of the English coast – over 550 miles – thanks to Enterprise Neptune, a campaign begun in 1964. See the informative and richly illustrated history by Merlin Waterson: *The National Trust. The First Hundred Years* (1995).

Members pay an annual subscription, for which they can visit all the houses, gardens and other properties free of charge. Headquarters of The National Trust are at 42-44 Queen Anne's Gate, London SW1H 9AS, tel. 020 7222 9251, fax. 020 7222 5097, www.nationaltrust.org.uk. Americans can join the Royal Oak Foundation to support the trust's work, www.royal-oak.org.

Overseas visitors can buy one or two week passes for one, two or a family - very reasonably priced but only available online.

Riding The Downs and the New Forest are the best areas for holidays on horseback, with riding lessons and pony trekking on offer at farms and accredited riding schools. Polo is also taught at the Mid-Forest Trekking Centre in the New Forest. For further information contact: The British Horse Society, National Equestrian Centre, Stoneleigh Deer Park, Kenilworth, Warwickshire, tel. 0870 120 2244, fax. 01926 707800, www.bhs.org.uk.

Walking 'Why make walks? To clear the mind, thoughts drifting effortless to the surface like tea leaves,' says walk artist Hamish Fulton (see p. 50). Not every walker can be an artist, but anyone can

Hikers

perform the works of Fulton or his Bristolian fellow artist Richard Long in their own way as they extend their walking experience.

Southern England is rich with good walks, especially along the Downs in Kent, Surrey and Sussex, as well as along the cliffs. Two of the finest long distance walks are the North Downs Way (153 miles from Farnham to Dover) and the South Downs Way (110 miles from Winchester to Beachy Head). For further information about these and other national trails consult www.nationaltrails.gov.uk. The walkers' organisation is The Ramblers' Association (the umbrella organisation for some 400 British associations) at its London office, 2/F Camelford House, 87-90 Albert Embankment, London SE1 7TW, tel. 020 7339 8500, fax. 020 7339 8501, www.ramblers.org.uk.

Websites Far too many to list, but always a good way to start looking up information. Try the official British Tourist authority site, www.visitbritain.com. Other general sites include www.aboutbritaincom; www.enjoybritain.com

Woodland Trust The Woodland Trust campaigns to protect ancient woodlands and to encourage more trees to be planted. One of its most spectacular plans is to replant 200,000 trees on a 600 acre estate near Maidstone where the farmer had so hated trees that he defied court orders and felled them by the tens of thousands, creating the featureless landscape now so prevalent in England. For information about woodlands under their protection or about their campaigns contact The Woodland Trust, Autumn Park, Grantham, Lincolnshire, NG31 6LL, tel: 01476 581111, fax: 01476 590808; www. woodland-trust.org.uk

Youth Hostels For addresses and information, contact: Youth Hostels Association (YHA), Trevelyan House, Dimple Road, Matlock, Derbyshire DE4 3YH, tel. 01629 592600, fax. 01629 592702, www.yha. org.uk.

Places to See, with Opening Times

This section gives summary details of many of the places worth seeing in south-east England. For major sites, see the description in the main text.

Opening times are always liable to change at short notice (particularly over holiday periods), so ring ahead or check a website. Groups should book. Most places are closed at Christmas, and many at New Year and on Good Friday. To avoid unnecessary disappointment, sites with a stated policy of having a 'last admission time' are listed with this as their closing time.

Most English Heritage properties are open daily Apr-Sept 10-6, Oct 10-5; Nov-Mar 10-4, and are closed 24-26 Dec and 1 Jan.

NT = National Trust, EH = English Heritage, P = Private, TIC = Tourist Information Centre, BH = Bank Holiday.

For further information, some essential books are of course *The Buildings of England*, originally edited by Nikolaus Pevsner, no longer, alas, pocket sized; John Betjeman's *Parish Churches of England and Wales*; Simon Jenkins' *England's Thousand Best Churches* and *England's Thousand Best Houses*; Gwyn Headley and Wim Meulenkamp's *Follies, Grottoes and Garden Buildings*

Kent

Appledore (10 m SSW of Ashford) Attractive village with good Romney Marsh church, St Peter and St Paul

Ashford (13 m SW of Canterbury) Now a commuter town thanks to the Channel Tunnel. Major Roman shanty town recently uncovered.
St Mary: fine medieval church

Aylesford (near Maidstone) Carmelite Monastery The Friars, 13th C.; nearby, ruins of Roman villa and prehistoric burial site (Kits Coty House). Tel. 01622 712272, www.thefriars.org.uk.

Badlesmere (5 m S of Faversham) St Leonard: unchanged interior 'of rare beauty' (Betjeman)

Barfreston (6 m N of Dover) St Nicholas: exquisitely decorated 12th C church with elaborate door. 'A casket of Norman art' (Simon Jenkins)

Bedgebury Pinetum (3 m S of Goudhurst) Finest collection of conifers in the world. Open every day, Mar-Oct 10-5, Nov-Feb 10-4

Bekesbourne (3 m S of Canterbury) Howletts Wild Animal Park: gorillas, tigers and elephants, held in original way;

www.howletts.net. Open daily except Christmas 10-5; tel. 01303 264647

Belmont (4 m SW of Faversham, A251) Late 18th-C. manor house by Samuel Wyatt. Indian colonial history, clock collection. April-Sep: Sat, Sun & BH Mon 2-5 and by appointment Mon-Thurs. Tel. 01795 890202; www.belmont-house.org

Beltring (nr Paddock Wood, B2015/ B2017, NE of Tunbridge Wells) The Hop Farm Country Farm: Victorian oast houses, history of hops industry, Shire Horse Centre etc. Open all year, summer 10-6, winter 10-4. Tel. 01622 872068, fax 01622 872630.

Belvedere (3 m N of Bexley) Crossness Pumping Station by Joseph Bazalgette, one of the wonders of Victorian England. Spectacular interiors. World's largest rotative beam engines recently restored; special steaming days. For visiting details, tel. 020 8311 3711 or www.crossness.org.uk

Bexleyheath (1 m N of Bexley) Red House: William Morris's first house, built with Philip Webb and intended to be centre of an artist's community. An icon of arts and crafts, recently acquired by the National Trust. Tel. 01494 755588 for opening hours (currently pre-booked tours only); www.friends-red-house.co.uk
   Christchurch: superb Victorian church

Biddenden (4 m NNW of Tenterden) Memorable, if short, village street

Biggin Hill (7 m NW of Sevenoaks) Famous for its Second World War aerodrome where air displays etc. are still held. Site of a famous party in 1943 to celebrate 1000 enemy kills. Chapel of Remembrance open daily 10-4, tel. 01959 570353.

Otherwise unattractive.

Birchington (W of Margate) Quex House, Quex Park: manor house (1813) with Powell-Cotton Museum, zoological and ethnographic collections from Africa and Asia, many in original cases. Apr-Oct, Tues-Thurs, Sun & BH Mon, garden and museum 11-5, house 2-4.30. Mar & Nov museum & garden, Sun only. Tel. 01843 42168, fax. 01843 84661, e-mail powell-cotton.museum@virgin.net
   In park, Waterloo Tower (1819) with battlements and open cast-iron helm, a kind of proto-Eiffel Tower.

Boughton Aluph (4 m NE of Ashford) All Saints, fine church with glass, isolated in 'lovely slope of downland' (Betjeman)

Boughton Monchelsea Place (5 m S of Maidstone) Elizabethan country house (1567-1575) with Regency alterations. Disappointing house but fine views of landscape garden and Weald. Open for group visits by appointment only Mon-Thurs 10-4. Tel. 01622 743120, fax. 01622 741168, www.boughtonmonchelseaplace. co.uk

Brabourne (10 m S of Canterbury) Prettily sited village. St Mary, with some 12C glass and monuments to Scot family, including fine brasses: 'a collection of considerable eccentricity' (Pevsner).

Brasted (5 m W of Sevenoaks) Brasted Place, fine villa by Robert Adam, c. 1784-5; home of Napoleon III in 1840, and his pet symbolic eagle

Brenzett (6 m NE of Rye) St Eanswith: delightful and isolated Romney Marsh church. Aeronautical Museum, with Second World War memorabilia,

Ivychurch Rd, tel. 01797 344747.

Broadstairs (3 m N of Ramsgate) Pleasant seaside resort.

Bleak House, Church Road: Dickens' summer house, where he wrote some of the eponymous novel. Gardens and memorabilia; museum of smuggling

Dickens House Museum, Victoria Parade: open daily in season, tel. 01843 861232 for exact times; www.dickens house.co.uk

Broomhill (Southborough, N of Tunbridge Wells) Victorian country house by Sir David Salomons and Sir David Lionel Salomons, scientist and designer. First house in England to use electricty. Wood-panelled Edwardian concert hall, briefly used for a people's opera festival. Extraordinary stables and watertower. Now training centre. For further information check www.salomonscentre.org.uk

Brook (4 m NE of Ashford) St Mary, one of the earliest Norman churches, with a spectacular tower (not always open) enclosing a chapel, in the German *west-werk* tradition. Early wall paintings

Brookland (5 m NE of Rye) St Augustine, wonderful detached belfry, a shingle-covered triple-layered cone. Early lead font, unrestored interior

Broome Park (1¼ m SE of Barham) 17th C house. 'There is no more amazing display of 17th C cut and moulded brickwork' (Pevsner). Depressingly surrounded by a golf course

Canterbury Centre of the Anglican world and most visited cathedral city in Britain.

Cathedral: Open 9-6.30 in summer, 4.30 in winter. Sung Eucharist 11.30 and

Evensong 3.15 on Sundays; Evensong 5.30 on weekdays. Tel. 01227 762862, www.canterbury-cathedral.org

Museum of Canterbury, Stour St, CT1 2NR. Open all year Mon-Sat 10.30-4, Sun 1.30-4. Tel. 01227 452747, www.canterbury-museums.co.uk

The Canterbury Tales, St Margaret's Street. Interactive visitor experience, open daily except Christmas. Tel. 01227 479227

Eastbridge Hospital, High St.: medieval almshouse, still in use. Refectory with 13th C mural. Mon-Sat 10-5, and for services.

Roman Museum, Butchery Lane. Mon-Sat 10-4, and Suns June-Oct 1.30-4.

Royal Museum and Art Gallery, High Street. Mon-Sat 10-4.45. Tel: 01227 452747. Includes numerous paintings by England's leading painter of cows, T. S. Cooper, and some stained glass. Housed in fine Victorian library building.

St Augustine's Abbey, Longport (near Cathedral): Daily Apr-Oct 10-6, Nov-Mar 10-4. EH

St Dunstan, St Dunstan's St: Interesting medieval parish church in front of Westgate. In a niche of Roper family vault is the head of the executed Sir Thomas More.

St Martin: earliest church in continuous use in England. Norman font.

West Gate Towers, St Peter's Street, fine medieval fortified gatehouse, Mon-Sat 11-12.15 and 1.30-3.15, tel. 01227 789876

Charing (12 m SE of Maidstone) Pretty village. St Peter and St Paul: set in ruins of archbishop's palace, grand tower and fine tracery. Vamping Horn

Chartham (5 m SW of Canterbury) St Mary's: showpiece of 'Kentish tracery' with split cusping: 'as if three fireworks had shot skywards at once to explode as a starburst' (Simon Jenkins); fine Rysbrack monument; one of Britain's earliest and finest brasses, to Sir Roger Septvans (note the 'fans' of his punning heraldry); good decorative glass

Chartwell (W of Sevenoaks, 1½ m S of Westerham, off B2026) Churchill's country house. House, garden and studio open Apr-June, Sep-Oct daily except Mon (inc. BH Mon) & Tues; July & August, daily except Mon 11-5. NT. Tel. 01732 866368

Chatham (2 m E of Rochester) Historic dockyard, with 47 listed monuments in 80 acres. Museum open daily Apr-Oct 11.30-4.30; Wed, Sat & Sun 11.30-4.30 in Feb, Mar & Nov; Double Ropehouse 1135 foot long, Feb-Mar daily 10-3, Apr-Oct 10-4; www.chdt.org.uk

Chiddingstone (10 m NW of Tunbridge Wells, off B2027) Fine village street, 'in its way perfect' (Pevsner).
The Castle (originally High Street House) is a neo-Gothic country house by William Atkinson, a pupil of Wyatt. Fascinating collections put together by Denys Eyre Bower, bank clerk and antique dealer. Includes James II's heart, Egyptian mummified animals, Japanese lacquerwork and armour. Neo-gothic orangery and other garden buildings. Apr-May, BH only; June-Oct, Wed-Sat 2-5.30. Tel. 01892 870347; www.chiddingstone-castle.org.uk

Chiddingstone Causeway (2 m NE of Chiddingstone) St Luke by J. F. Bentley, designer of Westminster Cathedral, with exciting fittings

Chilham (5 m SW of Canterbury, A252) Picture-perfect village with interestng church and delightful medieval castle (one of only two octagonal keeps in the coun-

try; the other is Odiham in Hampshire) encased in Jacobean house. Landscape park by Capability Brown with Jacobean terrace garden by John Tradescant; Victorian topiary chessmen and fantastic birds. Now sadly closed to the public.
St Mary has fine monuments, many in local Bethersden marble ('like damask', Pevsner). Vicious Victorian restoration ruined setting of important monument by Nicholas Stone, still extant.

Cliffe (5 m N of Rochester) Splendid medieval church, St Helen, in unexpected setting. Touted as site for third London Airport, but the bird life is too important and too threatening to jet engines.

Cobham (3 m W of Rochester, A2) St Mary, church with finest collection of brasses in the country, and a magnificent Renaissance tomb chest
Cobham Hall: enormous and magnificent Elizabethan and later country house. Cricket associations. Repton park, site of Richard Dadd's murder of his father. Pyramidal mausoleum by James Wyatt (1783) for 3rd Earl of Darnley, converted by descendants into house. Other memorials include the Toe Monument. Hall is now girls' school; open in summer, tel. 01474 824319 for details
New College of Cobham, behind church: almshouse 1598, original foundation 1362.
Owletts, The Street: Charles II brick house 1684, with small garden. Former country home of Sir Herbert Baker. Apr-Sep, Wed & Thurs 2-5. NT. Tel. 01892 890651, fax. 01892 890110

Cooling (5 m N of Rochester) Wonderful castle gatehouse, the 'old castle' of Sir John Falstaff. Church associated with Dickens (and used as the setting for the first chapter of *Great Expectations*). Isolation of this part of Kentish coast would have been ruined by proposed airport

Cranbrook (12 m E of Tunbridge Wells) Capital of the Weald.

St Dunstan, fine church built by clothiers, with superb Green Man bosses. 18th C baptistery for full immersion

Dartford (18 m E of London) Home town of two pop heroes: the painter Peter Blake, and the Rolling Stone Mick Jagger.

Holy Trinity Church has memorial plaque to railway pioneer Richard Trevithick, who died here in 1833; extensive brass collection.

Christ Church, arts and crafts church by Caröe

Deal (8 m N of Dover, A258) Good seaside town. Important Henry VIII coastal fort, Apr-Sep 10-6; Nov-Mar, Wed-Sun 10-4. Closed 24-26 Dec and 1 Jan. EH. Tel. 01304 372762

Dover Point of entry into Britain for milennia; still a tremendous sight from a cross-Channel ferry, especially at dawn.

Castle: Norman with exceptional Saxon church, still impressive though much restored. Roman Pharos (lighthouse). Daily Apr-Sept 10-6, Oct 10-5; Nov-Mar 10-4. Closed 24-26 Dec and 1 Jan. EH. Tel. 01304 201628

Maison Dieu/Town Hall Biggin Street. Medieval hospital building enlarged in 19th C. Ring for opening hours. Tel. 01304 201200. Cinque Ports memorabilia.

Museum, Market Square. Town history and the Dover Bronze Age boat, the oldest surviving sea'going vessel (3000 BC). Mon-Sat 10-5.30. Tel. 01304 201066

Roman Painted House, New St. Most extensive Roman wall paintings north of the Alps, decorations dedicated to Bacchus. Apr-Sep, Tues-Sun 10-5. Tel. 01304 203279

White Cliffs Experience, New St: Apr-Oct, Tues-Sun 10-5. Tel. 01304 210101

Down House (Downe, near Bromley) Charles Darwin's family house. Most of the correspondence, experiments and writing that went into the *Origin of Species* happened here. Tel. 01689 859119. EH.

Dungeness (8 m E of Rye) Probably the greatest expanse of shingle in Europe, a desert home for rare migrant insects and birds, and specialised flora. Managed by the RSPB.

Derek Jarman's house and garden. P.

Elham (6 m NW of Folkestone) Pretty high street. St Mary the Blessed Virgin, 'to many the most beautiful church in Kent' (Betjeman), is almost entirely a restoration by F. C. Eden, with many fine modern fittings

Eltham Palace (8 m W of Dartford) Magnificent art deco interiors concocted for Stephen Courtauld in remains of medieval palace that includes the third largest great hall in Britain. Wed-Fri, Sun & BH Mon Apr-Set 10-6, Oct 10-5, Nov-Mar 10-4

Emmetts Garden (W of Sevenoaks, 1½ m S of A25, between Sundridge and Ide Hill) Hill garden, begun *c.*1890, esp. rhododendrons and azaleas; more modern rose and rock gardens. Apr-Jun: Wed-Sun and BH Mon 11-5; July-Oct: Sat, Sun, Wed and BH Mon 11-5. NT. Tel. 01732 750367/ 868381

Fairfield (5 m SE of Rye) St Thomas of

Canterbury. Tiny medieval church in middle of field, with good 18th C fittings

Faversham Delightful town. Abbey St with restored 16-18th-C. houses; No 80 'The House of Thomas Arden' (1540), mayor murdered in 1550, basis of the Tudor shocker *Arden of Feversham* (1592)

St Mary of Charity: one of the biggest churches in England. Magnificent aisled transepts and nave by George Dance the Elder, and exquisite late 18th C spire growing bizarrely out of 19th C tower. Fine wallpaintings (*c.* 1310), 14th-C. misericords, brasses and other tombs

Fawkham (5 m SE of Dartford) St Mary: prettily set in trees

Finchcocks (1¾ m SW of Goudhurst) Georgian Baroque house (1725). Home of pianist Richard Burnett since 1970: 'Living Museum of Music'. Collection of historic keyboard instruments; concerts and courses. Easter-Sept, Sun 2-6; Aug, Wed-Sun 2-6. Tel. 01580 211702; www.finchcocks.co.uk

Folkestone (6 m SW of Dover) The Victorian seaside town survives in the Leas, which were planned by Decimus Burton. Not one but three Martello towers.

St Mary and St Eanswyth: splendid 13th C chancel, otherwise good Victorian church lavishly fitted out.

Godinton Park (2 m NW of Ashford) Jacobean country house: paintings, furniture, porcelain, gardens with topiary. Mid-Apr–mid-Oct: gardens Thur-Mon 2-5.30; house Fri-Sun 2-5.30. Tel. 01233 620773, fax. 01233 632652, email ghpt@godinton.fsnet.co.uk

Goodnestone Park (8 m SE of Canterbury, ½ m E of B2046 between A257 and A2) 18th-C. house with Jane Austen connections. Only park and gardens open to public. 43 different sorts of clematis. End Mar-end Oct, Mon-Fri 11-5, Sun 12-6. Closed Tues & Sat. Open to pre-booked parties at any time. Tel/fax. 013304 840107

Goudhurst (8 m E of Tunbridge Wells) Elegant Wealden village with church on ridge. St Mary the Virgin, impressive monuments to ancient Culpeper family. See also *Finchcocks*

Greatstone-on-Sea (8 m E of Tunbridge Wells) Beach with Listening Wall, designed to amplify sounds of war from across the Channel

Graveney (3 m NE of Faversham) All Saints: pretty church, with Grinling Gibbons pulpit

Groombridge Place (4 m SW of Tunbridge Wells, A264/B2110) 17th-C. country house (not open); charming garden and adventure park by Ivan Hicks: Apr-Oct 9-6 or dusk. Tel. 01892 863999; www.groombridge.co.uk.

Church in village by John Packer of Groombridge Place

Hadlow (4 m NE of Tonbridge) Castle tower built in *c.* 1838. Close cousin of Fonthill Tower, but better built and so still standing. Currently in parlous condition nevertheless. Mausoleum of its builder, Walter Barton May, in churchyard.

Herne Bay (3 m E of Whitstable) Museum of local interest: Mon-Sat 10-4, Sun in July and Aug 1-4.

St Bartholomew: neo-gothic by Caröe 'at his larkiest' (Pevsner)

Hever (10 m NW of Tunbridge Wells) St. Peter, with exceptional brass to Sir Thomas Bullen, Anne Boleyn's father. Lectern of 'monstrous ingenuity' (Betjeman).

Castle: Bullen/Boleyn family fortified house restored by Astors. 'Nowhere is Edwardian craftsmanship displayed with more extravagant panache, yet without damaging the medieval exterior' (Pevsner). Spectacular gardens. Mar-Nov daily: gardens 11-6, castle 12-6; Marc & Nov castle and gardens close at 4. Tel. 01732 865224, fax. 01732 866796; www.hevercastle.co.uk

Higham (SE of Gravesend) St Mary: mellow church with fine early door

Gad's Hill: only house owned by Dickens, where he died. Now school. Open 1st Sun of each month & BH Sun, 2-5. Tel. 01474 822366

Higham Park (3 m SE of Canterbury) Vast Belle-Epoque cum Art Deco country house currently being restored. Home of original Chitty Chitty Bang Bang. Apr-Oct, Sun-Thurs, 11-5. Tel. 01227 830830

Hildenborough (near Tonbridge) St John: thrilling interior by Ewan Christian (1843-44)

Hythe (W of Folkestone) St Leonard's: Spectacular 13th C chancel, built like a cathedral. One of two surviving ossuaries in England; bones to play with.

Ightham Mote (4 m E of Sevenoaks, off A227) 14th-C. moated house. Heavily restored. House Apr-Oct daily exc. Tues & Sat 10-5.30. NT. Tel. 01732 810378/811145, fax. 01732 811029

Isle of Sheppey Tautological, 'sheppey' meaning 'isle of sheep'. Sheerness, sacked by the Dutch on the way to Chatham. Bird sanctuary unwelcoming to surfboarders. Queensferry: combined rail and road bridge, vertical raiser.

Ivychurch (3 m NW of New Romney) St George: Romney marsh at its best, empty and serene

Kemsing (3 m NE of Sevenoaks) St Mary, simple village church with exquisite 13th C stained glass roundel, and other interesting glass and medieval pieces. Superb fittings by Ninian Comper

Kilndown (8 m SE of Tunbridge Wells) Completely preserved Ecclesiological church, started by A. Salvin, fitted out 1840-45

Knole (E of Sevenoaks) Vast 15th C and later country house, home of the Sackvilles. Important art and furniture. House Apr-Oct Wed-Sun & BH Mon 11-4; park daily, for pedestrians only; garden first Wed of each month May-Sep only 11-4. NT. Tel. 01732 462100/450608, fax. 01732 465528

Leeds Castle (E of Tunbridge Wells, M20 exit 8, B2163) Medieval moated castle, with park and maze. Open daily exc. Christmas Day, 30 June & 7 July. Mar-Oct 10-5; Nov-Feb 10-3. Tel. 01622 765400, www.leeds-castle. co.uk

Lenham (10 m SE of Maidstone) Typical and delightful Kentish village and church, St Mary, with monument to the fertile Mary Honywood; good pulpit, stalls and wall painting

Lullingstone (3 m S of Swanley) Church and castle side by side in Darenth valley – a hidden delight. St Botolph has some fine monuments – medieval, renaissance and rococo; cupboard font, rood screen.

Roman Villa: important mosaics. Open daily Apr-Sep 10-6; Nov-Mar 10-4. EH. Tel. 01322 863467

Lydd (8 m E of Rye) All Saints: grand and huge Romney Marsh church with Saxon fragments; tower perhaps by mason of Canterbury Cathedral, restored following bomb damage

Lydden Down (5 m NW of Dover) Unchanged chalk downland with fine orchids

Lympne (3 m W of Hythe) St Stephen: good Norman church side by side with the Castle, a late medieval manor house, 15th C. but originally 11th-C. residence of Archdeacons of Canterbury. Easter-Sept 10.30-18. Tel. 01303 267571

Site of Roman town (Lemanis). *See also* Port Lympne, 1 mile W of Lympne.

Maidstone Once-pleasant town centre with fine medieval town church and tithe barn. All Saints has the widest nave in Engand and fine perpendicular decoration, as well as being part of a lovely group of medieval collegiate buildings. Traffic now a nuisance.

St Luke, St Luke's road: Art Nouveau church by W. H. Seth-Smith

Museum & Art Gallery, St Faith's St: interesting collection: local Saxon archaeology, 17th C Dutch and Italian paintings, and natural history, costumes, ceramics, other local artefacts, in a 16th C house. Mon-Sat 10-5. Sun 11-4. Tel. 01622 754497

Tyrwhitt-Drake Museum of Carriages (formerly Archbishop's stable), Mill St. Apr-Oct daily 10-4.30. Tel. 01622 754497

Museum of Kent Life, Cobtree, Lock Lane, Sandling. Commemoration of the history of hop-picking. Mar-Oct 10-5.30 daily. Tel. 01622 763936, fax. 01622 662024, www.museum-kentlife.co.uk

Marden (7 m S of Marden) St Michael and All Angels: stained glass by important modern maker Patrick Reyntiens, 1962, still influenced by Sutherland

Margate Now seedy seaside town, but has some attractive atchitecture. Beloved of J. M. W. Turner (to whom a strikingly obtrusive museum is to be built) and home town of Tracey Emin.

Shell Grotto, Grotto Hill: superb shell-encrusted grotto, probably 18th C though claimed to be earlier. Easter-Oct, 10-5, winter weekends 11-4

Mereworth (6 m W of Maidstone) Castle is one of the great monuments of English Palladianism

St Lawrence: spectacular but anonymous mid 18th C classical church, which retains its medieval monuments. Exterior 'a goulash of famous London churches' (Pevsner), interior superb

Mersham (3 m SE of Ashford) St John the Baptist: worth seeing for its extraordinary west window.

Mersham le Hatch: first house by Adam after his return from Rome. P.

Minster in Sheppey (N of Isle of Sheppey) St Mary and St Sexburga: considerable remains of late 7th C nunnery of St. Sexburga incorporated in medieval church

Minster in Thanet (5 m W of Ramsgate) St Mary : grand church with exquisite 13th C vaulted chancel: 'nothing short of majestic' (Jenkins); misericords

Mount Ephraim (Hernhill, 6 m W of Canterbury, between A2 and A299) Park *c.*1800, garden, 1912, with topiary and view of Thames. Gardens Easter–mid-Sept. 1-6, BH Mon 11-6. Group bookings in advance only. Tel. 01227 751496, fax. 01227 750940, www.mountephraimgardens.co.uk

Nettlestead (3 m SW of Maidstone) St. Mary, small but important 15th C church with some fine early glass; rebuilt after 1496 to hold collection of stained glass put together by John Pympe, lord of the next - door manor

New Romney (10 m E of Maidstone) St Nicholas: the principal church (and trading place) of the Cinque Ports before the disastrous storm of 1287. Its 'grave and satisfying simplicity' is the result of William Morris's campaign to prevent restoration by rebuilding: an early victory for his recently founded Society for the Preservation of Ancient Buildings – the 'Anti Scrape'. Reticulated windows 'a true high point in English art' (Jenkins)

Newington (3 m W of Sittingbourne) St. Mary the Virgin: well-known picturesque church in orchard setting with wall paintings and a giant font cover

Northfleet (2 m W of Gravesend) St Botolph; church of many periods in dramatic setting

Nurstead Court (2 m N of Meopham) Medieval hall house with Victorian additions; a faded and eccentric delight inside Tel. 0800 0934935 for opening times

Old Romney (8 m E of Rye) St Clement: a fine Romney Marsh church with extensive 18th C fittings

Ospringe (SW of Faversham) Maison Dieu: remains of medieval pilgrims' hospice; museum. Easter-Oct, Sat, Sun & BH Mon 2-5.

Owletts see under Cobham

Pashley Manor (near Ticehurst, NW of Hastings, A21) Tudor half-timbered house (1550) with Queen Anne rear façade (1720). Park and gardens: Apr-Sep, Tues-Thurs, Sat & BH Mon 11-5. Oct garden only Mon-Fri 11-4. Tel. 01580 200692

Patrixbourne (3 m SE of Canterbury) St Mary; gorgeous Norman doorway, collection of Swiss stained glass

Pattyndenne Manor (S of Goudhurst, E of Tunbridge Wells, A262, B2079) Fine 16th-C half-timbered house. Guided tour by owner, by appointment. Tel. 01580 211361

Penshurst (7 m NW of Tunbridge Wells, B2176) A Kentish village at its best.
    Penshurst Place: Medieval and later country house with toy museum. House Apr-Sept 12-5.30 (Sat till 4); garden 10.30-6; also weekends in March. Tel. 01892 870307, fax. 01892 870866, www.penshurstplace. com

Plaxtol (6 m E of Sevenoaks) Attractive village with rare Commonwealth church.
    Old Soar: stone house with solar, EH

Port Lympne (Lympne, 3 m W of Hythe, B2067) Sir Philip Sassoon's country house 1911-13, magnificently enlarged and redecorated in 1920's; later owned by John Aspinall. Terraced garden and zoo. Daily except Christmas Day, opens at 10. Tel. 01303 264647 *See also* Lympne

Queenborough (2 m S of Sheerness) Once a royal port; Holy Trinity church with fine views from tower

Quex House, see Birchington

Rainham (2 m E of Chatham) St Margaret; medieval church with exceptional fittings and decoration

Ramsgate Late Georgian and Victorian seaside town: cliffs and harbour.

St Augustine's: Pugin's own church (now a Benedictine abbey, and mutilated in wake of Vatican 2) next to his own house, The Grange (now Landmark Trust).

St George: spectacular Georgian Perpendicular revival church

Reculver (3 m E of Herne Bay) St Mary's Abbey: only two towers survive from the Augustinian church wantonly demolished in 1809. Remains of one of the earliest Roman fortresses

Richborough Roman Fort (1½ m N of Sandwich) Museum of Roman excavations. Apr-Sep 10-6 daily; Oct 10-5 daily; Nov Wed-Sun 10-4; Dec-Feb Sat & Sun 10-4; Mar Wed-Sun 10-4. Closed 24-26 Dec and 1 Jan. EH. Tel. 01304 612013

Rochester Ancient town with attractive High Street.

Cathedral: Venerable, loveable, but not magnificent Norman cathedral (do not see Canterbury on the same day) with charming 19th C turrets, E. English quire, beautiful doors and other fittings

Charles Dickens Centre, Eastgate House, High St. Oct-Mar 10-4; Apr-Sep 10-6, closed Christmas and Boxing Day. Tel. 01634 844176

Restoration House, 17-19 Crow Lane: Miss Havisham's house, recently restored. June-Sep, daily 10-5. Tel. 01634 848520, www.restorationhouse.co.uk

Rochester Castle: Norman Bishop's castle, Apr-Sep 10-6 daily; Oct 10-4 daily;

Nov-March 10-4 daily. Closed 24-26 Dec and 1 Jan. EH. Tel. 01634 402276

Rolvenden (3 m SW of Tenterden) Weatherboarded village; monument by Lutyens in St Mary the Virgin, a fine and typical Kentish church.

Great Maytham Hall. Lutyens house (1910) built around George I core. Secret garden that inspired Frances Hodgson Burnett. May-Sep, Wed & Thurs 2-5. Tel. 01580 241346.

Romney Marsh Unique flat landscape, quite unlike the fens or Holland. See *Lydd, Old Romney, New Romney, Brenzett, St Mary in the Marsh, etc. etc.*

St Margaret's at Cliffe (4 m NE of Dover) Once popular seaside resort, favourite of Noël Coward and Ian Fleming.

St Margaret of Antioch: Norman church with 'sumptuous' (Betjeman) carving

St Mary in the Marsh (2 m N of New Romney) Unrestored Romney Marsh church

St Nicholas at Wade (6 m W of Margate) Home of Poet Laureate Robert Bridges. Handsome church St Nicholas with good carving

Sandwich Miraculously preserved Cinque Port, famous for its second hand bookshops. Some fine churches (including St Clement, Norman and later, with angel-roof). Check www.open-sandwich.co.uk

Guildhall: guided tours Tue-Thurs, 11.30 and 2.30. Guildhall Museum Tues-Sat 10.30-4, closed 12.30-2 Tues, Wed & Fri; Sun 2-4.

The Salutation: country house in Queen Anne style by Edwin Lutyens, 1911, with garden by Gertrude Jekyll. P

Royal St George's Golf Club: celebrated course
See also Richborough Roman Fort

Scotney Castle (near Lamberhurst, 8 m S of Tunbridge Wells, A21) Ruins of moated castle set in Edwardian rose and rhododendron gardens. Garden: April–Oct Wed–Sun & BH Mon 11-6; open some days in March. Old castle buildings open same hours but only May–mid-Sep. Estate: car park and walks open all year. NT. 19th C house by Salvin private. NT. Tel. 01892 891081, fax. 01892 890110

Sevenoaks Pleasant town centre. H. G. Wells lived in 1894 at 23 Eardley Road, where he finished writing *The Time Machine*.
The Vine: one of the oldest cricket grounds in England, 1734.
Riverhill House (1 m S): Georgian country house in pretty gardens

Shoreham (5 m N of Sevenoaks, A225) Idyllic village in Darenth 'Valley of Vision', where the romantic landscape painter Samuel Palmer lived in Water House near bridge (1826-34), and painted surrounding villages as earthly paradise. Graham Sutherland lived in neighbouring village Trottiscliffe (1936 onwards).
St Peter and St Paul: good medieval church with one of the best rood screens in England

Sissinghurst Castle (16 m S of Maidstone, 2 m E of Cranbrook, A262) Tudor gatehouse surrounded by Vita Sackville-West's famous garden. Apr–mid Oct, Tues-Fri 1-6.30, Sat, Sun & Good Fri 10-6.30. Ticket office and exhibitions open at 12 Tues-Fri. NT. Tel. 01580 710700/ 710701

Smallhythe Place (N of Rye, B208 2 m S of Tenterden) Ellen Terry Museum, 16th-C. half-timbered country house, where the Shakespearian actress lived from 1903 until her death in 1928. Memorabilia of herself and other actors. May–mid Oct, Sat-Wed 1.30-6 or dusk if earlier; open Good Fri. NT. Tel. 01580 762334

Smarden (12 m SE of Maidstone) Picturesque village. St Michael, 'the Barn of Kent', with vast medieval nave

Speldhurst (2 m NW of Tunbridge Wells) Handsome village. St Mary neo-gothic with excellent Morris glass

Staplehurst (8 m S of Sevenoaks) All Saints has famous early door. Pretty farmhouses in vicinity

Stone (2 m E of Dartford) St Mary the Virgin: superb 13th C interior with some Victorian vaulting, in dismal setting

Stoneacre (Otham, 4 m E of Maidstone, A20) Fine half-timbered house in Weald, *c.*1480, restored 1920's by art historian Aymer Vallance. Farm garden, particularly beautiful in the spring. Apr–mid Oct, Wed, Sat & BH Mon 2-6. NT. Tel. 01622 862157

Tenterden (10 m SW of Ashford) Town with attractive houses. St Mildred has superb tower

Teynham (3 m E of Sittingbourne) 'The cherry garden and apple orchard of Kent' (Lambarde) with imposing church

Tonbridge Pleasant small town with medieval church, St Peter and St Paul, and remains of castle
Castle gatehouse *c.*1300. Open all year Mon-Sat 9-4; Sun & BH Mon 10.30-4; closed Christmas Day and New Year's

Day; grounds open all year. Tel. 01732 770929

Chequers Inn, High Street. 15th C. inn, tel. 01732 358957

Portreeve's House, East St. 16th C house

Tudeley (near Tonbridge) All Saints: unforgettable stained glass by Chagall

Tunbridge Wells Largely delightful town with good suburbs.

Pantiles: 17th C shopping precinct.

Church of King Charles the Martyr: important and beautiful 17th C church with superb plasterwork.

Museum and Art Gallery, Civic Centre, Mount Pleasant: town & regional history, Tunbridge Ware etc. Mon-Sat (not Easter Sat or BH Mon) 9.30-5. Tel. 01892 554171.

Upnor Castle (2 m NE of Rochester) Elizabethan coastal fort, 1559 near historic 18th C barracks. EH.

Walmer Castle Henry VIII coastal fort, 1540: Apr-Sept daily 10-6; Oct daily 10-5; Nov, Dec & Mar Wed-Sun 10-4; Jan-Feb Sat & Sun only 10-4. Closed 24-26 December and when Lord Warden is in residence. Tel. 01304 364288

Westerham (5 m W of Sevenoaks) Attractive small town with two interesting houses:

Quebec House: childhood home of General Wolfe, victor at Quebec (1759). Georgian interiors, memorabilia. Apr-Oct Tues & Sun 2-6. NT. Tel. 01372 453401

Squerryes Court: William and Mary House, 1681: park, formal garden and topiary. Apr-Sep, Wed, Sat, Sun & BH Mon, gardens 12-5.30, house 1.30-5. Tel. 01959 562345/563118, fax. 01959 565949

Westgate (1½ m E of Margate) Victorian seaside town preserved in aspic. Site of first bungalows built in England (named after tea planters' houses in Bengal).

Westwell (3 m N of Ashford) St Mary: ordinary looking village church, but inside 'a village cathedral' (Betjeman). Beautiful 13th C vaulted chancel, triple-arched screen, 'gothic at is most diverting and beautiful (Jenkins)

Wingham (6 m E of Canterbury) Village with fine houses. St Mary has seen vicissitudes but has fine monuments

Woodchurch (4 m E of Tenterden) Pretty Kentish village houses and green. All Saints 'one of the most beautiful churches in Kent' (Betjeman) – a plain nave with light-filled chancel

Wrotham (8 m N of Tonbridge) St George: interesting porch, screen and fine brasses. Lady Chapel by Comper

Wye (4 m NW of Ashford) Pretty market town.

St Gregory and St Mark, church in pleasant medieval grouping of buildings, light and elegant Georgian interior

NCC reserve: – one of the most important chalk grassland habitats, particularly fine orchids. 5 m NW is the superb chalk woodland of Yockletts Bank

Surrey

Albury Park (1½ m E of Albury, A25/A248 E of Guildford) Astonishingly restored country house, with Pugin sweeping away earlier work. Park with tulip tree etc. Garden originally by the Evelyn family, 1655-58, with terraces and water-tunnel. In park, delightful church with fervent Pugin decorations, 1839 and later. May-Sept, Wed & Thurs 2-4.30. Tel. 01483 202964

Box Hill (2 m E of Dorking) Superb, if over-popular, chalk downland with yew and box and other trees. Colonies of edible snails. Wonderful views. NT

Brooklands Museum (off B374, between Weybridge and Byfleet) Museum of car racing and aircraft. Tues-Sun & BH Mon, winter 10-3, summer 10-4 Tel 01932 857381.

Brookwood Cemetery (2 m W of Woking) Once largest cemetery in the world. Houses remains of St Edward the Martyr and Rebecca West, amongst many, many others. Fine trees. Guided tours, tel. Margaret Hobbs (secretary of Brookwood Cemetery Society) on 01344 891041

Burpham Court Farm Park (off A320 near Guildford) Rare breeds farm. Daily 10-6, check beforehand in winter. Tel. 01483 576089

Carshalton (1 m E of Sutton) Carshalton House with Rococo decoration, now girl's school. Occasionally open.

Little Holland House, 40 Beeches Avenue. Perfectly preserved Arts and Crafts house built by Frank Dickinson and furnished for himself. Tel. 8770 4781

Cheam (1 m SW of Sutton) Now London suburb.

Nonsuch Mansion, near site of Henry VIII's palace, by Wyattville, occasionally open.

Whitehall, small Tudor house kitted out as museum of interiors. Wed-Sun & BH Mon 2-5, Sat 10-5.

Chertsey (3 m NW of Weybridge) Museum, with good textile collection, Tues-Fri 12.30-4.30, Sat 11-4.

St Peter: chancel medieval but rest a 'repellent bit of Gothick' (Pevsner)

St Ann's Hill: famous views from iron age hill fort and park once owned by Charles James Fox, sadly spoilt by adjacent M3

Chilworth (3 m SE of Guildford, A248) St Thomas: wonderful Arts and Crafts church.

Manor: 17th-C. park and terrace garden, probably copied from Albury. Mysterious prehistoric circular monuments. Open one weekend a month between Apr-Jul. Tel. 01483 561414

Clandon Park (West Clandon, 3 m E of Guildford, A247) Neo-Palladian country house with astounding hall and outstanding porcelain collection and park. Apr-Oct, Tues-Thurs, Sun & BH Mon, house and garden 11-5; museum 12-5 NT. Tel. 01483 222482

Claremont (near Esher, A307) 18th C. country house by Capability Brown and Henry Holland (with his pupil John Soane), now boarding school. Tours by appointment. Tel. 01372 467841; www.claremont-school.co.uk. Of the original house by Vanbrugh the Belvedere alone survives.

Claremont Landscape Garden,

Portsmouth Rd: early, historically important garden by William Kent and remodelled by Capability Brown. Summer daily 10-6, Winter 10-5 but closed Mon. NT. Tel. 01372 469421

Compton (2 m SW of Guildford) The Watts Gallery: paintings by Victorian G. F. Watts, who is buried in nearby graveyard overlooked by his wife's astonishing Chapel. Daily exc. Thurs 2-6; Oct-Apr additionally open 11-1 on Wed & Sat. Tel. 01483 810235, www.wattsgallery.org.uk. Chapel open daily all day

St Nicholas: Norman church with only surviving two-storey sanctuary in England, with a railing that may be 'the oldest architectural wood carving in an English church' (Jenkins)

Cranleigh (6 m S of Guildford) Pretty iron village, now submerged in modern housing etc.

Brooking Home Study Collection, 44 The Drive: collection of architectural details (main section now with University of Greenwich) put together entirely by the efforts of Charles Brooking. Open by appointment: contact 01483 274203, and during Heritage Open Days

Crosswater Farm (Crosswater Lane, Churt, A27 between Farnham & Haslemere) Six acres of woodland garden; over 500 different types of rhododendron. May-mid June 10-5. Tel. 01252 792698; www. rhododendrons.co.uk

Croydon Always an important suburb of London, though it prefers to see itself as an associated city; proud of its increasingly metropolitan architecture and tram system.

St Michael, Poplar Walk: magnificent church by Pearson.

Archbishop's Palace: favoured summer residence of Archbishops of Canterbury in middle ages. Open Heritage Days only.

Devil's Punchbowl (3 m N of Haslemere) Dramatic natural site, fine walks.

Egham (5 m NE of Chertsey) St John the Baptist: superb Denham monuments.

Royal Holloway College: magnificent Victorian French Renaissance buildings, and small but superb art collection, sadly reduced by wanton selling. Tel. 01784 443004 for visiting details

Epsom (3 m E of Leatherhead) Racing open to public; Tel. 01372 726311. Museum now closed. Occasional antique fairs. www.epsomderby. co.uk.

Esher (4 m SW of Kingston) Pleasant small town with a 'most lovable' (Betjeman), 'most endearing' (Pevsner, so often thought to be the antithesis of the poet in his taste) church, St George, with superb family pews and monuments to Princess Charlotte (who died at nearby Claremont)

On Esher Green the remaining gatehouse of a palace of a medieval bishop of Winchester, encased by William Kent in early Gothick.

Farnham (A287) Attractive small town with handsome main street.

Castle a seat of the Bishops of Winchester since 12th C. Guided tours for groups, by arrangement. Wed 1-4, except over Christmas. The Keep is EH: Apr-Sep 10-6; Oct 10-5. Tel. 01252 713393; www. farnhamcastle.com

Museum of Farnham, in George I Wilmer House, West St. Paintings, Cobbett memorabilia. Very child-friendly. Tues-Sat 10-5

Rural Life Centre, Tilford: largest collection of its kind in the south. Particularly strong on wheelwrighting. Arboretum. Mar-Oct. Wed-Sun & BH Mon 10-5; Nov-Feb Wed & Sun 11-4. Tel. 01252 795571; www.rural-life.org.uk

Frensham (4 m S of Farnham) Country Park: good example of Surrey heathland, Great Lake

Gatton (2 m N of Redhill) St Andrew, 'an involuntary museum from the attentions of someone who went on the Grand Tour with an acquisitive eye' (Pevsner). Family pew complete with fireplace. Gothick makeover, much Flemish woodwork.

Gatton Park, now a school, with the 'Town Hall' – a small 18thC pavilion where 'elections' for this notorious rotten borough were held

Godalming (4 m S of Guildford) Delightful small town, bijou Town Hall, and good medieval church (Sts Peter and Paul). Overlooked by Charterhouse School, magnificent if forbidding Victorian pile by Hardwick. Fine chapel by Sir Giles Gilbert Scott

Goddards (Abinger Common, 4 m SW of Dorking) Edwardian country house by Lutyens, 1898-1910. Garden originally by Gertrude Jekyll. Headquarters of Lutyens Trust. Only by appointment. Tel. 01306 730487; www.lutyenstrust.org.uk

Grafham (6 m S of Guildford) St Andrew: own parish church of architect Woodyer, who overcame Bishop Sumner's refusal to consecrate churches with screens by making the one here into the structural support of the roof

Great Bookham (3 m SW of Leatherhead) St Nicholas: weatherboarded tower and fine monuments

Guildford Town with steep High Street with some fine buildings (especially Guildhall) and views of the Hog's Back. Second hand bookshops and record shop. Outskirts well stocked with villas by Shaw, Voysey and Lutyens.

Abbot's Hospital: Fine Jacobean almshouses with many original fittings. P.

Castle, 11-12thC, in well-bedded municipal flower gardens

Cathedral, visible from afar, by Sir Edward Maufe (formerly Muff).

Guildford House Gallery, 155 High St: exemplary town house c. 1660; changing exhibitions of art and handicrafts, Tues-Sat 10-4.45. Tel. 01483 444740; www.guildfordhouse.co.uk

Guildford Museum, Castle Arch. Local collections, including much about Gertrude Jekyll. Mon-Sat 11-5. Tel. 01483 444751

Holy Trinity: dramatically broad church, monument to Archbishop Abbot, (founder of the Hospital) with columns on pedestals shaped as piles of books

Hascombe (4 m SE of Godalming) Picturesquely pretty village, centre of Lutyens country, with many early houses; one of the finest is his remodelling of Winkworth Farm, ½ m N of church.

St Peter: superbly preserved Victorian church (Woodyer)

Hatchlands Park (East Clandon, 4 m NE of Guildford, A246) Country house of Admiral Boscawen, c.1750, with interiors by Robert Adam. Collection of old keyboard instruments, paintings & furniture. Garden by Humphrey Repton & Gertrude Jekyll. Apr-Oct, Tue-Thur, Sun & BH Mon 2-5.30. NT. Tel. 01483 222482

Lingfield (4 m N of East Grinstead) St Peter and St Paul: 15th C church with fine monuments to Cobham family

Limpsfield (5 m W of Sevenoaks) Burial place of Delius, not for any local connection but because he wanted to lie in an English country churchyard. He was followed by Beecham and other musicians

Loseley House (3 m SW of Guildford) Tudor house with decorations from Henry VIII's ruined Nonsuch Palace, and hangings from Henry's banqueting tents. May-Sept, Wed-Sat 1-5. Tel. 01483 304440; www.loseley-park.com

Lower Kingswood (2 m N of Crawley, by Gatwick airport) St Michael: beautiful and entertaining church by William Burges

Lowfield Heath (2 m N of Reigate) Church of the Wisdom of God: Byzantine-style Victorian church with genuine Byzantine spolia

Munstead Wood (Heath Lane, Busbridge, S of Godalming, B2130) Home of Gertrude Jekyll, designed by Lutyens, 1896. Garden now being restored. Only by appointment. Tel. 01483 419618

Ockham (6 m NE of Guildford) All Saints: fine medieval church in delightful parkland setting. Monuments by Rysbrack and Voysey. Birthplace of William of Ockham, he of the razor

Ockley (6 m S of Dorking) Hanah Peschar Sculpture Garden, Black and White Cottage, Standen Lane, Ockley. Beautiful water gardens with sculptures, many for sale. Tel. 01306 627269

Oxenford (near Peper Harrow, 1½ m W of Godalming) Superb barn and gatehouse by Pugin, 'among his best buildings' (Pevsner). Also enlarged St Nicholas which has a fine 17th C monument,

Painshill Park (near Cobham, A245) Classical landscape park by Charles Hamilton. Lakes and many pavilions; wonderful grotto. All in process of restoration. Apr-Oct, Tues-Sun & BH Mon 10.30-6; Nov-Mar Tues-Sun exc Fri but inc BH Mon 11-4. Tel. 01932 868113 & 866743; www.painshill.co.uk

Polesden Lacey (3 m NW of Dorking) Country house with Edwardian interiors and Old Master paintings, superb park & gardens. House: Mar, Sat & Sun 1.30-4.30; Apr-end Oct, Wed-Sun 1.30-5.30. Park: 11-6. NT. Tel. 01372 458203/452408

Shere (5 m E of Guildford) Picture postcard village

Stanwell (near Heathrow) St Mary: fine monument (1622) by Nicholas Stone

Stoke d'Abernon (2 km SE of Cobham) Church in a lovely setting, 'possibly the classic example of bad restoration' (Pevsner). Britain's oldest brass. Pulpit with hour glass

Sutton Place (3 m N of Guildford) Tudor country house with park & gardens by Sir Geoffrey Jellicoe. Only by appointment. Tel. 01483 504455

Thursley (2 m N of Hindhead) St Michael: Victorianized church with extraordinary 15th C belfry construction. Monuments, including by Lutyens.

Beautiful dry and wet heath reserve, with superb bird and insect life

Titsey (2 m N of Oxted) Regency country house in heavily wooded landscape, with amusing interiors

Vann (8 m S of Guildford, A283, between

Hambledon & Chiddingfold) Gardens with water garden by Gertrude Jekyll, 1911. Open under the National Gardens Scheme for three weeks a year between Easter Monday and mid June; and by appointment. Tel. 01428 683413

Virginia Water (2 m SW of Egham) Beautiful lake, designed by the painter Thomas Sandby, with ruins (including columns from Leptis Magna) and a totem pole. Fine walks. Expensive suburbia, now including the Holloway Sanatorium, turned into flats. Fort Belvedere, an 18th C folly, was Edward VIII's favourite house.

Waverley (2 m SE of Farnham) Abbey: ruins of the first Cistercian abbey in England; attractive setting
   Crooksbury House: one of Lutyens' best, and earliest houses

Winkworth Arboretum (2 m SE of Godalming, B2130) Park on spectacular site, with rare trees and shrubs. All year till dusk. NT. Tel. 01483 208477.

Wisley Gardens (7 m NE of Guildford, A3) Royal Horticultural Society garden. Display of vast selection of plants and garden shrubs. Mon-Sat 10-7. Tel. 01483 224234

Witley (3 m S of Godalming) Highly picturesque village, typical Surrey vernacular. Witley Court (now a conference centre) famous for its underwater ballroom.

Wotton (3 m SW of Dorking) Picturesque church, St John, in pretty country. John Evelyn buried here; his family occupied Wotton House, where the gardens, although not the house, largely survive. Garden buildings include the ruined Tortoise House.

Sussex

Alfriston (near Seaford, B2108) Attractive village elegant 14th C church, St Andrew, and fine houses, including the 14th C Clergy House, the very first property acquired by NT. Apr-Oct daily except Tues & Fri 10-5; Nov-Dec Wed-Sun 11-4; Mar. weekends 11-4. Tel. 01323 870001

Amberley (3 m N of Arundel) 'One of the best show villages of Sussex' (Pevsner)
   Magnificent 13-14thC castle (see also Hotels)

Arlington (8 m E of Lewes) St Pancras has elements of all styles from Anglo-Saxon to Perpendicular

Arundel (10 m E of Chichester) Pleasant town dominated by castle, allegedly inspiration for Mervyn Peake's Gormenghast.
   Castle: Victorian family seat of Dukes of Norfolk. Art & furniture. St Nicholas, magnificent but divided church with fine tombs in the Fitzalan chapel, visited from the castle. Apr-Oct 11-5, daily exc. Sat. Tel. 01903 883136; www.arundelcastle.org
   St Philip Neri: the imitation French medieval church which dominates views of Arundel.

Bateman's (NW of Hastings, A265, ½ m S of Burwash) Country house of Rudyard Kipling. Apr-Oct 11-5 daily, exc. Thurs & Fri. Garden also open weekends in March, 11-4. NT. Tel. 01435 882302

Battle Abbey (7 m N of Hastings, B2100) Scene of so-called Battle of Hastings. Summer 10-6. EH. Tel. 01424 773792. Splendid but fragmentary remains of the Abbey erected in 1070. Pleasant town.

Bayham Abbey (3 m N of Wadhurst)

Extensive ruin of Premonstatensian Abbey in picturesque setting (Gothick villa etc.) EH

Beachy Head (3 m SW of Eastbourne) NT. Grandest cliff in the south-east. Magnificent views and walks along crumbling chalk. England's favourite suicide spot: at least one a month.

Bentley (near Halland, 7 m NE of Lewes, B2192) Tudor house, extended in 1960's by Raymond Erith. Park, gardens, wild duck reserve. Apr-Oct 10.30-4.30; Nov-Dec, Feb-Mar, Sat & Sun only. Closed Jan. Tel. 01825 840573

Bexhill-on-Sea (4 m SW of Hastings) De La Warr Pavilion (on beach) by Erich Mendelsohn & Serge Chermayeff, 1933-36 – a famous and exciting piece of modernism now at long last restored

Bignor (between Petworth and Arundel) Small village with 'exhilarating view near the church into an amphitheatre of the Downs' (Pevsner), and exemplary 15-C cottage, 'The Old Shop'.
Roman villa with 4th C mosaic floors. Mar-Oct 10-6 daily exc Mon, tel. 01798 869259

Bodiam Castle (3 m S of Hawkhurst, E of A229) Unusually well preserved medieval moated castle (1385-89) restored by Lord Curzon, then Viceroy of India, given to NT in 1925. Mid Feb-Oct daily 10-6; Nov-mid Feb Sat & Sun 10-4. Tel. 01580 830436

Bosham (3 m W of Chichester) Holy Trinity: grand Anglo-Saxon parish church with later additions

Boxgrove (5 m E of Chichester, A27) Benedictine Priory church with important

Early English choir, delightful Tudor painting in the vaults (c. 1550). De La Warr chantry chapel (1532)

Bramber (N of Worthing, A283) Ruined castle. St Mary's House and garden: 15th-C. half-timbered house with Elizabethan painted rooms and collections relating to the poet Thomas Hood, May-Sep, Thur, Sun & BH Mon 2-5.30, Sun 10-6. Tel. 01903 816205

Brightling (5 m NW of Battle) St Thomas Becket: distinguished by the Fuller Mausoleum (Smirke); nearby Brightling Park rejoices in a number of Fuller's other follies

Brighton Busy but still pleasant seaside town, with many interesting buildings; famous for antique shops.
Museum and Art Gallery, Church St: important ethnological collection, Dalí's Mae West sofa, art nouveau and art deco furniture, porcelain, Old Master, Victorian and modern paintings, including a collection by the local artist Glyn Philpot. Tues 10-7, Wed-Sat & BH Mon 10-5, Sun 2-5. Tel. 01273 290900
Booth Museum of Natural History, 194 Dyke Road. Victorian collection of stuffed birds in picturesque building, now augmented with much other natural history. Tel. 01273 292777
Preston Manor, Preston Park: Georgian house of 1738 with alterations 1905. Edwardian household items. Mon-Sat except Thursday 10-5, Sun 2-5. Tel. 01273 290900
The Royal Pavilion: April-Sep: daily 9.30-5; Oct-March daily 10-5. Tel. 01273 298822; www.royalpavilion.org.uk
Theatre Royal, New Road. Tel. 01273 328488; www.theambassadors.com/theatre royal

St Bartholomew, Ann St: 'an unforgettable experience' (Pevsner) – an immense neo-gothic church of the highest quality, plain but richly furnished. Designed to the Biblical specifications of Noah's Ark.

St Martin, Lewes Rd: finely fitted out Victorian church

St Michael, Victoria Rd: follows designs first by Bodley and then, grandiose, by Burges; much Pre-Raphaelite glass and decoration

St Paul, West St: reredos by Burne-Jones

St Peter, Victoria Gardens: early church by Sir Charles Barry

Camber (1¼ m S of Rye) One of the deepest beaches in the south; Tudor dodecagonal castle

Castle Goring (1½ m N of Goring) Superb and surprising Gothick-Palladian house by Biagio Rebecca. In parlous condition, but may be rescued

Charleston Farmhouse (Firle, 6 m E of Lewes, A27) Country home of Vanessa Bell and Duncan Grant, meeting-place of the Bloomsbury Group. Apr, May, Sep, Oct, Wed-Sun & BH Mon 2-5; July & Aug, Wed-Sat 11.30-5, Sun & BH Mon 2-5. Tel. 01323 811266; www. charleston. org.uk

Chichester Attractive medieval town with 'the most typical English cathedral' (Pevsner), unforgettably dominating the landscape. Evensong 5.30 (exc. Wed), Sun 3.30

Chichester Festival Theatre, Oaklands Park. Exciting building by Powell and Moya; celebrated theatre festival. Tel. 01243 781312

Pallant House Gallery, 9 North Pallant: Queen Anne town house with Georgian furniture, porcelain, 20th-C. British art. May be enlarged by the architect St John Wilson to house his collection of modern art; it is to be hoped that this will not be a provincial version of his 'academy for secret policemen', the British Library. Temporary exhibitions. Tue-Sat 10-5, Sun 12.30-5. Tel. 01243 774557, www.pallant-housegallery.com

St Mary's Hospital, St Martin's Square: medival almshouse still in operation

The Mechanical Music and Doll Collection, Church Rd, Portfield: musical boxes, barrel organs, pianolas, phonographs etc. June-Sep, Wed 1-4. Tel. 01243 372646

Clayton (6 m N of Brighton) St John the Baptist: 11th-13th C church with very fine wall paintings

Cowfold (5 m S of Horsham) Pretty village, with one of Britain's finest brasses in St Peter

Cuckfield (9 m SE of Horsham) Modest and pretty village. Holy Trinity, large medieval church attractively restored.

See *Borde Hill* and *Nymans*'

Denmans Garden (Fontwell, A27 between Chichester and Arundel) 20th-C. garden. Mar-Oct daily 9-5. Tel. 01243 542808; www.denmans-garden.co.uk

Ditchling (N of Brighton) Former artists' colony run by Eric Gill, documented in Ditchling Museum, Church Lane. Tue-Sat 10.30-5, Sun 2-5. Tel. 01273 844744

Anne of Cleves House: 'eminently picturesque' (Pevsner)

East Grinstead (12 m W of Tunbridge Wells) Picturesque town centre. Longest continuous run of 14th C timber-framed buildings in England

Sackville College: 17th C almshouses with hammerbeam roof. Mid-June to Mid-Sep, Wed-Sat 2-5. Tel. 01892 770179

St Margaret's Convent: one of the pioneer works of the Ecclesiological movement, by G. E. Street

Saint Hill Manor (2 m SE): Georgian house with entertaining relics of several owners, including the Maharajah of Jaipur and L. Ron Hubbard. Now part of Church of Scientology. Open daily 2-5

East Guldeford (1 m NE of Rye) St Mary: only Romney Marsh church in Sussex

Eastbourne Old fashioned seaside town; grand seafront with famous Grand Hotel.

Towner Art Gallery, Manor Gardens, High St: 19th & 20th-C. British art, changing exhibitions, regional history. Tues-Sat 10-5, Sun & BH Mon 2-5. Tel. 01323 411688

Firle Place (5 m E of Lewes, A27) Country home of Gage family since 15th C; Tudor house altered c.1730, important art and furniture collections. June-Sep, Wed, Thur, Sun & BH Mon 1.45-4.15. Tel. 01273 858335; www.firlestreet.freeserve.co.uk

Fishbourne (near Chichester) Roman Villa & Museum with famous mosaics: Feb, Nov and first half Dec daily 10-4; Mar-July, Sep-Oct daily 10-5; Aug daily 10-6; Jan Sat & Sun only 10-4. Tel. 01243 785859

Glynde Place (3 m E of Lewes) Country house of 1579 with art collection. May Sun & BH Mon, June-Sept, Wed, Sun & BH Mon 2-5. Tel. 01273 858224

Glyndebourne (3 m E of Lewes) Unattractive house now joined to equally unattractive opera house, in blissful setting. Great opera, and, less well-known, fine paintings in the beautiful Organ Room. Inside, the opera house has superb acoustics and sight lines, and as it is now much larger, there is always a good chance for return tickets or even standing room. Season lasts most of the summer, and there are recitals in the winter. Ring 01273 813813 for further details

Goodwood House (4 m NE of Chichester) Country house of Duke of Richmond, large art and furniture collections (magnificent Canaletti, Stubbs etc.). Easter & May-Oct, Sun & Mon 2-5; Aug, Tue-Thur 2-5. Tel. 01243 755000, www.goodwood.co.uk

Goodwood Races. Tel. 01243 774107

Sculpture at Goodwood: Hat Hill Sculpture Foundation Changing open-air exhibition of contemporary British sculpture, information centre, lectures etc. Mar-Oct Thur-Sat 10.30-4.30. Tel. 01243 538449

Hammerwood Park (3 m E of East Grinstead A264) Beautifully restored late Georgian country house, 'a demonstration of primeval force' (Pevsner) built 1792 by Benjamin H. Latrobe, architect of the Capitol in Washington and the cathedral in Baltimore. Led Zeppelin lived here. June-Sep, Wed, Sat & BH Mon 2-5.30. Tel. 01342 850594

Hamsey (2 m N of Lewes) St Peter: handsome, isolated medieval church, relatively unrestored

Hardham (1 m S of Pulborough) St Botolph: Saxon church with 12th-C wall paintings, possibly the earliest in Enland, rather faded.

Hardham Priory: exquisite fragment in beautiful setting

Hastings Cinque Port in constant decline since the 12th C, with some recovery with advent of sea-bathing. Now, with adjoining St Leonards (created by Decimus Burton's father) a seaside town with old churches and ruined castle. St Mary in the Castle, based on the Pantheon, partly dug out of the rock. Holy Trinity, Robertson St, a virtuoso display by Teulon

Haywards Heath (11 m N of Brighton) Commuter town. Borde Hill Gardens, Balcombe Road: superb historical-botanical collections. Tel. 01444 412151

Herstmontceux Castle (Hailsham, A27 N of Eastbourne) 15th C. Renaissance moated castle. Science centre in former Observatory. International Study Centre of Queen's University, Ontario since 1993. Park & garden: April-Sep 10-5, Oct 10-4 Science centre. Guided tours of the castle. available, tel. 01323 832816

Hove (W of Brighton) Grand but more genteel continuation of Brighton. Proposals to build new and enormous tower blocks by Frank Gehry
13 Brunswick Square: Regency Town House: museum of Brighton life and architecture from its golden period; currently only guided tours, check www.regency-town-house.org.uk

Hurstpierpoint (9 m N of Brighton) Georgian houses in village.
Danny, 1 m S: Elizabethan mansion, now used as residential flats for the elderly; collection of shoes. May-Sep, Wed-Thurs afternoons. Tel 01273 833000

Lancing College (near Shoreham, W of Brighton, A259) Private school founded 1848, with monumental neo-gothic chapel, begun 1868 (R. H. Carpenter). Check first for visiting times. Tel. 01273 452213; www.lancingcollege. co.uk

Leonardslee Gardens (Lower Beeding, 5 m SE of Horsham, A281/A279) Begun 1889, magnificent collection of rhododendrons, azaleas, camellias, magnolias. Apr-Oct daily 9.30-4.30. Tel. 01403 891212

Lewes (6 m E of Brighton) Highly picturesque country town, with many bookshops. Castle & Museum, High St: archaeological finds. Mon-Sat 10-5.30 (closed Mon in Jan), Sun & BH Mon 10-5.30 . Tel. 01273 486290
Anne of Cleves House Museum, 169 High St: 16thC half-timbered museum of local history. Mar-Oct Mon-Sat 10-5, Sun 12-5; Nov-Feb Tues-Sat 10-5. Tel. 01273 474610
Market Day: Monday

Littlehampton (W of Worthing) 'Miniature Belgravia' (Pevsner) for a few streets of seaside terraces. Titular town of Osbert Lancaster's celebrated Countess, Maudie

Mayfield (8 m S of Tunbridge Wells) Pretty village. Mayfield Palace, a seat of the Archbishops of Canterbury and later of Sir Thomas Gresham, is now a school. The superb Great Hall is the school chapel. Ring 01435 874600 for visiting details.
Braylsham Castle: beautiful neo-Gothic moated house built in the 1990's. P.

Michelham Priory (7 m N of Eastbourne, B2108) Remains of Augustinian monastery (1229) with Elizabethan alterations, 14th-C. gatehouse, musical instruments, Sussex wrought iron. Mar-Oct 11-5.30; Feb & Nov 11-4. Tel. 01323 844224

Midhurst (6 m W of Petworth) Large village full of attractive houses from all periods.

Just to the NE is Cowdray Castle, a grand ruined Tudor house, only visible from outside. World-famous polo all summer; see www.cowdraypolo.co.uk, or tel. 01730 813257

Newtimber Place (4½ m S of Hurstpierpoint) Moated 16th C house with striking neoclassical murals

Northiam (6 m NW of Rye, A268) Pretty weatherboarded village.

Brickwall House 17th C country house, garden with historical plants and modern topiary chessmen. Stables by Smirke. Now a college. Open by appointment. Tel. 01797 253388

Great Dixter: 15th-C half-timbered country house, restored by Lutyens (1910), with imported period extensions. Gardens 1910 and later, originally by Nathaniel Lloyd, author of *Garden Craftsmanship in Yew and Box* (standard work on topiary), enlarged by son Christopher, one of Britain's most famous garden writers (*The Well-Tempered Gardener, etc. etc*). Apr-Oct 14-5 daily exc. Mon. Tel. 01797 252878; www.greatdixter. co.uk

Nymans Garden (Handcross, 4 m S of Crawley, A23/B2114) One of England's loveliest gardens. Mar-Oct, Wed-Sun & BH Mon 11-6; Nov-Mar Sat-Sun 11-4. NT. Tel. 01444 400321. House mostly ruined, Lady Rosse's library and drawing room built in her 'potting sheds'

Parham House (3½ m S of Pulborough, A283) Tudor country house with art collection, park and maze. House: April-Sep, Wed, Thurs, Sun & BH Mon; also Tues and Fri in Aug, 2-5. Park: 12-5. Tel. 019103 742021

Regothicized medieval church, St Peter, in park.

Petworth (15 m NE of of Chichester, A272/A283) Petworth House: grand 17th-C. house on Downs with dazzling art collection and park by Capability Brown. House Apr-Oct, Sat-Wed 11-5.30, Sat & Sun 1-5.30. Park: 8 till dusk. NT. Tel. 01798 342207

Small and charming town nestles around the house's walls. Antique shops.

Cottage Museum, 346 High St: memorial to life of the estate workers at the beginning of the 20th C

Pevensey Castle (NE of Eastbourne) Impressive Roman and medieval fortress, parts of which were discreetly converted to modern military use in the War. Apr-Oct 10-6; Nov-Mar, Wed-Sun 10-4. EH, Tel. 01323 762604

Playden (1 m N of Rye) St Michael: landmark church with interesting screens

Rodmell (4 m SE of Lewes) Monk's House, home of Leonard & Virginia Woolf. Apr-Oct, Wed & Sat 2-5.30. NT. Tel. 01372 453401

Rotherfield (5 m N of Heathfield) St Denys, unspoilt church with early wall paintings and attractive furniture; outstanding Burne-Jones glass

Rye Delightful but popular Cinque Port town with literary connections. Grand medieval church (St Mary) with 16th C clock.

Lamb House, West St: home of Henry James, and E. F. Benson. Apr-Oct, Wed & Sat 2-6. NT. Tel. 01372 453401

Rye Art Gallery, 107 High St and Ockman Lane: 20th-C. British art (Burra,

Epstein, Sutherland etc.) Changing exhibitions. 10.30-1, 2-5. Tel. 01797 223218

Rye Museum, Ypres Tower: local history in 13th-C. tower. Easter-Oct 10.30-1, 2-5. Tel. 01797 226728

Selham (3 m E of Midhurst) St James, with interesting capitals

Sheffield Park Garden (between Lewes and East Grinstead, A275) Park by Capability Brown and Humphrey Repton. Mar-Oct Tues-Sun 10.30-5; Nov-Dec Tues-Sun 10.30-3; Jan-Feb Sat & Sun 10.30-3. NT. Tel. 01825 790231. The house, by James Wyatt, is private.

Shipley (S of Horsham) Good Norman church in tiny village. Pretty country. Fine windmill

Shoreham-by-Sea (between Brighton & Worthing) Little harbour town with two exceptional Norman churches: St Mary de Haura (i.e. Le Havre) and St Nicholas

Singleton (6 m N of Chichester, A286) Weald and Downland Open Air Museum with approx 40 houses 14th-19th C. Rare breed days, activity days for children. Mar-Oct 10.30-6; Nov-Feb Wed, Sat & Sun 10.30-1. Tel. 01243 811348/811363, www. wealddown.co.uk

Sompting (2 m NE of Worthing) St Mary: Unique 11th C tower with 'Rhenish helm', tower arch with almost Ionic capitals: 'it is somehow incredibly moving, this fumbling recognition of the classical past which was already so many centuries ago' (Pevsner)

South Harting (12 m NW of Chichester) St Mary and St Gabrield: interesting church in fine village position; roofs 'an anthology of Elizabethan carpentry' (Pevsner)

Standen (2 m S of East Grinstead, B2110) Former country home of London lawyer, designed by Philip Webb 1892-94. Superb interiors by Morris & Co. Late Victorian garden. House: Apr-Oct, Wed-Sun & BH Mon 1-5. Garden open till 6, and also 113 Nov- mid Dec. NT. Tel. 01342 323029

Steyning (5 m N of Worthing) Good large village with Norman church (St. Andrew) with very fine interior.

Local museum, daily Tues-Wed, Fri-Sat 10.30-12.30 & 2.30-4, or 4.30 in summer; Sun & BH Mon in afternoons only

Tortington (2 m SW of Arundel) St Thomas: charming rustic church with Norman carving

Trotton (3 m W of Midhurst) St George: simple church with important brasses

Upmarden (8 m NW of Chichester) St Michael, remote church of great simplicity; 'everything is just right' (Betjeman)

Uppark (near South Harting, B2146, between Petersfield and Chichester) Meticulously restored country house, c. 1690. Gardens. Landscape park by Humphrey Repton. Apr-Oct Sun-Thurs 1-5, garden 11-5. NT. Tel. 01730 825857

Wakehurst Place Garden (near Ardingly, B2028, north of Haywards Heath) Rare exotic trees and plants, special collection of birches. Outpost of Royal Botanic Gardens, Kew. Elizabethan manor house. Daily Apr-Sept 10-7; Oct 10-5; Nov-Jan 10-4; Feb 10-5; Mar 10-6. NT. Tel. 01444 894066

West Chiltington (11 m N of Worthing) St Mary: unspoilt church with good medieval wall paintings

West Dean (5 m N of Chichester, A286) Former country home of collector Edward James, now college of art, handicrafts and restoration. Courses for diploma, summer school, conferences. Tel. 01243 811301. Only the park, gardens & arboretum are open to public: Mar, Apr & Oct 11-5; May-Sep 10-5. Tel. 01243 818210; www.westdean. org.uk

West Hoathly (7 m N of Haywards Heath) Pretty village. The Priest's House, a medieval cottage, is now a museum of Sussex life. Mar-Oct Tue-Sat & BH Mon 10.30-5.30, Sun 12-5.30

Winchelsea (2 m SE of Rye) Charming remains of planned medieval town, with superb early 14thC church

Withyham (3 m WSW of Groombridge) St Michael: medieval church rebuilt in 17th C and including superb Sackville chapel: monuments by Cibber, Flaxman, Chantrey. Gatehouse of Sackville seat of Old Buckhurst survives just to the south

Worth (3 m E of Crawley) St Nicholas: superbly preserved Saxon church, chancel arch largest of its period to survive

Hampshire

Alton (8 m W of Farnham) Allen Gallery: excellent ceramics collection and other decorative arts (ask to see the Tichborne Spoons). Tue-Sat 10-5. Tel. 01420 82802

Ampfield (5 m SW of Winchester) Sir Harold Hillier Gardens: Garden and arboretum begun in 1953 with 40,000 different plants 'greatest collection of hardy trees and shrubs in the world'. Apr-Oct 10.30-5 or one hour before dusk. Tel. 01794 368787; www.hilliergardens.org.uk

Ashmansworth (9 m NNE of Andover) St James: unrestored church of various periods. 13th C wall paintings. Memorial window to Gerald Finzi by Laurence Whistler, and memorial stone by Reynolds Stone

Avington (6 m NE of Winchester) St Mary: perfect Georgian church.
Avington Park: Fine 17th and 18th-C. country house, with beautiful painted rooms. May-Sept Sun & BH Mon 2.30-5.30. Tel. 01962 779260

Basing (2 m E of Basingstoke) St Mary: fine medieval church, built by the Paulet fal War. Basing House, which stood nearby, was destroyed in that war, and Inigo Jones taken prisoner

Beaulieu (13 m S of Southampton) Ruined Cistercian Abbey. Palace House: country house built into gateway of abbey. National Motor Museum (founded 1952). Open daily 10-6. Tel. 01590 612345

Bishop's Waltham (9 m NE of Southampton) Pleasant, if cramped, medieval town with ruins of palace of Bishops of Winchester.

St Peter: ancient minster, much rebuilt, with 17th C gothic additions. Pulpit donated by the great 17th C preacher Lancelot Andrews

Boarhunt (3 m NE of Fareham) St Nicholas: isolated church built just before the Norman conquest, in amazingly complete condition

Bournemouth Luxuriously laid out seaside town on pine-covered slopes with exceptional Victorian churches: St Augustine's by Butterfield; St Stephen's by Pearson; St Michael's and St Swithun's both by Norman Shaw; St James' by Street.

Bramley (5 m N of Basingstoke) St James: rare medieval mural of Thomas à Becket; transept by Soane; fine furnishings

Bramshill House (5 m NW of Fleet) Spectacular Jacobean house. Now Police College and so regrettably closed to the public

Breamore (3 m N of Fordingbridge) St Mary's: Anglo-Saxon church (c.1000) in exceptional condition, with remains of Rood damaged by iconoclasts
    Breamore House: Late Elizabethan country house (1583) with paintings, furniture, tapestries by Teniers, agriculture and coach museum, early Mexican paintings. Museum 1-5.30, house 2-5.30. May-Sep daily exc. Mon & Fri; Easter to end Apr, Tue & Sun; May-July & Sep daily exc. Mon & Fri; Aug, daily.Tel. 01725 512233

Broadlands (nr. Romsey, 7½ m S of Southampton, 3057) Country house on the Test, extended by Capability Brown (1767) and Henry Holland (1788); superb plasterwork. Birthplace of Lord Palmerston, later home of Earl Mountbatten, uncle by marriage of Elizabeth II, who began her honeymoon here. Mountbatten was First Sea Lord and last Viceroy of India, and as symbol of imperial Britain was killed in 1979 by IRA bomb. June-Aug daily 12-4. Tel. 01794 505010

Bucklers Hard (2½ m S of Beaulieu, off B3054) Maritime Museum with models of Nelson's fleet, built here; workmen's cottages. March-May 10-5, June-Sept 10-6, Oct-February 10-4.30. Tel. 01590 616203

Burghclere (4 m S of Newbury, A34) Sandham Memorial Chapel, with unforgettable paintings by Stanley Spencer. NT. Apr-Oct, Wed & Sun 11.30-5; Nov & Mar, Sat & Sun 11.30-4. NT

Chawton (1½ m S of Alton, A31/32) Jane Austen's house from 1809 until her final illness in 1817. Mar-Nov daily 11-4; Dec-Feb, Sat & Sun 11-4. Tel. 01420 83262
    Chawton House: Elizabethan house, heavily rebuilt, once owned by Jane Austen's relations. Now study centre for women's literature. Tel. 01420 541010 for visits and other information. www.chawton.org

Christchurch (5 m ENE of Bournemouth) Important Augustinian priory, now longest parish church in the country. Spectacular Norman arcading, famous stair turret, Superb reredos and fine misericords, chantry chapels and monuments.

Corhampton (4 m WSW of East Meon) Delightful Saxon church with medieval wall paintings (possibly 11th-C, *pace* Pevsner)

Crondall (3 m NW of Farnham) All Saints: 'noble Norman-transitional interior' (Betjeman) and fine setting

Damerham (3 m NW of Fordingbridge) St George: unusually attractive Norman and later church

East Meon (5 m W of Petersfield) Pretty high street. All Saints: exceptional Norman church ('one of the most thrilling in Hampshire' – Pevsner) with fine Tournai marble font. Fittings by Comper

Ellingham (3 m N of Ringwood) St Mary, charmingly furnished village church Reredos sometimes ascribed to Grinling Gibbons

Elvetham Hall (1 m SE of Hartley Wintney) Astonishing Victorian mansion by S. S. Teulon, now conference centre and hotel

Emsworth (2 m E of Havant) Yachting centre. Home of P. G. Wodehouse; display in local museum, above the fire station. Fri, Sat & BH Mon 10.30-4.30, Sun 2.30-4.30

Empshott (7 m SE of Alton) Holy Rood: 'a complete 13th C church' (Pevsner) set in woodland

Exbury Gardens (15 m SW of Southampton, off B3054) Park and garden of Baron Edmund de Rothschild's country house (1965). Over 1 million rhododendrons. Park only: March-Oct daily 10-5.30; Nov weekends 10-4. Tel. 02380 891203; www.exbury.co.uk

Farnborough (3 m N of Aldershot) Famous for its air show. Every other July; www.farnborough.com
St Michael's Abbey: chaste French neo-gothic mausoleum built by the Empress Eugénie (d. 1920) for the family of Napoleon III, and the abbey founded to serve it. Regular masses for members of the imperial family, including Napoleon I. Open at some services. Guided tours every Sat at 3.30. www.farnboroughabbey.org

Farringdon (3 m S of Alton, N of Portsmouth, A32) All Saints: frescoes of Last Judgement, mid 14th-15th C.
Massey's Folly: enormous village hall built by the rector with his own hands (and those of a solitary other labourer)

Fawley (10 m SE of Southampton) All Saints: Norman church surrounded by oil refinery

Fleet (3 m NW of Aldershot) All Saints: Grand but restrained church by Burges

Fosbury (½ mile W of Vernham Dean) Typical Iron Age hill fort in relatively unspoilt Hampshire country

Froyle (4 m NE of Alton) Church of the Assumption: Attractive church with fine furnishings in harmonious setting

Gosport (W of Portsmouth) Naval town with much official architecture, including series of Palmerston forts designed to ward off the French invasion feared in the 1850's. Station 'one of the finest pieces of station architecture from the beginning of the railway age' (Pevsner). St Mary: fine High Victorian church by Henry Woodyer. Holy Trinity, a 17thC church lightly restored inside but thoroughly Italianized out by Blomfield (who added the campanile). Handel's organ from Canons, where he was organist to the Duke of Chandos.
The Hovercraft Trust, 15 St Mark's Rd. 48 hovercraft inc. cross-channel and world's fastest, the SRN Swift. Occasional open days. Tel. 01705 601310

Hale (9 m N of Ringwood) Hale House: country home of the baroque architect Thomas Archer, and possibly by him. Idiosyncratic village church, St Mary, certainly by Archer. Fine monuments

Hambledon (10 m N of Portsmouth) Georgian village, home of cricket.
St Peter and St Paul: 'a textbook of medieval parish church architecture' (Pevsner)

Hartley Wespall (6 m NE of Basingstoke) St Mary: worth seeing for amazing timber framework of W wall

Hawkley (4 m N of Petersfield) St Peter and St Paul: Vigorous church by Teulon with a Rhenish helm (cf. Sompting)

Highclere Castle (4½ m S of Newbury, A34) Largest country house in Hampshire, by Barry and Allom; perfect park by Capability Brown, 1774-77 and later Victorianized, Old Masters, Egyptian collection. July-Aug Tue-Sun 11-5. Tel. 01635 253210

Highcliffe Castle (9 m E of Bournemouth) Spectacular Victorian Gothic mansion incorporating much French medieval stonework. Tel. 01425 278807 for visiting times.

Hinton Ampner (7½ m E of Winchester, A272) Neo-Georgian country house, Regency furniture, paintings, resident ghost, beautiful 20th-C formal gardens. Gardens Apr-Sept Sat-Wed 11-5; house Tues & Wed only, 1.30-5, and also Sat & Sun in Aug. NT. Tel. 01962 771305

Houghton Lodge (W of Winchester, 1½ m S of A30 near Stockbridge) Gothick cottage orné on the Test.. Picturesque architecture

and setting. Kitchen garden with Hampshire Hydroponicum: 'an exhibition of soilless horticulture with biological control of greenhouse pests'. Mar-Sept, Mon, Tues, Thur & Fri, 2-5; Sat & Sun, 10-5. Tel. 01264 810502; www.houghtonlodge.co.uk

Hursley (4 m SW of Winchester) All Saints: textbook Ecclesiological church built for John Keble. Superb glass, designed by Butterfield

Hurst Castle Island fortress in Solent, 1542-44, part of Henry VIII's coastal defences. Surrounded by saltmarsh and mudflats rich in plant and bird life. Apr, June, Sept & Oct 10-4.30; July & Aug 10-5.15. (Ferry from Keyhaven). EH. Tel. 01590 642344

Idsworth (7 m S of Petersfield) St Hubert: atmospheric church in isolated position, very fine wall paintings

Lyndhurst (8 m ESE of Southampton) New Forest town, famous for its meat. St Michael: eccentric church by Victorian master of coloured brick, William White; furnishings by Leighton and Flaxman, superb stained glass by William Morris

King's Somborne (7 m W of Winchester) Marsh Court: country house of Edwardian stockbroker above the Test, 1901-04, by Lutyens, garden by Gertrude Jekyll. 'Full of Lutyens faerie' (Pevsner). P

Kingsclere (11 m NE of Basingstoke) St Mary: rebuilt Norman church distinguished by louse weathervane associated with King John

Micheldever (7 m N of Winchester) Site of controversially large housing development (a town bigger than Winchester) threatened by Eagle Star Insurance. Thus far held at bay; see www.deversociety.org.

St Mary: octagonal church by George Dance, with three Baring monuments by Flaxman

Minstead (3 m NW of Lyndhurst, A31) All Saints: medieval church with untouched Georgian interior; burial place of Conan Doyle.

Furzey Gardens: famous picturesque gardens (since 1922), daily 10-5. Tel. 02380 812464

Mottisfont Abbey (4 m N of Romsey, A3057) Augustinian monastery founded 1201, manor house since Reformation. Drawing room spectacularly decorated by Rex Whistler. Park and rose garden, 19thC French roses a speciality. Garden: April-Oct, Sat-Wed, 11-6; June 11-8.30. House: Apr-Oct, Tues & Sat 1-5. NT. Tel. 01794 341220/ 340757

Netley Abbey (2 m SE of Southampton) Ruined Cistercian Abbey. Any reasonable time. EH. Tel. 01703 453076

New Forest Ancient forest, with largest spread of lowland woodland in north-west Europe, and one of Britain's richest natural habitats (heath and bogs as well as trees). Deer and birds in abundance. Museum and visitor centre at Lyndhurst. Re-opens during 2004; tel 023 8028 3444

North Baddesley (3 m E of Romsey) St John: charming church in fine setting

Northington (5 m NE of Winchester) The Grange: shell of grand neo-Grecian house by William Wilkins, 1804-9, home of the Baring family whose superb mausoleum by Westmacott is in the church. EH. The ruins of the house are now used for opera per-formances in summer; tel. 020 730 5408

Pamber End (4 m N of Basingstoke) Priory Church : chancel and crossing tower of 12th C priory, 'a serenely beautiful composition' (Betjeman)

Portchester Castle (near Portsmouth, ½ mile S of A27) Roman fortification with Norman castle and refined Norman church, a set piece of French Romanesque. Daily Apr-Sept 10-6, Oct 10-5; Nov-Mar 10-4. Closed 24-26 Dec and 1 Jan. EH. Tel. 01705 378291

Portsmouth Only British city on an island site. Chief naval base of the kingdom since 17th C. Very badly bombed in consequence and dismally rebuilt.

Cathedral: overgrown parish church of great charm, all periods from 13th to 20th C. Magnificent weathervane, 'The Golden Barque'

Royal Garrison Church, originally medieval hospital with beautiful 13th-C chancel, and fittings by Street

City Museum and Art Gallery, Museum Rd: English furniture, ceramics and glass, paintings and town history. Apr-Oct 10-5, Nov-Mar 10-4.30. Tel. 02392 827261 www.portsmouthmuseums.co.uk

Charles Dickens Museum, 393 Old Commercial Rd: Dickens' birthplace. Apr-Oct 10-5; ring for details of out of season openings. Tel. 023 9282 7261; www. charlesdickensbirthplace.co.uk

Natural History Museum, April-Oct daily 10-5.30, Nov-Mar daily 10-4. www.portsmouthnaturalhistory.co.uk

Southsea Castle, Clarence Esplanade: Henry VIII coastal fortress, military and archaeological collection and D-Day Museum with Overlord embroidery. April-Sep daily 10-5. Tel. 02392 827261; www.southseacastle.co.uk

Portsmouth Historic Dockyard: a dockyard from the 12th C, with the world's first dry dock (1495), much expanded in 17th C, especially by Samuel Pepys. Some magnificent military buildings. Nelson's flagship HMS *Victory*, Nelson memorabilia, model ships and figureheads; the *Mary Rose* (1510-11) Henry VIII's flagship, salvaged from harbour where it sank in 1545 (disappointing but dramatic); and the HMS *Warrior*, England's first iron warship, 1860. Apr-Oct 10-4.30, Nov-Mar 10-4. 10-5.30. Tel. 023 92 86 1533; www.royalnaval museum. org

Amongst the interesting churches:

St Agatha, off Charlotte St: one of the few buildings to survive the devastating bombing of Landport; superb Victorian church with sgraffito decoration by Heywood Sumner

St Philip, Hawthorn Crescent, Cosham: one of the most acclaimed churches by Ninian Comper

Rockbourne (3 m NW of Fordingbridge, W of A338) Pretty village with five long barrows in vicinity.

Roman farm with museum. Apr-Sep, daily 10.30-6. Tel. 01725 518541

Romsey (10 m SW of Winchester) Important Saxon abbey rebuilt by the conquerors: 'here is great Norman architecture, grand in scale and rich in detail' (Betjeman). Fine Saxon and later carvings.

King John's House, Church Court: 13th C house – not King John's – with medieval graffiti.

Bath House, 91 Middle Bridge St 'decorated by a maniac or an advertising monumental mason' (Pevsner).

See also Broadlands

Rowland's Castle (4m NNE of Havant) Attractive village

Stansted Park: 18th and 20th C country house with fine paintings, walled gardens, park and arboretum, but alas no longer Ivan Hicks' surreal 'Garden of the Mind'. 'Disarming' (Pevsner) Gothick chapel with bright decoration aimed at the conversion of the Jews. July-Sept, Sun-Tue 2-5. Tel. 02392412265; www.stanstedpark.co.uk

St Mary Bourne (5 m NW of Andover) St Peter: early church with superb Tournai marble font and fine tombs in churchyard

Sandham Memorial Chapel see Burghclere

Selborne (SE of Alton, B3006) Delightful village with Gilbert White Museum, home and garden of classic 18th-C. naturalist at 'The Wakes'. Apr-Oct 11-5. Tel. 01420 511275. His church (and burial place) set over a ravine, is most attractive Norman and later; restored by his great-nephew William White

Shedfield (9 m E of Southampton) New Place: fine Lutyens house built around 17C rooms salvaged from Bristol

Silchester (6 m N of Basingstoke) Roman walls of camp still standing. Open any reasonable time. EH. Attractive church, St Mary, next to the walls

Southampton Important port in middle ages (hence superb fortifications, including the Bargate), and again in 20th C; merely a watering town in intervening period. Badly bombed.

Art Gallery, Civic Centre: Old Masters, 19thC French artists, and esp. 19th (Burne-Jones) & 20th-C. English painting. Tue-Sat 10-5, Sun 1-4. Tel. 023 8083 2277

John Hansard Gallery, University Campus at Highfield: Contemporary art gallery (inc. photography), founded 1979. Tue-Sat 11-5, Sat 11-4. Tel. 023 8059 2158

Maritime Museum, Town Quay, in 14th C wool warehouse: 'Titanic' exhibition. Tues-Fri 10-1 & 2-5, Sat 10-1 & 2-6, Sun 2-5. Tel. 023 8063 5904

Mayflower Theatre, Commercial Rd: Well known provincial theatre. Tel. 02380 711811, www.the-mayflower.com

Medieval Merchant's House, 58 French St (between Castle Way and Town Quay): 14th-C. Apr-Sep 10-6; Oct 10-5. EH

Tudor House Museum, St Michael's Square: 15th-C house, with collection from town's history. Tel. 02380 332515. Currently closed.

St Mary: grand steeple by Street

St Michael: originally Norman church with fine furnishings

Pilgrim Father's Monument: 50-foot high lighthouse in the Royal Docks

University: in great part by Basil Spence. South Stoneham House, now a hall of residence, probably by Hawksmoor

South Hayling (Hayling Island, by Portsmouth) St Mary: very fine 13th C church

Southwick (3 m N of Portsmouth) HMS Dryad, Eisenhower's HQ, where final orders for D-Day were given

St James: largely unrestored 16th C church

Steep (2 m N of Petersfield) Home of Edward Thomas; memorial windows in the church by Laurence Whistler

Stockbridge (7 m S of Andover) Pretty one-street village, original end of the A272

Stoke Charity (7 m N of Winchester) St Mary and St Michael: fascinating collection of tombs

Stratfield Saye House (A33, between Basingstoke and Reading) Country seat of the Dukes of Wellington since 1817. Park. Easter weekend and July. Weekdays gates open 11.30-3.30, weekends 10.30-3.30. Guided tours only. Tel. 01256 882882; www.stratfield-saye.co.uk

Sway (3 m NW of Lymington, New Forest) Peterson's Tower: Concrete tower 218 foot high, built 1879-85 by Andrew Thomas Peterson, retired judge from Calcutta, as his mausoleum. 13-storey folly.

Tichborne (6 m E of Winchester) Home of eponymous claimant, whose family also owned the Tichborne Worthies, the only set of secular 'Apostle' spoons in existence (now Allen Gallery, Alton).

St Andrew, lovely church, mishmash of periods

Titchfield (2 m WSW of Fareham) Attractive ancient port town, now mostly Georgian.

St Peter, has fine Elizabeth tombs of the Earls of Southampton (Shakespeare's patron is a small child on one of them). 'Spectacular' (Pevsner) Tudor gatehouse of former Southampton seat, built within nave of former abbey

Upton Grey (6 m SE of Basingstoke) The Manor House: garden by Gertrude Jekyll, 1908, restored according to her original plans. Arts and Crafts house built for editor of *The Studio*, 1907. Mon-Fri by appointment only. Tel. 01256 862827

The Vyne (4 m N of Basingstoke) Fascinating Tudor country house with later alterations. Open daily Apr-Oct Sat-Wed 11-5; grounds with pavilion also open Feb-Mar Sat & Sun 11-5. NT. Tel. 01256 881337

Wickham (2 m N of Fareham)'Finest village in Hampshire, and one of the best in the south of England' (Pevsner), mostly Georgian

Winchester Capital of Wessex, and England's second capital for centuries. Spoilt by 1970's pedestrianisation, but with many pretty buildings.

Cathedral: Until the 19th C the largest building in England, and one of the largest in Europe; magnificent monuments. Surrounded by attractive buildings. Mon-Sat 8.30-6; Sun 8.30-5. Tel. 01962 857200; www.winchester-cathedral.org.uk

City Museum, The Square: archaeological and city history collection. Apr-Oct Mon-Sat 10-5, Sun 2-5; Nov-mar Tues-Sat 10-4, Sun 12-4. Tel. 01962 848269

Great Hall of Winchester Castle, High St: magnificent medieval hall, with Round Table. All year 10-5. Tel. 01962 846476

Hospital of St Cross: Unique medieval hospital founded 1136 and with large12-13 C church. Present hospital buildings 15th C. Footpath through water meadows. April-Oct Mon-Sat 9.30-5; Nov-Mar 10.30-3.30. Tel. 01962 851375; www.stcross hospital.co.uk

St Catherine's Hill: Iron Age hillfort and medieval maze. Interesting plant life and butterflies.

Winchester College, 77 Kingsgate St: Founded 1382, and much survives from this early phase. Ring for details of tours. Tel. 01962 621100

Winchfield (3 m W of Fleet) St Mary: impressive 12th C church, 'Norman of a singular ferocity' (Pevsner)

Wolverton (7 m NW of Basingstoke) St Catherine: well-preserved 18th C church

Isle of Wight

Appledurcombe (2 m NNW of Ventnor) Terrific ruins of Vanbrugh-influenced house. EH

Arreton (3 m SE of Newport) St George: Saxon and later church with interesting monuments, some by Westmacott.

Manor: 17th-C. country house with wireless museum & toy and doll collection. Apr-Oct, Mon-Fri 10-6, Sun 12-6. Tel. 01983 528134

Bembridge (B3395) Windmill, Georgian, 1700, the only one left on the island. Apr-Jun & Sep-Oct daily exc. sat 10-5, July-Aug daily 10-5. NT. Tel. 01983 873945

Brading (5 m S of Ryde) St Mary: large early church with remarkable retro tomb of Sir John Oglander.

Roman villa with exceptional mosaics: daily 10-5.30.

Carisbrooke (2 m SW of Newport) St Mary: Norman priory church with magnificent Perp. tower.

Castle: Norman castle where Charles I was imprisoned. Local museum. Daily Apr-Sept 10-6, Oct 10-5; Nov-Mar 10-4. Closed 24-26 Dec and 1 Jan. EH. Tel. 01983 522107

Compton Down (SE of Freshwater) Beautifully flowered chalk grassland with wonderful views

Cowes (4 m N of Newport) Home of yacht racing. St. Mary has bizarre tower by John Nash (who is buried in another of his churches here, St James). Castle by James Wyatt

Dimbola Lodge (Freshwater Bay, Terrace Lane) Home of photographer Julia Margaret Cameron. Tues-Sun & BH Mon 10-5. Tel. 01983 756814; www.dimbola. co.uk

Godshill (5 m SSE of Newport) Famously pretty village. St Lawrence: fine monuments to Worsleys of Appledurcombe, and famous 15th C wall painting, the 'Lily Crucifix'

Mottistone Manor (SE of Freshwater, B3399) Elizabethan house (1567). Garden: Apr-Oct, Tue & Wed 11-5.30, Sun & BH Mon 2-5.30. House: Aug. BH Mon 2-5.30 and by appointment. NT. Tel. 01983 741302

The Needles Old Battery (SW of Freshwater) Palmerston coastal fort, 1862, spectacular cliff view. Apr-June & Sep-Oct, Sun-Thur 10.30-5; July & Aug daily 10.30-5. NT. Tel. 01983 754772

Newport Main town of island; Nash buildings; Victorian atmosphere
St Thomas, the town church, though Victorian, has superb 17th C pulpit

Nunwell House (¾ m W of Brading) 17th/18th-C., with park and garden. July-Sept Mon, Tues & Wed 1-5. Tel. 01983 407240

Osborne House (2 m SE of East Cowes) Queen Victoria's favourite house, designed by Prince Albert. Daily Apr-Sep 10-6, Oct 10-5. EH. Tel. 01983 200002

Quarr (4 m NE of Newport) Abbey buildings by Dom Paul Bellot, 'a virtuoso in brick' (Pevsner)

Ryde (7 m NE of Newport) Attractive early Victorian seaside town

Sandown Museum of Isle of Wight Geology, High St: incl. rich fossil collection. Apr-Oct, daily 10-6, Nov-Mar daily 10-4. Tel. 01983 404344

Shorwell (5 m SW of Newport) Famously pretty village of thatched cottages, with fine Perpendicular church, St Peter, with monuments and wall painting of St Christopher ('entertaining fishes and ships' – Pevsner).

Whippingham (1 m SW of Osborne) St Mildred, royal church

Yarmouth St James: Jacobean church with contemporary statue of Louis XIV
Castle: Henry VIII coastal fort (1547). Apr-Sep 10-6, Oct 10-5. EH. Tel. 01983 760678

Hotels and Restaurants

H = Hotel, B & B = Bed and Breakfast, R = Restaurant, GF = Good Food

*'There is nothing which has yet
been contrived by man by which
so much happiness is produced as by
a good tavern or inn'
(Dr Samuel Johnson, 1776)*

Kent

Boughton Lees (4 m N of Ashford, A251)
Eastwell Manor: Edwardian country
house, H & GF. Tel. 01233 213000,
www.eastwellmanor.co.uk

Boughton Monchelsea (5 m S of
Maidstone, off B2163) Tanyard, Wierton
Hill: 14th C timber-framed house, country
guest house, H & R. Tel. 01622 744705

Canterbury Debenham's Crypt
Restaurant, St George's St: snack-bar in
cellar built in 1395 as dormitory for pilgrims
Sully's County Hotel, High St: H & GF.
Tel. 01227 766266
Tuo e Mio, 16 The Borough: Italian
restaurant, GF. Tel. 01227 761471.
www.tuoemio.com

Chartham Hatch (5 m W of Canterbury,
A28) Howfield Manor: small country
house hotel, H & R. Tel. 01227 738294

Chilham White Horse: 15th C inn near
church (Chantrey monument) on former
Pilgrim's Way: pub sign copy of Stubbs'
'White Horse' (Tate Gallery) Tel. 01227
730355

Chilston Park Extremely attractive country house hotel . Tel. 01622 859803

Dover Number One Guesthouse, 1 Castle
St: Georgian B & B, below castle. Tel.
01304 202007, www.number1guesthouse.
co.uk

Fordwich (3 m NE of Canterbury, A28)
George & Dragon, King St.: old guesthouse on Stour, B & B. & R, specialising in
seafood. Tel. 01227 710661

Ivy Hatch (E of Sevenoaks, A227) The
Plough, High Cross Rd: GF. Tel. 01732
810268

Lamberhurst (SE of Tunbridge Wells,
A21) Brown Trout: village pub with garden, GF. Tel. 01892 890312

Smarden (8 m W of Ashford) The Bell, Bell
Lane, one of the best pubs in Kent. R & B
& B. Tel. 01233 770283

Speldhurst George and Dragon Inn, timber-framed house of 1212, third oldest pub
in England (landlord says it's the oldest):
farmhouse cheese and cider from the vat.
Tel. 01892 863125; www.george-and-
dragon-speldhurst.co.uk

St Margaret's at Cliffe (3 m N of Dover, B2058) Wallett's Court, West Cliffe: small country house hotel and spa, H & GF. Tel. 01304 852424, www. wallettscourt.com

Tunbridge Wells Cheevers, 56 High St: GF. Tel. 01892 545524

Calverley, Crescent Rd: Hotel in home of Decimus Burton (1828ff.), H & R. Tel. 01892 526455; www.tunbridge-wells.com/hotels

Sankey's, 39 Mount Ephraim: Fish restaurant, GF. Tel. 01892 511422

The Spa Hotel, Mount Ephraim: Georgian spa hotel, H & R. Tel. 01892 520331, www.spahotel.co.uk

Thackeray's House, 85 London Rd: Restaurant on ground floor of novelist's home, bistro in cellar, GF. Tel. 01892 5119121

Whitstable (N of Canterbury, A290) Whitstable is the setting of Somerset Maugham's novel about his childhood, *Cales and Ale* (1930)

Whitstable Oyster Fishery Co, Horsebridge Beach: Fish restaurant with own cinema, own oyster farm, and over 50 types of British fish; popular day trip from London. GF & H (also fishermen's huts). Tel. 01227 276856, hotel 01227 280280; www.oysterfishery.co.uk

Wye (NE of Ashford, A28) Wife of Bath, 4 Upper Bridge St: gourmet restaurant, ideal place to drink toast to Aphra Behn (1640-89), first English authoress to earn her living and make her name from writing. She came from Wye and is buried in Westminster Abbey. GF. Tel. 01233 812540; www.w-o-b.demon.co.uk

Surrey

Box Hill (N of Dorking, A24) Burford Bridge Hotel: Keats, Stevenson, Nelson were among its guests, H & R. Tel. 01306 884561

Ewhurst (near Cranleigh, SE of Guildford, B2127) Windmill Inn, Pitch Hill: pub with garden and view. R. Tel. 01483 267444

Haslemere (SW of Guildford, A3/A286) Lythe Hill Hotel, Petworth Rd, timber-framed house, small luxury hotel with park and tennis, H & R. Tel. 01428 651251, www.lythehill.co.uk

Morels, 25-27 Lower St: GF. Tel. 01428 651462

Ripley (5 m NE of Guildford, A3) Michel's, 13 High St: GF. Tel. 01483 224777

Selsdon Park (SE of Croydon) Selsdon Park Hotel, Addington Rd, Sanderstead: haunted country house hotel in suburbia; golf course, H & R. Tel. 020 8657 8811

Tadworth (S of Epsom) Gemini, Station Approach: GF. Tel. 01737 812179; www.gemini-restaurant.com

Walton-on-Thames Le Pêcheur at the Anglers, Riverside restaurant specializing in fish: GF. Tel. 01932 227423

Witley (3 m SE of Godalming, A283) The White Hart: picturesque pub (George Eliot's local). R. Tel. 01428 683695

Sussex

Alfriston (B2108) Star Inn, timber-framed house (c. 1520) in picturesque village on Downs. H & R. Tel. 0870 400 8102

Amberley (NE of Chichester, A29/B2139) Amberley Castle, H & GF. Tel. 01798 831992, www.amberleycastle. co.uk

Bosham (4 m W of Chichester, A259) Millstream Hotel, comfortable country hotel, H & R. Tel. 01243 573234, www.millstream-hotel.co.uk

Brighton Black Chapati, 12 Circus Parade, New England Rd: GF. Tel. 01273 699011

Food for Friends, 17-18 Prince Albert St, The Lanes: health food restaurant, R. Tel. 01273 202310; www.foodforfriends. com

Langan's Bistro, 1 Paston Place: started by late London restaurateur Peter Langan, GF. Tel. 01273 606933

Terre à Terre, 71 East St: vegetarian cuisine, GF. Tel. 01273 729051

The Grand, King's Rd: Victorian hotel (1864), H & R. Tel. 01273 224300; www.grandbrighton.co.uk

Topps Hotel, 17 Regency Square: small Regency hotel opposite West Pier, H & GF. 01273 729334

The Twenty One, 21 Charlotte St: Victorian guesthouse in elegant Kemp Town, H & R. Tel. 01273 686450

Burpham (N of Littlehampton, A27, E of Arundel) George and Dragon, 18thC pub on South Downs, GF. Tel. 01903 883131

Chichester Droveway, 30A Southgate: GF. Tel. 01243 528832

Little London Restaurant, 38 Little London/East St: GF. Tel. 01243 537550

Ship Hotel, North St: Georgian house with Adam staircase and naval tradition. H & R. Tel. 01243 778000, www.shiphotel. com

Chilgrove (7 m N of Chichester, B2141)

White Horse Inn, restaurant on Downs with exquisite wine list, GF & B&B. Tel. 01243 59219; www.whitehorse chilgrove.co.uk

Climping (W of Littlehampton, E of Chichester, A259) Bailiffscourt: luxury country house hotel with garden and private beach, H & R. Tel. 01903 723511

Coolham (3 m SW of Billingshurst, A272) Blue Idol Guest House: 16thC farmhouse, where William Penn used to meet the Quakers; still used as a Friends' meeting house. B & B. Tel. 01403 741241

Cuckfield (11 m N of Brighton, A272) Ockenden Manor, Ockenden Lane: luxury country house hotel (1520). H & GF. Tel. 01444 416111

Eastbourne Grand Hotel, Jevington Gardens. Victorian hotel where Claude Debussy spent summer 1905 with his mistress Emma Bardac, H & GF. Tel. 01323 412345, www.grandeastbourne. co.uk

East Grinstead Gravetye Manor, Vowels Lane (5 m SW of E.G., B2028): Elizabethan country house, former residence of pioneering Victorian gardener William Robinson, whose own garden is one of the pleasures of this luxury hotel, along with organic vegetables, H & GF. Tel 01342 810567; www.gravetyemanor.co.uk

Herstmonceux (N of Eastbourne, A271) Sundial, Gardner St: GF. Tel. 01323 832217

Jevington (nr Eastbourne, B2105) Hungry Monk: gourmet restaurant on Downs, home of the banoffee pie. GF. Tel. 01323 482178; www.hungrymonk.co.uk

Little Horsted (S of Uckfield, NE of Lewes, A26) Horsted Place: luxury Victorian country house hotel with golf course, tennis etc., H & GF. Tel. 01825 750240, www.horstedplace.co.uk

Lower Beeding (SE of Horsham, A281/279) Jeremy's at the Crabtree, Brighton Rd: pub, GF. Tel. 01403 891257

Midhurst (11 m N of Chichester, A286) The Angel Hotel, North St, 16thC country hotel, H & GF. Tel. 01730 812421

Netherfield (nr Battle, NW of Hastings, B2096) Netherfield Place: small 1920's country house hotel, H & GF. Tel. 01424 774455, www.netherfieldplace.co.uk

Northchapel (near Petworth) Half Moon Inn, once owned by one of the greatest early cricketers, Noah Mann. GF. Tel. 01428 702270

Pulborough (between Chichester and Horsham, A29) Stane Street Hollow, Codmore Hill: cottage restaurant, GF. Tel. 01798 872819

Rye Jeake's House, Mermaid St: 17thC house in Rye's picturebook main street, comfortable B & B. Tel. 01797 222828
   Landgate Bistro, 5-6 Landgate: GF. Tel. 01797 222829
   The Mermaid, Mermaid St: 15thC timber-framed house with legendary reputation, H & R. Tel. 01797 223065
   The Old Vicarage, 66 Church Square (near St Mary's), B & B. Tel. 01797 222119

Seaford (W of Eastbourne, A259) Quincy's, 42 High St: GF. Tel. 01323 895490

Thakeham (N of Worthing, A24) Little

Thakeham, Merrywood Lane, Storrington: country house by Lutyens (1902), now luxury hotel, H & R. Tel. 01903 744416

Wilmington (NW of Eastbourne, A27) The Crossways, Lewes Rd: regional cuisine, H & GF. Tel. 01323 482455, www.crosswayshotel.co.uk

Wych Cross (S of East Grinstead, A22/A275) Ashdown Park Hotel, Forest Row: Victorian country house hotel on edge of Ashdown Forest, former convent, H & R. Tel. 01342 824988, www.ashdownpark.co.uk

Hampshire

Brockenhurst (SW of Southampton, A337) Le Poussin, The Courtyard, Brookley Rd: gourmet restaurant on edge of New Forest, local dishes (mushrooms!), GF. Tel. 01590 623063
   The Snake Catcher: pub named after the local celebrity Brusher Mills

Emsworth (E of Portsmouth, A27) Spencers, 36 North St: GF. Tel. 01243 372744
   36 on the Quay, 47 South St: popular quayside restaurant, R. Tel. 01243 375592

Eversley (S of Reading, A327/B3348) New Mill, Riverside restaurant, GF. Tel. 0118 973 2277; www.thenewmill.co.uk

Hurstbourne Tarrant (8 m N of Andover, A343) Esseborne Manor, small country house hotel, H & GF. Tel. 01264 736444, www.esseborne-manor.com

Longstock (S of Andover, A3057) Peat Spade Inn, GF. Tel. 01264 810612

Lymington (9 m E of Bournemouth, A337) Limpets, Gosport St: GF. Tel. 01590 675595; www.limpets-lymington.co.uk

Middle Wallop (NE of Salisbury, A30/A343) Fifehead Manor, small country house hotel, H & GF. Tel. 01264 781565

Milford on Sea (E of Bournemouth, A337/B3058) Rocher's, 69 High St, GF. Tel. 01590 642340

Westover Hall, Park Lane: country house hotel with sea view, built in 1897 for Alexander Siemens, H & R. Tel. 01590 643044, www.newforest-online.co.uk/westoverhall

New Milton (E of Bournemouth) Chewton Glen Hotel, Christchurch Rd: super-luxury country house hotel on edge of New Forest – keep-fit, riding, hunting facilities, H & GF. Tel. 01425 275341, www.chewtonglen.com

Portsmouth Bistro Montparnasse, 103 Palmerston Rd, Southsea: GF. Tel. 023 9281 6754; www.bistromontparnasse.co.uk

Romsey (NW of Southampton, A27/A3057) Old Manor House, 21 Palmerston St: GF. Tel. 01794 517353

Southampton Browns Brasserie, Frobisher House, Nelson Gate: GF. Tel. 01703 332615

Wickham (A32, 8 m NW of Portsmouth) The Old House: Georgian hotel, H & GF. Tel. 01329 833049

Winchester Wykeham Arms, 75 Kingsgate St: 18thC inn. H & GF. Tel. 01962 853834

Hunters, 5 Jewry St: GF. Tel. 01962 860006

Hotel du Vin & Bistro, 14 Southgate St: GF. Tel. 01962 841414; www.hotelduvin.com

Woolton Hill (3 m S of Newbury, A343) Hollington House Hotel, Church Rd: country house hotel with garden: H & GF. Tel. 01635 255100

Isle of Wight

Bonchurch (near Ventnor) Peacock Vane, Regency country house, family H & R. Tel. 01983 852019

Winterbourne Hotel, country house with Dickens associations. ('The prettiest place I ever saw in my life at home or abroad.'), H & R. Tel. 01983 852535

Calbourne (E of Freshwater, B3401) Swainston Manor: H & R. Tel. 01983 521121

Chale (8 m S of Newport, B3399) Clarendon Hotel, family guest house, near Wight Mouse Inn, H & R. Tel. 01983 730431

Freshwater Farringford Hotel, Tennyson's former home. H & R. Tel. 01983 752500

Seaview (3 m E of Ryde) Seaview Hotel, High St: Victorian hotel on seafront, H & R. Tel. 01983 612711, www.seaviewhotel.co.uk

Quarr Abbey (W of Ryde, A3054) Benedictine monastery, B & B (men only!). Tel. 01983 882420

Events and Local Customs

February

Shrove Tuesday: pancake race in Bodiam (Sussex), open only to women

Portsmouth Music Festival: till April; www.portsmouthmusicfestival.co.uk

March

Dole Distribution in Biddenden (Kent): bread and cheese for the needy: Easter Monday

April

Menuhin International Violin Competition, Folkestone (Kent); www.this-isfolkestone.co.uk/yehudimenuhin.htm

May

Theatre Festival, Chichester (Sussex) till September; www.cft.org.uk

Brighton Festival: theatre, music, art: 1-3 week; www.brighton-festival.org.uk

Charleston Festival: readings by authors, lectures etc, Charleston Farmhouse, Firle (Sussex); www.charleston.org.uk

Surrey County Show, Guildford

Opera Festival, Glyndebourne (Sussex): till August; www.glyndebourne.com

June

Dickens festival in Broadstairs (Kent): exhibitions, concerts: middle of June; www.broadstairs.gove.uk

Dickens festival in Rochester, with parade in historical costumes: first week

Derby and Oaks: racing in Epsom (Surrey): beginning of June; www.directracing.com

Golf tournament in Sandwich (Kent)

Isle of Wight Festival: mid June till beginning of July; www.isleofwightfestivals.com

Round the Island Yacht Race, Cowes (Isle of Wight): last week; www.cowes.co.uk

July

Dolmetsch Music Festival in Haslemere (Surrey): old chamber music on old instruments

Royal International Horse Show Hickstead (West Sussex); www.hickstead.co.uk

Glorious Goodwood: racing in Goodwood (Sussex): end July; www.gloriousgoodwood.co.uk

Polo tournament at Cowdray Park, Midhurst (Sussex); www.cowdraypolo.co.uk

Kent County Show, Maidstone (Kent): mid July; www.kentshowground.co.uk

August

Cricket week in Canterbury (Kent): 1st week

Greyhound Racing: The Regency Final, Brighton

Cowes Week: climax of sailing regatta, Isle of Wight: beginning of August; www.cowesweek.co.uk

Southern English Church Music Festival: choral and organ concerts in different cathedrals every year: Chichester, Salisbury and Winchester

Knighthood of the Old Green, Southampton: since 1775 club members in frock coats and top hats play tournament on England's oldest bowling green (13th C.)

September
Arundel Festival (Sussex): classical and modern music; www.arundelfestival.co.uk

English Wine Festival, Alfriston (Sussex): 1st week

Rye Festival (Sussex): theatre and music; www.ryefestival.co.uk

October
Canterbury Festival: theatre, music, dance, art

Bellringers' Feast in Twyford (Hampshire): 7 October

November
Guy Fawkes Day, commemorating Gunpowder Plot (1605) to blow up parliament and James I. Bonfires and fireworks, especially worth seeing in Lewes and Rye (Sussex): 5 November

London-Brighton Rally: vintage cars: 1st Sunday

Tudeley Festival: early church and chamber music, Tudeley (Kent)

December
Dickensian Christmas Festival, Rochester: first weekend

Picture Credits

Peter Sager: front cover flap & back cover flap; pp. 4, 5, 48, 49, 53, 67, 84, 86, 108, 118, 120, 123, 127, 132, 143, 153, 158, 161, 172, 184, 185, 188, 193, 194, 195, 202, 206, 209, 212, 215 & 216; colour plates 2, 9, 10, 14, 16, 20, 25, 27, 29, 30, 32, 34, 37, 38, 39, 40, 42, 44, 47, 54, 55, 56, 57, 70 & 74
Ashmolean Museum: p. 117
Michael Bengel: front cover, colour plates 69 & 81
Bodleian Library: p. 90
Pieter and Rita Boogaart: colour plates 35, 64 & 65
British Library: p. 1
Country Houses Association, courtesy of Humberts Leisure: colour plates 17, 18, 19 & 58
John Crook, Winchester: colour plate 71
Dover Museum: p. 16
English Heritage: pp. 6 (below), 21, 35, 164, 226 & 227; colour plates 6, 7, 12, 13, 22, 23, 67, 73, 78 & 79
Famous Fishing: colour plate 63
Loseley House: colour plates 59, 60 & 61
David Lyons: colour plates 24, 31, 75, 76 & 77
Renate von Mangold: p. 39
Florian Monheim: pp. 2, 6 (above); colour plates 1, 3, 4, 11, 28 & 72
National Portrait Gallery: p. 224; colour plate 48
Painshill Park Trust: p. 168 & colour plate 46
Dirk Reinartz: p. 7
Royal Collection: colour plate 8
Royal Horticultural Society, Wisley: colour plates 52 & 53
Sculpture at Goodwood: back cover; p. 107; colour plate 41
Tate Gallery: colour plates 45, 49 & 62
The Trustees of the Edward James Foundation: p. 103
Ullstein Bilderdienst: p. 29

All other images from the author's or the publishers' collections.

Index

Figures in **bold** refer to principal entries
Figures in *italic* refer to illustrations

Front cover: Leeds Castle, by Michael Bengel
Inside front cover: Great Dixter, by Peter Sager
Back Cover: Marc Quinn's *The Overwhelming World of Desire*,
    courtesy Sculpture at Goodwood
Inside back cover: The Pantiles, Tunbridge Wells, by Peter Sager
Frontispiece: Canterbury Cathedral, the Crossing, called Great Harry,
    by Florian Monheim

Pallas Athene would like to thank Sebastian Wormell, Pieter and Rita Boogaart,
    Graham Daw, and Demi Ross, Mike and Svetlana at Olympic Press.
    Particular thanks also to Barbara Fyjis-Walker, for her devoted ferretting
    out of errant quotations and to Christopher Wright for his careful reading of
    the Places to See. David Henry Wilson as well as making an inspired and
    exemplary translation, remains the rock on which these books are built

The book is part of the Pallas Guides series, published by
    Pallas Athene, 42 Spencer Rise, London NW5 1AP.
If you would like further information about the series,
    please write to us at the above address,
    or visit our website, **www.pallasathene.co.uk**
Series editor: Alexander Fyjis-Walker
Series assistant: Barbara Fyjis-Walker
Series designer: James Sutton
Editorial assistants: Jenny Wilson, Ava Li, Rosanna Kelly

This English edition, with updatings and revisions,
    first published 2004 by Pallas Athene
Translation, adaptation, revisions, updatings and all additional material
    © Pallas Athene 2004
German edition first published 1996 by DuMont Buchverlag GmbH & Co.,
    Cologne © 1996 DuMont Buchverlag GmbH & Co

ISBN 1 873429 09 6

Printed in China